Vertical Reference

Vertical Reference

THE LIFE OF LEGENDARY MOUNTAIN HELICOPTER RESCUE PILOT JIM DAVIES

by Kathy Calvert

RMB

For information on purchasing bulk quantities of this book, or to obtain media excerpts or invite the author to speak at an event, please visit rmbooks.com and select the "Contact" tab.

RMB | Rocky Mountain Books Ltd.
rmbooks.com
@rmbooks
facebook.com/rmbooks

Cataloguing data available from Library and Archives Canada
ISBN 9781771604154 (paperback)
ISBN 9781771604161 (electronic)

Cover photo: Bell 206B Jet Ranger by Dale Portman

Printed and bound in Canada

We would like to also take this opportunity to acknowledge the traditional territories upon which we live and work. In Calgary, Alberta, we acknowledge the Niitsítapi (Blackfoot) and the people of the Treaty 7 region in Southern Alberta, which includes the Siksika, the Piikuni, the Kainai, the Tsuut'ina and the Stoney Nakoda First Nations, including Chiniki, Bearpaw, and Wesley First Nations. The City of Calgary is also home to Métis Nation of Alberta, Region III. In Victoria, British Columbia, we acknowledge the traditional territories of the Lkwungen (Esquimalt, and Songhees), Malahat, Pacheedaht, Scia'new, T'Sou-ke and W̱SÁNEĆ (Pauquachin, Tsartlip, Tsawout, Tseycum) peoples.

We acknowledge the financial support of the Government of Canada through the Canada Book Fund and the Canada Council for the Arts, and of the province of British Columbia through the British Columbia Arts Council and the Book Publishing Tax Credit.

Vertical reference flying is the ability to look out and down, or out and back rather than using the natural horizon that you've been taught from day one to use. It's just an extremely unnatural way to fly a helicopter. It's probably the hardest flying you'll ever do.

—ANDRE HUTCHINGS, DIRECTOR OF OPERATIONS
AT VOLO MISSION HELICOPTERS

Contents

Foreword   ix

Acknowledgements   xiii

1   Growing Up   1

2   A Glimpse of the World   21

3   Birth of Heli-Skiing in the Bugaboos   51

4   Changes: From Bugaboos to Banff   85

5   Permission or Forgiveness   115

6   Development of the Public Safety Program   137

7   Eclectic Use of the Helicopter   175

8   The Contract   205

9   No Lack of Work   229

10   The Coast and Home Again   255

Appendix: Public Safety in Parks Today   281

Endnotes   295

Bibliography   303

Foreword

by Peter Fuhrmann

"Dreaming is part of life."
—RAINER MARIA RILKE

"If you don't do it with passion it is not worth doing."
—JACK LEMMON

The sling rope was tight as the helicopter hovered above. Jim called, "I can't lift you. I'm in a downdraft. Not enough power." "Listen, Jim, the four army guys here will lift the stretcher, with the guy in it, who has a hole in his head, and at the count of three they will throw the stretcher out from the wall into the void and I will jump with it and you fly." We are on Mt. Edith's east face, 3,000 ft. up on the wall. Now we are falling 1,000–2,000 ft. but we finally settle under the helicopter as it establishes lift and levels off over the highway. As we pass over Vermilion Lakes, Jim calls, "Where do we go? Answer – front of the hospital. Ask them to bring out a stretcher." The victim is taken into emergency. The doctor says, "We can't do anything for him, he needs a neurosurgeon. He needs to be taken to Calgary by ambulance." My adrenaline level is reduced. As I drive down Banff Avenue, I find out the ambulance's front tire has fallen off. Into my station wagon he goes and we fly at high speed toward Calgary. The ambulance from Calgary intercepts us at Scott Lake Hill. Six months later the young guy who had a hole in his head is back with his unit. Can you believe this? It was reality. We saved his life and we did it with passion and luck! Now how did we get there? It was the evolution of alpine rescue, from rope to steel cable and finally helicopter sling rescue.

The wall was big. Avalanches were roaring down on all sides. Sixteen students and their teacher were screaming for help from the middle of the face. Even the Himalayan superstars standing there were helpless. Wiggerl Gramminger and his crew went to the top and with ropes knotted together were able to lower him down. He was lowered many hundreds of feet, and then they brought them up one after the other, 16 times. On the 17th trip, it was the teacher.

"Knotted ropes, wouldn't a cable be better?" everyone wondered. Wasti Mariner and Wiggerl Gramminger developed the cable rescue system, which included a harness, winches, brake blocks, swivels and frogs (cable clamps). One of the first uses was the spectacular rescue of Claudio Corti off the north face of the Eiger in 1957. The rescuer was lowered 1,000 ft. and then raised the same distance, saving the famous climber's life.

The dreaming went on. The advent of helicopter sling equipment was around the corner. They slung cows in special harnesses to safety from alpine meadows; why not rescuers and victims? Paula Gramminger, Wiggerl's wife, was sewing rescue harnesses, and I brought a couple back to Canada in 1970. The nexus for all this rescue capability was the Swiss Rega (air rescue), whose systems were becoming recognized internationally.

I met Dr. Fritz Buehler of the Swiss Rega at an ICAR

(International Commission for Alpine Rescue) conference in Czechoslovakia in 1973 and he told me this story. I think it happened a year earlier, in 1972. The victim had fallen into the Grand Canyon onto a ledge that was impossible to get to conventionally. Fritz read about the ordeal playing out in Arizona in the local Zurich newspaper. He phoned the US Park Service and offered his assistance. His crew flew to Flagstaff, Arizona, in his Lear jet, rented a helicopter and flew to the lip of the canyon. From there they slung a rescuer down into the canyon, retrieved the injured climber and flew back to Switzerland. You would think America would have embraced this new rescue capability, but they failed to act. It was Canada that led its development in North America.

In 1971, Eric Friedle, the president of ICAR, organized an international helicopter conference located above Grindelwald, Switzerland. People from 18 nations participated, including me, Willi (Pfisterer) and Jim (Davies). There were heli-slinging demonstrations being conducted near Kleine Scheidegg. A number of helicopters could be seen parked in front of the hotel located just below the Eiger north face, including an Agusta Bell 206A, an Alouette III SA, an SA 315B Lama and a Bell 407 amongst others. There were several demonstrations displaying the usefulness of helicopters in rescue work. There were demonstrations on direct hookups, use of winches, and electrical versus hydraulic hookups, but the greatest was a rescuer hanging 600 ft. below a Lama helicopter, being dropped off in the middle of the Eiger north face and then being picked up again. We were all impressed.

Jim was there sitting amidst all the European helicopter pilots telling them how difficult it was to fly a rescue in the wild Canadian Rockies while using underpowered machines. Some of these pilots flew up to five missions a day. The exchange of ideas was superb for Jim and we thanked them for all the information they provided. This was the beginning of a dynamic rescue system in Canada and Jim was a big part of it.

So, you hang suspended below a helicopter flying through the air. Is it exciting? Intoxicating? We are flying to an accident site high up on the mountain where we will find survivors or something worse. Who is flying above? It's Jim. He is flying the machine. He is special – he is pedantic (meticulous). Before we took off, he checked fuel, oil, every bolt and nut to make sure all was right. And now he listens to the sound of the engine and the transmission. He's a pro – 15,000 hours on helicopters and I now hang 100 ft. below him. I am the founder of the Association of Canadian Mountain Guides, a member of the Federation of Alpine Guides – we are a team! What Jim does, and what I do once I arrive at the accident site, keeps us alive. We have a bond. We trust each other. The rope that connects him with me is the spiritual link that even surpasses friendship.

Acknowledgements

First and foremost, I would like to thank Jim Davies for his un-stinting support for this book by providing candid interviews, photographs and, most important, the pilot log books (though terse) that gave an unfailing record of his many exploits as a pilot, both fixed wing and in the helicopter.

No book is complete without another set of eyes to spot the inconsistencies, from unanswered questions to mistakes in punc-tuation – essentially the job of an editor. I was very fortunate in having this ominous task undertaken by my sister Susan Forest, a freelance editor with several editing awards in her resume. Thank you, Susan, for this contribution, which has made the book so much better.

Different sources were used to mine the numerous stories that define Jim, but the most insightful came from those who knew him best. Thank you, Roy Andersen, for your time and insight into this story. Thank you also for your reading of the first draft, which gave me confidence to continue with the numerous tasks involved in completing a book. I would also like to thank Bruce McTrowe for his push to see this project started. He had long believed that Jim's story was an integral part of Banff's history and needed to be told. His multi-dimensional familiarity with Jim's life opened up numerous avenues for discovery beyond that of a rescue pilot.

I likewise would like to thank those people who contributed insights and stories that could not be found in any book or document. Thank you, Eddie Amann, George Capel, Leo and Linda Grillmair, Cliff White, Eric Langshaw, Nelda Sharp, Morgan Davies, Marg Gmoser, Freda Odenthal, Mark Adams, Todd Cooper, Paul Maloney, Linda Cooper, Grace Mickle and Peter Fuhrmann.

I would like to add that much of the information for Jim's book came from an earlier book, *Guardians of the Peaks*, published in 2006. The present book was aided by the many interviews taken prior to this year which provided access to those no longer with us. In this category, I would like to posthumously thank Tim Auger, Lance Cooper, Willi Pfisterer and Jim Sime.

It is not possible to get a book published without a publisher. I am fortunate in having the long-time support of Rocky Mountain Books, who have been there since I first started writing. It is a true luxury to be able to phone up Don Gorman at RMB and say, "I have a great story – will you publish it?" The answer has always been, "Sure – when can you have the first draft in?" Thank you, RMB, for engaging so fully in the life, heritage and culture of our Rocky Mountains.

Finally, the project would have been far more drawn out without the support of my husband, Dale Portman. His help with the research and editing was invaluable in writing this book with much enjoyment.

Growing Up

On January 29, 1938, the temperature in Banff hovered around minus 30 degrees Celsius, accompanied by a weather front laden with snow.

The area from Lake Louise to Saskatchewan River Crossing was even colder, taking the brunt of the storm. The snowfall was heavy and deep, making travel difficult. The constant barrage from snow falling from the trees added to the discomfort of the trip. Under these conditions the weary traveller often felt the impact of these snowy balls when they landed on their head or neck, soaking their clothing. Such was the case on that January day as Bert Davies slogged up the unbroken trail leading to the Bow Summit warden cabin.

Bert, the district warden from Saskatchewan River Crossing, still had good weather when Banff dispatch announced over the phone line that Lila, Bert's wife, had gone into labour with their first child. Before asking Bert when to expect him in Banff, dispatch also warned him of a major storm developing that would hit the Lake Louise district later that afternoon.

Fay Nowlin, the district park warden for Bow Summit, was waiting for Bert to accompany him the rest of the way to the railway station at Laggan (Lake Louise). The distance from Saskatchewan River Crossing to Bow Summit is 44 km, but Bert stayed in a small line cabin used mainly for shelter when needed.

Bert had already made good time despite having to face more difficult travelling conditions once he reached the pass. He was tired and grateful when he saw Fay on the porch and the door open to the warmth within. Both Fay and Bert expected the storm would have blown itself out by morning, hoping for better travelling conditions. To their dismay, it was worse. But Bert was determined to go even if it meant only reaching the Hector Lake line cabin. Fay had an added reason to reach Banff, as Lila was his sister.

It had only been a day or so earlier when Bert answered the regularly scheduled radio call that came every morning at 8:00. He had been getting updates on the progression of the pregnancy, since it was Lila's first baby. The forestry phone line was put in when the line cabins were built, linking all the backcountry warden cabins together. The phone system was designed to allow headquarters to ensure everyone staying in the backcountry was still alive and healthy. It was amazing that a forestry phone even existed in that remote area of the park. Mostly it was used to order supplies, communicate travel plans and just plain provide some social interaction to relieve the solitary months the wardens spent in the bush.

The two wardens spent a restless night in the Bow Summit warden cabin feeding wood into the stove every few hours as the temperature dropped. They left as soon as it was light, strapped into their ungainly wooden skis, secured the cabin and then hoisted up their heavy packs and hoped they would make it to the train station at Lake Louise before dark. At least the next section was mostly downhill, and they made better time with two men to break trail. But the conditions were still difficult, and to Bert's frustration they spent another night out at the Hector Lake line cabin.

Bert Davies in army uniform
(JIM DAVIES COLLECTION).

Bert finally reached Laggan Station, where he hopped on the first train heading east to Banff. His wife, Lila, was staying on Cougar Street in her mother's house during the pregnancy, as Bert had been largely absent during her last trimester. But Bert did not stop long at the house; he went straight to the hospital, where he was relieved to find both mother and son doing well.

Before he left, however, they settled on the name Jim, which was of no consequence to the infant, who only cared about nursing, being warm and sleeping. He did not know that he would grow up surrounded by the scenic mountains that cradled the small town of Banff. At that time, Banff was connected to Calgary by the 1A Highway, which was not a major road. People who came to visit Banff back then found a small town whose principal attraction was the Banff Mineral Hot Springs and the

Banff Springs Hotel. But they may have been a bit intimidated by the dense surrounding wilderness that was a stone's throw from the edge of town. Black bears wandered freely throughout the town checking out the open garbage cans. Elk and deer, also casual residents, checked the yards for sweet edible flowers or settled for the rich lawn grass. Efforts to chase them off were not always successful.

Bert Davies was born in Edmonton's Royal Alexandra Hospital in 1907. His parents had a small farm near Vermilion where they made a living from grain crops and cattle. They had no running water aside from an outdoor well, no electricity or phone connection. Heat for the house came from wood cut and stacked in the fall, and light came from kerosene lanterns. They had no car – nothing short of a tank stood a chance against the primitive roads that turned to gumbo whenever it rained. But the Davieses were close friends with neighbours who had a car that they borrowed to make the bumpy ride to Edmonton.

As a child, Bert attended the one-room schoolhouse in Vermilion, which only taught elementary and junior high school classes. Most children were considered old enough to start working on the farm after grade 8 and had little use for higher education. From then on, they were educated in the art of running a farm.

Bert's dad, Hubert, was more open minded about the value of higher education, however, and decided Bert should at least get his high school diploma. Since that was not possible in Vermilion, he sent his son to finish high school in Banff while living with his uncle, chief park warden Jack Warren. It was a pivotal decision that would eventually lead to Jim's pioneering work as a helicopter pilot.

Bert liked the mountains and had good connections with the

park warden service through his uncle. It did not take much encouragement for him to apply for the job of park warden once he finished school. Banff was a tourist town where the main employment was either with the government or with a business tied to tourism. As a farm boy, Bert had the skills to work in the backcountry with horses and take care of a warden district. Though he was lonely at times, he loved the demands of keeping a well-managed backcountry district. He ensured the district cabin and line cabins were clean and ready for use, along with the trails. The trails were most important, as that was where the backcountry telephone lines usually ran. Too frequently, a tree would fall across the line, or the line would wear out. A lot of time was spent just keeping the line in repair.

With so much time spent in the bush, social activities were limited. Most of Bert's short time off was spent catching up with the family and having a drink at the King Edward Hotel with old friends. However, in the late 1930s, a bar was not the best place to meet girls, especially with the strict drinking laws of the time. The few mixed events in Banff townsite always seemed to be held when he was in the bush. Fortunately, the bars did allow young women to work as waitresses, and that was where he met Lila Nowlin.

Lila's parents, George and Amelda Nowlin, were originally from Salt Lake City in Utah but soon relocated to Idaho Falls, where they bought a small ranch and raised their children as Mormons. Finding land for a farm of their own was expensive, with most of the good land already settled. This precipitated their next move to Canada. In 1908 they joined a large group of 57 families who faced the same problem and were moving to Alberta, where farmland was cheaper. Another incentive to do this was to avoid the persecution that dogged fellow Mormons in the United States.

Canada passed the Homestead Act in 1872, aimed mainly at the prairies, which the government wanted to actively colonize to prevent it from being claimed by the United Sates. The Act gave a claimant 160 acres for free, charging only $10 as an administration fee. The only other requirement was to be over 21 years of age and show signs of developing the property within three years.

It was quite an expedition, with a train of 18 rail cars carrying the 57 families, their belongings and all the animals they could afford to take. Many of the group settled in different areas, but the Nowlins pressed on to Claresholm. Here they lived on a small farm where they raised four children: Floyd, Fay, Tim and Lila.

The farm was too small to make a good living, and when George had an opportunity to work as night watchman for the fire department in Banff in 1936, he took it. Accompanied by Lila and Fay, he rented a small house and settled into the Banff community until they moved to Calgary in 1955. Fay thought the best job in town was with the warden service and soon joined up. He became an accomplished skier and eventually taught winter survival techniques and skiing to American and British soldiers at the Columbia Icefield and Bow Summit.

Bert and Fay became good friends when they shared adjoining backcountry districts of Bow Summit and Saskatchewan River Crossing. They were adept at winter travel and would often go on long winter ski patrols throughout the district. Just getting in and out of their districts was a challenge. Bert's district cabin at Saskatchewan River Crossing was four arduous days from Lake Louise on skis in the winter. It was a bit shorter in summer when

Bert and Lila's wedding picture
(JIM DAVIES COLLECTION).

the road from Laggan Station to the summit became usable after the snow was gone. It was barely a road, however, and was a major challenge to truck horses over.

Neither Fay nor Lila embraced all the restrictions of their faith and had no qualms about smoking or drinking. Knowing little about the Church of Jesus Christ of Latter-day Saints, Bert was not put off by such lapses. He was probably more concerned about who else this lively young woman might meet, when he was in the bush for such long periods. Apparently, he managed to get to town frequently enough to catch her eye. With so few young, unattached women around, Bert decided he should marry her before someone else did.

Bert and Lila were married in 1937 and she was soon pregnant with Jim. Lila had grown up on a farm not far from Claresholm and was already a good rider. This self-reliant, independent spirit would manifest itself in Jim, who definitely took the "road less travelled" throughout his life.

Bert and Lila also made some special friends in the early years of their marriage when Lila joined him at the Crossing for the summer. Jim remembers visiting Silas Abraham, a Stoney (Nakoda) Chief who lived with his family downstream from the crossing on the Kootenay Plains. Silas was a small, peaceful man who was always glad to see them. When Silas went to Banff for supplies, he and his family would visit Bert and Lila at their warden cabin. Silas's wife would sit silently, patiently working on her latest creation of clothing made from moosehide while Lila served copious cups of tea to the men and Bert caught up with Silas regarding wildlife sightings or changes in the district. The trip to Banff was not one Silas made often, so Bert would pack in extra supplies in the summer in anticipation of Silas visiting his warden cabin. Silas and his wife loved canned food, especially tomatoes, and would give Bert unique handmade moosehide jackets, gloves and moccasins in exchange for the coveted food. Both men would think they got the better of a deal that was, in fact, mutually beneficial.

Jim spent summers growing up at the remote station. Lila enjoyed the summers there too and missed Bert when he stayed on in the winter. Jim, and later Tad, his younger brother, had more freedom than most parents would be comfortable with today. As a child, he found the environment around him was often his teacher. With nothing else to compare his life to, Jim does not remember any feeling of isolation, but he was happy when his brother Tad was born four years later.

Bert loved being a district warden, especially when his family was with him. At the end of any day or patrol he would always tell the kids about what he'd seen, remarking on spotting his favourite bear that day, or how many elk were feeding on the high

The Davies family in Banff
(JIM DAVIES COLLECTION).

alpine slopes. It was a rare day he saw nothing to remark upon. He also often took Jim with him, just for a ride on the front of his saddle, to a fire lookout or some other nearby destination.

The Icefields Parkway road connecting Lake Louise to Jasper began construction in 1931 and was completed in 1940. It ran right by the warden station at Saskatchewan River Crossing where Bert was stationed. With the construction, a small hotel and gas station were established on the other side of the river. Jim remembers getting into trouble when he crossed the narrow bridge above the North Saskatchewan River leading to the motel, which was too high for his mother's comfort. But, after a while, she gave up trying to temper her son, particularly after they put him to work pumping gas at the motel.

The time Jim's family spent at Saskatchewan River Crossing was cut short when the Second World War broke out and Jim's father was drafted into the army. Bert didn't get far, however, as he did not pass the physical due to kidney problems. Like most men not sent overseas, Bert was disappointed to find he was to remain in Ontario, teaching the troops to drive all kinds of vehicles, and hoping they wouldn't kill themselves before being deployed to Europe. He was not there long before he was transferred back to Banff as a guard to supervise a prisoner of war camp on the Morley Flats, just east of the mountains.

Lila and the children stayed at her mother's house in Banff after Bert was drafted. In 1943 Jim turned 5 and began schooling, starting with kindergarten. The move to Banff was fine for Lila and the boys, but when Bert was discharged from the army, he was not happy with the new situation. He joined Lila and the boys at her mother's house the first year, and then rented a house on Marmot Street. Bert was now a town warden, which was uninspiring as there was little to do but enforce the National Parks Act, which usually amounted to rounding up stray dogs. Bears were not a problem during the winter and did not cause much fuss with the locals in the summer. Townsfolk treated them as a nuisance and often just took a broom to them rather than call for help. Tourists were a little less prepared for serious encounters, but threat from bear attacks did not deter them from chasing the animals all over the place for a picture. But the main problem for Bert was an antagonistic relationship with Bruce Mitchell, the chief park warden.

Jim was surprised to be enrolled for kindergarten in the Mountain School, founded by Margaret and Henry Greenham in the mid-1920s. Margaret Greenham was a free thinker and ahead of her time. She believed learning consisted of more than the three Rs and encouraged outdoor activities as well as an interest in the arts and drama. The school expanded over the years, adding dormitory cabins to accommodate students from the rest of the province. It reached its greatest capacity

Mountain School, now Banff Centre

(JIM DAVIES COLLECTION).

following the war but closed shortly thereafter when the Greenhams retired in 1947.

Although the Mountain School had an excellent reputation (it is now part of the Banff Centre, and the Margaret Greenham Theatre is named after her), Jim could not figure out why he was in an all-girls' school. He wasn't sure if he wanted to don the official school uniform of green tunic, blazer and hat. As far as he was concerned, he would never fit in with this crowd. He was caught off guard on his first day at school when the students all assembled for a picture. Jim was the one standing all by himself trying to hide behind a tree.

To his relief, Jim only attended this school for kindergarten, and moved to the regular elementary school in Banff for grade 1. It's possible Jim was temporarily sent to the Mountain School to alleviate the overcrowding during the war.

One thing both Jim and George Capel, an early friend of Jim's, remembered was the elementary school principal, whose idea of discipline seemed particularly severe. He did not give the strap on the hand to the child who misbehaved, but rather applied it to the tender tummy – and it hurt like hell. But despite the discipline, Jim was happy to be among children his own age. He soon made friendships that lasted his entire life. John Derrick, Ian Nelson and George Capel all became members of the Banff Ski Runners, and later all three coached kids in skiing and eventually racing.

Another early friend of Jim's was David Neish. David was the nephew of the famous Bill Neish, who helped the RCMP in the apprehension of three fugitives from Saskatchewan in 1935. The outlaws were Russian Doukhobors who had already shot two RCMP officers when they were stopped on suspicion of robbery. They did not really have an escape plan; they simply drove west until they hit the east gate of Banff National Park. But they didn't even have two dollars to get into the park. By then a manhunt was under way and the fugitives were finally stopped just east of the gate, where a gunfight ended with two more officers killed. The three men then took off into the bush. One was shot that evening, and the next day Dale, an RCMP dog, was brought in to track the other two. As the day progressed, outraged citizens came in droves to help the police. The situation escalated when hand grenades and gas guns appeared. Once they heard a track was found by the dog, various small groups of volunteers combed the dense bush bordering the road. The RCMP tried to close the road before the scene turned to chaos and someone else got shot. In one group of searchers was Bill Neish, a Banff park warden at that time. With deadly aim he wounded the two remaining men, who soon died of their injuries.

Bill's story got around town, and time polished his image as the hero of the gunfight. Bill reported to Ottawa he'd been on patrol to the east gate and "shot two bandits." Parks officials in Ottawa could not understand how such an incredible incident only warranted three words, "shot two bandits." They asked for more details so Bill replied, "Snowing like hell."

Bill had a colourful history before he joined the warden service, having served in the Canadian Army during the First World War, and four years with the RCMP. One is left with the impression that Bill's parting of the ways from the RCMP was mutual – but not amiable. The warden service probably suited Bill better, being a less formal law enforcement unit that allowed members a lot of freedom in carrying out their duties. He was a loner and the warden service gave him lots of time to be alone.

The Neish family lived on Beaver Street, directly across the alley from Muskrat Street where Jim lived. Kids roamed the streets with little supervision in that gracious era when people left their doors open and did not worry about strangers. One day, David was cruising down the back alley and happened to look up to see Jim looking down from a loft in his family's garage. They "exchanged niceties" and Jim came down to engage in the social conformities of young children. Jim was David's first acquaintance in Banff, and their rapport turned into a lifelong friendship.

Jim and David were both active kids whose imaginations, and often daring escapades, kept their mothers happy to see them come home at the end of the day. One stunt they almost attempted would probably have put them in the hospital, if not the grave. David's relatives from Scotland had sent the family a wartime parachute. They were probably thinking his mother could use it to sew clothes for the family. Before she got the chance, though, David brought it over for Jim to see, with the grand idea they could hike to the top of Tunnel Mountain and jump off to find out if it really worked. They hauled the messy load of silk and strings to the highest part of the mountain and peered over the edge. Fortunately, one look at the cliff plummeting to the small town below gave them second thoughts. Besides, they could not figure out how to get the thing in the air as it lay in a white heap in the pines with not a breeze to even ruffle the light silk.

Another pastime for Jim and his friends that almost became a ritual was pestering the wildlife in town. In the early years, Banff residents were used to seeing bears, elk and deer wander freely throughout the town with an implicit understanding of "if you leave me alone, I'll leave you alone." That worked for most people as long as the tulips weren't eaten. The main attraction for bears and sometimes elk were the unprotected garbage cans left in back alleys.[1] The bears in town were fair game for the boys. Every Friday night, Jim and his buddies would roam back alleys, looking for bears with their heads in the light aluminum trashcans. It was great fun to run up behind them and give a swift kick to the black hind end sticking out of the battered cans.

A bear's response was predictable for the most part. Most bears would jump further in, then bolt down the alley until the can finally fell off.

On one occasion, though, the prank did not go as expected. The bear in question was in the alley behind the commercial enterprises lining Banff Avenue, at the Adrianne Restaurant. Forgetting the layout of the alley, the boys spooked the bear gobbling away on rich restaurant leavings. The bear took off as expected but ran the wrong way. It ended up trapped in a fenced-in area behind the restaurant.

Now the youngsters had a problem. The bear's only way out was back through the middle of his young tormentors not far behind him. The boys quickly realized their mistake but there was little they could do. Suddenly the bear spotted the open door that led to the kitchen. Without hesitation the bear charged into the kitchen that led to the restaurant.

Now thoroughly confused, the bear charged past cooks forced to leap onto countertops, and through the swinging doors to the dining area, where the patrons were eating dinner. One man had the presence of mind to comment, "The bear was only as high as the table."

The bear did a circuit of the crowded tables but retreated before the diners were all up in arms. The terrified animal had not bargained for this nightmare. He finally ran back past the cooks (who wisely had not moved) and out the open back door. The boys, by now, were long gone, hoping they wouldn't get caught.

The bear probably set a record getting out of town.

Though local residents were used to four-legged intrusions, animal presence became a real problem once tourists began to arrive in greater numbers. The park staff became less tolerant of habituated animals that kept them busy dealing with animal/human conflicts.

Two other diversions for the kids were Banff Indian Days in the summer and the Banff Winter Carnival in January. The Winter Carnival was especially fun during the dark cold days, so far from the months of summer. There was a lot to see and do, but one highlight for Jim was creating an ice sculpture of a seal juggling a ball, which won him first prize, despite competition from renowned artists like Rick de Grandmaison.

But for sheer excitement, nothing could beat grabbing the end of a rope attached to the saddle horn of an Indian pony, in a winter race down Banff Avenue put on by the Stoneys. As Jim remembers, there was a lot of bumping and wild swinging on the snow, and being plastered by snow, dirt and horse manure flung from the hooves of the galloping ponies. The first pony across the finish line with a kid still intact won the race.

The summer Banff Indian Days were just as anticipated as the Winter Carnival, and the whole town got involved. One memory lingers in Jim's mind: the Stoneys' drum dance they performed in their camps on the plain just north of town. The scene was lit by a dying sun and numerous bonfires. The flames flickered light on the beautifully decorated costumes of men and women dancing before their ceremonial teepees. The dancers, silhouetted against the dying light, flashed colourfully as darkness set in.

As Jim got older, downhill skiing became the highlight of his life, but he and his friends had to economize on lift tickets. The cost was two bits for six runs on the Norquay rope tow. The way David saw it, if they had to pay all the time, their skiing would barely last an hour. Instead, they rode the upper half of the rope tow by picking up a ride midway and stopped skiing before they reached the bottom and had to pay the ticket puncher. As their prowess and stamina grew, the kids often skied the runout gully that took them to the bottom of the ski hill road, then hitched a ride in a car or truck back to the top. Some days it took a while to get a ride.

When the kids couldn't get to the ski hill, they flew down a small ski jump they built near the old cemetery in town. As winter

Jim's early ski days at Mt. Norquay
(JIM DAVIES COLLECTION).

wore on, the jump became bigger and bigger, giving anyone interested in becoming an Olympic ski jumper an early opportunity to see if such a career was worth pursuing. The adults didn't
object as long as the kids stayed on the runout and didn't get
flipped onto any of the gravestones.

Skiing soon became a main event for many kids in town – one
of the big benefits of living in Banff. The kids were able to take
the bus from town up to Mt. Norquay, ski all day, then take the
runout down to the highway. From there they would trudge
home, often in the dark, with their skis over their shoulders.

Every Sunday, the Norquay operators held a race, either in

slalom, giant slalom or downhill skiing. Jim proved to be quite athletic and was soon winning most of the races.

Jim also skied at Sunshine ski hill, which was known to have excellent snow from early winter until late into the spring. The Sunshine road was closed to public cars, so skiers accessed the area via a bus from Banff's King Edward Hotel. Only the ski bus, staff and park wardens going to the Healy Creek warden station had access. This meant skiers had to make the last bus down or be trapped on the mountain. There was a ski-out trail that reached the warden cabin, but it was still a long trip back to Banff.

Taking the bus had its own perils, as the road passed through a number of avalanche paths en route to the village, but the ski operators set up a primitive warning system. A trigger device placed high in the avalanche starting zone sent a signal down to the road, causing a red light to flash so the driver could stop before entering the path of an oncoming avalanche. Sunshine Village had bulldozers on hand to clear the road, but it was rare to see the rush of snow plunge down the hill. Certainly, the system seemed to work, as there are no records of anyone being caught in these slides.

× × ×

By 1951, Bert's dislike of being a town warden and conflicts with the chief park warden had him looking around for another means to support his family. At that time, considerably more snow fell in Banff each winter than presently does, and most people shovelled their driveways almost every day. This job was time consuming and never really adequately done. Bert decided to buy a tractor with a front-end loader and fill this overlooked niche. Everyone told him he was crazy, that he was foolish to invest in expensive equipment. But that winter, the snow was exceptionally heavy, and work piled up, making Bert's business very profitable. The following summer he increased his operation, buying a cat and two trucks. It was the right time to get into the trucking business; Calgary Power had started building the Spray and Barrier dams and roads were being improved. This provided Bert with as much work as he could handle.

When Jim saw the tractor, he developed an instant fascination with machines and how to make them run. He had a knack for mechanics and spent hours fiddling or fixing the vehicles for maximum performance. By the time Jim was 16, Bert put him to work during the summer months. This love of machines was to be an important element of Jim's world for the rest of his life.

Jim was never a stellar academic student but managed well enough. One thing he was sure of: schoolwork was no competition for skiing or running a cat.

In his teen years, it was skiing that mattered the most to Jim, particularly after he went to the Canadian Championships held at Grouse Mountain, with future ski coach Doug Robinson, Jim and Patsy McKenzie and Wayne Ferguson, to race. At that time there was no recognized national ski team in Canada; the championship races simply sent the best skier from the various ski clubs across Canada to the competition. At 17, Jim won a silver and three gold medals and was considered the best junior skier in Canada. Ironically, he did not get the gold in the downhill race, his strongest event, as he was forced to come to a full stop partway down the course when a group of women wandered onto the course; but even with this handicap, he still placed second.

After a race

(JIM DAVIES COLLECTION).

Had there been a recognized national team to send to the Olympics in Europe, Jim's life might have taken a different course. He would have been a serious contender to join the Canadian Olympic ski team, founded only few years later.

2

A Glimpse of the World

Although Jim went through all the years of schooling required by the government, it did not seem to lead him into a future that attracted him. By grade 12, he had chosen no career. However, for a quiet and undemonstrative person, he was remarkably prone to spontaneously taking advantage of opportunities that appealed to him.

One afternoon, a casual conversation over coffee with John Derrick, with whom he had often skied, led Jim to radically alter his life's direction. John had made arrangements to ski in Europe and was leaving the next day, with the thought of going on to further travels. For some reason he had decided he wanted to see the Pope.

Without a second thought, Jim asked if he would like a companion. They agreed to go together, but Jim had some hustling to do, to line up his travel arrangements.

First, he told his parents he was going. Not only was he only 17 – and had never travelled much beyond Alberta and BC – but a trip to Europe meant pulling out of school without graduating. Jim was not surprised when his parents objected.

But Jim didn't care about academic achievement or attending university. He had worked for his father and living at home had enabled him to save most of his earnings. In the late 1950s, Europe was still amazingly cheap, and with care, Jim felt he could afford a few months there. One unexpected source of support came from Catherine Whyte,[2] who gave him $25 with the stipulation that he have a really good meal on her. With Catherine's support his parents reluctantly agreed, knowing Jim would probably go no matter what they said.

It took a few days for Jim to round up his gear and money, but John was willing to wait. The first leg of the trip was by train to Chicago, connecting to New York. These cosmopolitan cities were nothing like what they'd seen in Canada. After a few days in both Chicago and New York, they took a boat to Southampton, England, and then hopped a boat across the English Channel to France. Jim was more or less tagging along with John, whose destination was Wengen, Switzerland, which could only be reached by train. The whole trip was exciting for both of them.

Wengen was the epitome of a beautiful, picturesque Swiss mountain town, clinging high up on a mountainside, below the stunning peaks of the Oberland summits. The north face of the Eiger next to the Jungfrau and the Monarch were a few of the more dramatic peaks surrounding the town. The boys quickly found accommodation in the staff quarters of the Molitor ski boot factory, a short walk from the ski lifts that would spirit them to the many high cols that accessed ski runs to other small towns such as Grindelwald. They had unlimited skiing in great conditions that they took full advantage of. They could scarcely believe that all this skiing was available to them for a mere $24/month.

Jim's mastery of skiing accelerated with this daily exposure and he began to look at racing more seriously, entering the Lauberhorn downhill race, at that time considered one of the hardest in the world. In order to win the Lauberhorn, the skiers needed not only courage and ability to take risks, but perfect wax, technique and stamina. At over 4.4 km (2.7 mi.), this course remains the longest in the world.

Jim entered the Lauberhorn as a representative of Canada. Other countries participating were Switzerland, Austria, France, Italy and Germany. Jim's competition included world-class skiers, among them Toni Sailer from Austria, the legendary Olympic champion (who won). To Jim's credit, he came 18th out of 100 participants. Even after the Canadians began to send a national team over, this was a very good showing; it would be a while before the Canadians began to get better results.

What caught Jim's attention was how many pairs of skis Toni had brought to the start of the race. When he asked why, Toni's coaches said each set of skis was waxed for different conditions. Jim knew nothing about waxing skis, but soon realized waxing technique was a closely guarded secret from team to team. In fact, the skis were given different layers of wax for different parts of the hill. For the colder conditions found near the top, they used a colder gliding wax. As the skier approached the middle to bottom section of the course, warmer wax would be exposed, if the colder wax had worn off. It was the lack of mastery of this old art that kept the Canadians (and probably Americans) from doing as well as their European counterparts in the first years they went to the Olympics.

Though racing in the Lauberhorn was a high point of Jim's trip, another incident impacted him far more.

One day, the two young men took the train from Wengen to a pass between the Jungfrau and the Lauberhorn peaks to ski the Kleine Scheidegg, a popular ski area famous for incredible

Jim skiing in the Lauberhorn race
(JIM DAVIES COLLECTION).

views of the Oberland peaks. Impressive Swiss railway engineering allowed the train to take passengers to the pass between the Jungfrau and Lauberhorn peaks.

It was a beautiful day as Jim and John debated what to ski first. They were interrupted by the unfamiliar sound of an engine rising up from the valley. Jim was entranced at the sight of a small plane that abruptly came into view, heading straight for them. He could have been "toppled by a feather" as he watched how gently the pilot came in for a landing on this postage-stamp-sized patch of snow. The pilot edged into the pass and landed on a slightly elevated slope, testing it for stability. Jim had never seen anything like it but was keenly aware of the precision it took to complete such a delicate manoeuvre.

A group of people sprang from the plane, gathering their skis from an outside basket, and ran for cover. The pilot then swung sharply around and gracefully lifted off over the steep cliffs below and back to town. Jim was struck by the competence of the pilot and the difficulty of flying such a machine into such a tight place at that altitude. It was a challenge Jim could not ignore; he knew he had found a goal that offered more than the limited world of ski racing. Even though he was still young enough to improve his skiing, the sport in Canada was too far behind in training and support to reach the calibre of international competition.

×　×　×

By early spring, Jim was ready to return home. John had plans to touch the Pope and continue travelling in Europe, leaving Jim to head home alone by boat to Montreal. From there he took the train to Gray Rocks ski hill, close to Mont Tremblant north of Montreal, where he met up with Jerry Johnson, who ran the ski school there. His old friend George Capel was also there and together they found good accommodation at Gray Rocks.

Jerry asked Jim to help teach novices to ski – a job Jim did not like at all. He knew how to ski but had never taught anyone else and had no idea how to go about it. After six weeks, the snow was going and he'd had enough. One bright lining to it all, though, was the opportunity to train at Mont Tremblant for a downhill race. The Austrians were coming for the race, which was a significant event, as Canada was getting some recognition for the quality of its snow and ski hills. Jim didn't win the race, but he came very close.

With the ski season over, Jim drove back to Banff with Jerry Johnson and spent the next three years working for his dad. The government was twinning the Trans-Canada Highway and completing the Icefields Parkway, so Jim spent much of his time working out of Lake Louise. This was fine for him as he enjoyed the work and quickly reacquainted himself with his interest in machinery.

Also, Jim did not have to give up skiing, as the toe of Victoria Glacier still extended well into the valley and provided great skiing into the summer. A group of skiers could be seen traipsing up the trail on long summer evenings and on most weekends with their skis on their backs. It was a carefree time, when rules were loose, and the summer was beautiful. He lived in the present and did not worry too much about his future.

Home life in the Davies household was harmonious, and Jim and his younger brother, Tad, developed a bond typical for siblings in the days where the only entertainment was found outside. Nevertheless, Jim was not close to Tad in these years, for a number of reasons. The four-year age difference dictated who their friends were, which led to different pursuits. In their younger years, Jim was in Boy Scouts at the same time Tad was in Cubs. Also, when Tad was starting high school, Jim was off in Europe, a significant separation. And if Jim and Tad quarrelled, it was usually over Tad's smoking.

Part of Jim's attitude toward smoking may have come from an early experience with Jim's cousin Nelda Sharp. They were out picking berries on a hot summer day, when she produced some cigarettes. She teased Jim to try one, which she lit and smoked with ease, passing it to him. Although Jim's parents were both smokers, he took the butt as if it was a lit stick of dynamite. He warily puffed on what remained. He was mildly sick from the nicotine but had a violent reaction to the smoke. He flung the thing to the ground and, announcing it was terrible, asked, how could she smoke those things anyway?

Another reason for their lack of closeness might have been that Tad never picked up skiing the way Jim did, possibly because he could never keep up with Jim's success. Nelda Sharp recalls

Tad at 14
(COURTESY OF NELDA SHARP).

that Tad wanted to be as good a skier as Jim but just wasn't old enough to ski that well. There was a bit of hero worship on Tad's part, but also competition.

Nelda, closer to Tad in age, did not know Jim as well, but recalls a third reason: there was a big difference in their personalities. To Tad, Jim seemed aloof and always out with a small group of close friends or trying to earn money, collecting golf balls and selling them back to the golfers at a cut rate. Tad had a mischievous, outgoing personality and made friends easily. Nelda loved doing things with Tad, whose sense of humour made everything fun.

Colleen Coggins, a friend of Tad's who tagged along when she could,[3] remembers that Banff was quite cliquish in those days. The business crowd, a bit richer and advocating for change that would improve business, was different from the more reserved, underpaid government workers there to uphold the ideals of the national parks. School, though, broke down some of these social barriers and kids of similar age tended to stick together. Colleen did not engage in any of Tad's pranks, but she was aware of them.

By age 16, Tad was developing into a handsome young man with a winning smile and open personality that made him popular in school. Still, as he grew older, he always seemed to be under Jim's shadow, especially when Jim was winning all the big ski races. Banff was decidedly a ski town and took pride in turning out some of the best skiers in Canada through the Banff Ski Runners racing program.

Tad skied, but he was no star. He had to find his own individual path that did not always bring up a comparison with Jim. After some thought, he chose to join the navy. The navy took men as young as 16 with parental consent, so that was where he applied. Bert was proud of Tad's decision and supported him.

Tad was on top of the world with such encouragement from his family. He was finally on a course that had nothing to do with skiing and would allow him to become his own man with an identity separate from his brother and father. Just after turning 17, he went east, to Halifax.

Before he knew it, Tad was swabbing decks and other jobs on the ships in dry dock. The work was very demanding, leaving him exhausted by the end of each day. But after a month, he was doing whatever he could to avoid heavy work, feeling worse and worse as days went by.

He wasn't getting fit; he was getting sick.

The hard-nosed senior naval staff thought Tad was shirking his duty. They admonished him constantly to shape up and complete his assigned duties. When this proved impossible, he was given a dishonourable discharge and sent home.

When Tad returned to Banff, Lila took one look at him and knew something was radically wrong. She took him to the General Hospital in Calgary, where the doctor asked if Tad had been exposed to German measles (rubella) or scarlet fever when he was a baby. As in most small communities in the 1940s, vaccination was not mandated, and few people were aware of its importance. The doctor realized Tad had Bright's disease, a failure of the kidneys and other major internal organs, such as the liver and gall bladder, from exposure to measles as a boy. In Tad, the disease had progressed to the point where all his organs were failing. Nothing could be done but keep him as comfortable as possible.

Jim was working up north when he got the call from his parents telling him Tad was ill with an incurable kidney disease. Jim remembers this moment vividly, his memory flooding back to Tad getting accepted in the navy and how proud his father was. His brother had looked fine in the spring.

Jim returned home immediately to be with his brother, still finding it hard to believe Tad was dying. Sitting with Tad in the hospital room rocked Jim to his core. He could do nothing for his brother, wracked with pain. If the doctor was giving Tad pain medication it seemed to have no effect on his suffering.[4]

Tad's parents and friends stayed with him to the end, which he knew was coming. One of Tad's wishes was to see Nelda before he died. She lived north of Calgary with her husband and child and could not drive. Her husband refused to let her go, not realizing how important it was to her.

Bert was furious when he found out Tad had been given a dishonourable discharge from the navy. With the help of the doctor, he fought to have the discharge amended to "discharged for medical reasons."

But Tad did not linger long. By the end of the week he was dead at the age of 18, and his mother was sunk in a grief that she would endure until she died. Bert bore the loss more stoically, somehow burying it deep enough to support his wife and get restitution for Tad.

The funeral was held in Banff, and Nelda was able to attend along with other family relatives. Nelda felt Lila never got over the loss of her son. Whereas Bert could throw himself into his business and Jim returned to the demands of becoming a pilot, there was no escape for her.

× × ×

When Jim returned from Europe, he put aside any thought of returning to school. His dad, however, appreciated the determination his own father had shown when it came to education, and was soon nagging Jim about finishing his schooling, so Jim headed for the Southern Alberta Institute of Technology (SAIT) in Calgary. He was at the registrar's office to pick up an application for an electronics certificate when two very pretty young women joined him in line. After they left, Jim asked the fellow behind the desk what they were applying for. He replied, "commercial art." Jim looked at the man for a minute, then said, "Give me that form." He filled it out and trotted after the girls. He now reflects that if he'd arrived half an hour later, he would have become an electrician.

Since Calgary was too far to commute to from Banff, Jim had to find accommodation in the city, which he found in a small basement suite. In the late 1950s, Calgary was not the cosmopolitan city it is today; the culture was western, with an unsophisticated view of the world. For Jim, who had been exposed to cities like Chicago, New York and Marseilles, which he visited when not skiing at Wengen, the only real attraction outside of school was the Calgary Flying Club – though the girls did turn out to be a lot of fun. But Jim still missed the mountains and went home to ski on holidays, weekends and winter breaks.

One of the people with whom Jim skied in Banff was Eddie Amann, who was instrumental in Jim's early flying carrier.

Eddie was part of the European migration to Canada that started soon after the end of the war. Those who came from the Alps (Switzerland, Germany, Italy and Austria) tended to head for the Canadian Rockies, where they felt at home. These immigrants brought a new level of mountaineering and skiing skill to Canada that ultimately led to a more European approach to mountain rescue.

Eddie was a qualified mechanic, but he did not qualify for immigration unless he put down "farmer" as his occupation. This was a surprise to Eddie, who thought most countries would be crying for trained mechanics. He was certainly no farmer. He arrived at Quebec City, with his skis, boots and poles, intending to take the train to Calgary and thence to the mountains, but to his surprise his ticket took him to Edmonton, where there were no mountains in sight. The trip across Canada impressed him with the vastness of the country, and he worried the mountains might be a long way from Edmonton.

There was no job waiting for him in Edmonton, but through luck he met a farmer who needed a hired hand. The farm was near Drayton Valley, which, to Eddie's disappointment, had only low, tree-covered hills and flat open fields. One of the first things the farmer's wife asked was, "Can you milk a cow?"

Eddie stayed on the farm, where he was employed in all kinds of jobs, got to know the family well and worked hard to learn English. Their youngest daughter, Freda, teased him about being taller than him and wondered why he'd lugged a set of skis all the way from Austria. The young Freda would meet him again when she moved to Banff with her husband, Heinz Odenthal, who ran a service station there. When she thought back to the time Eddie spent with the family, she could see the connection. All Eddie wanted was to do was get to the mountains. Through age-old supplementary communication, Eddie stayed on, hoping to get to the mountains after the haying season.

When Eddie figured out the geography of Alberta and picked up some English and a bit of cash, he announced he wished to work in the mountains. Freda's dad offered to drive him to Edmonton. Upon reaching the highway west of Edmonton, her dad felt Eddie would have trouble getting much farther on his own and decided to drive him west, to Edson. Once they got there, they could see the foothills leading into the mountains beyond. Again, Freda's father thought he might not get a ride very easily and eventually drove him all the way to Jasper. It was probably the farthest he'd been from the farm, but it was worth it just to see the mountains for the first time.

The irrepressible young Austrian soon found work in Jasper at Papa George's Mountain Motors garage, fixing taxis and Volkswagen vans, despite being hampered by his skimpy knowledge of English. Working at Mountain Motors forced him to polish up his English, which he picked up more easily with other mechanics with their common knowledge of machinery. Once the vans were running each evening, he would take midnight tours to Edith Cavell Tea House, Maligne Canyon and Jasper Park Lodge.

In the early 1950s, the Marmot Basin ski hill had not yet been established, so Eddie had to contend with ski-touring near Whistlers Mountain, where there was a rope tow.[5] This was popular with the locals, whom he impressed with his advanced ability to ski. It was also a great way to meet people and work on his English "ski speak."

Eddie liked Jasper and the people he worked with, but his objective had always been Banff, where he felt the community was more supportive of the ski industry. When he finally met two fellows from Banff, his English was good enough to convey to them that his real desire was to move there. The fact that he had lugged his skis, boots and poles all the way from Austria impressed his new friends. But timing is everything. They informed him that the Banff Chairlift Corporation had been given the go-ahead to build ski lifts at Norquay and Sunshine. Furthermore, the projects would be starting that fall and they were now in the process of hiring men for the job. With his improved English, Eddie wasted no time getting to Banff even if it meant going via Edmonton and Calgary.

Eddie had no problem finding work on the construction crew building lifts at Mount Norquay, until it got too cold to work.

He followed this up with a winter job at Sunshine, maintaining the Snowcats[6] and Bombardiers used to keep the road free and haul people to the top of the ski runs. Though the lifts had not been built there yet, a day lodge had been established to serve food, and it was here that Eddie became friends with Jim – then a high school student – who worked as a bus boy in the cafeteria. It wasn't long before the two found common ground in their fascination with engines. Eddie had more skiing experience than Jim and they skied together when not working. Jim particularly benefited from this association, as the best way to become a good skier is to ski with someone better than you. This early mentorship helped Jim to win races and he was soon one of the best junior skiers in Canada.

When the highway construction work was finished the following spring, Eddie headed to Whitehorse, where he hoped to find one of the high-paying jobs rumoured to be in abundance in the North. But he was unable to find work in Yukon, so it was back to Jasper and his old job with Papa George.

One thing Eddie cradled in his heart was a secret passion to fly airplanes. He never spoke about it, however, because the likelihood of that becoming a reality seemed like a pipe dream. But he was in a young, emerging land that was just beginning to crack open the doors to opportunity. Not long after returning to Jasper, he was sent out to the Palisades located east of the townsite to pick up the crew flying helicopters for the Trans Mountain Pipeline that ran from Edmonton to Vancouver. He had observed helicopters flying low through the mountain passes but had no idea what they were doing. Eddie could hardly contain his excitement when he had the opportunity to get close to one of the helicopters parked near the fuel pumping station at the Palisades and ask the men what they were doing. Apparently, they flew along the pipeline looking for gas leaks, which could be detected by swarms of flies attracted to the methane. Methane gas is also given off by decomposing animals, which helps the fly locate the carcass.

The pilots flying for Okanagan Helicopter made the most of their stay in Jasper, and parties in their motel were lively, especially if other pilots were working in the area. Eddie was invited to some of these parties, as he made friends easily and had a great interest in helicopters.

With his foot in the door after getting acquainted with the pilots, Eddie had no qualms about asking the men how to get a job flying helicopters. It may have surprised them to get such a question from a young man newly arrived from Austria and struggling with the language, but they took him seriously enough to ask their boss if Okanagan Helicopters was looking for pilots – then assured him the company was definitely hiring. All he had to do was get to Vancouver. Becoming a helicopter pilot was beginning to look more complicated than Eddie expected. But flying helicopters was new and exciting and could easily turn into a lifelong occupation.[7]

Eddie solved the problem of getting to Vancouver by hitching rides on the Canadian National Railway (CNR). He had already made friends with the engineers on the trains and asked their advice on how best to get to Vancouver. Despite the fact that Jasper was in a national park, it was primarily a railway town. At the engineers' invitation, he rode in the caboose to Kamloops, and from there he got a ride to Vancouver. He had the address and a contact name for Okanagan Helicopters, but the promised assurance of jobs waiting was not quite accurate. In fact, they were not hiring pilots at all – even qualified ones. This did not discourage Eddie. He'd been a certified mechanic in Austria and suggested they hire him as apprentice mechanic to become licensed in Canada. It was fortunate that Eddie liked the work, as it took a few years to get his licence.

Slowly, the demand for pilots started growing as big exploration companies began to realize helicopters could be put to many uses. Eddie was encouraged to obtain his fixed-wing private licence, enabling him to move on to obtaining a commercial fixed-wing pilot's licence – a prerequisite for helicopter training. Okanagan was behind him and leased him a fixed-wing plane to fly for the company. This gave him a chance to make money while accruing the necessary flying hours to get his commercial licence. The government also wanted more pilots and sponsored a program of donating $200 to the required $450 needed to pay for the licence.

Most of Eddie's flying was done in northern British Columbia, where he made friends with a helicopter pilot flying a Bell 47 with dual controls. The pilot asked him if he wanted to try it out for an hour. That hour led to 30 more, and by the time he got back to Vancouver, Eddie was prepared to write the exam for his helicopter licence.

During this time, Eddie had kept up his skiing at Grouse Mountain and was there when Jim – now a high school senior – was winning most of the alpine ski races during the Canadian National Championships. Eddie was not surprised at how well Jim was doing, as he was already one of the best skiers in Banff when Eddie first met him. When they got together to catch up, Jim was surprised to learn that Eddie was working on qualifying as a helicopter pilot. At that point,

Jim was dedicated to skiing rather than flying, little anticipating that his goals would change – though he was interested in both flying and helicopters. He was intrigued that Eddie, who had immigrated with very little money, was making strong headway in a new field after overcoming a significant language barrier, showing Jim what could be done if you truly wanted something.

Eddie did get his commercial fixed-wing licence and moved on to flying geologists in northern Alberta and Saskatchewan. It was good money and gave him many qualifying hours as a helicopter pilot, but like a boomerang he always came back to the mountains – which, to Eddie, meant Banff. During this period, Eddie made enough money, with the help of another pilot, to buy a Norseman (fixed wing) from Pacific Western Airlines (PWA). The two returned to Calgary and did well flying on varied contracts out of that city.

At the same time, Eddie was also flying helicopters for Bullock Wings & Rotors. This was where Eddie wanted to be, simply because this company was the most experienced in flying helicopters in mountainous terrain. In order to do so, however, he had to take an advanced course in mountain flying from Evan Bullock in Banff. Another friend realized this meant a lot of driving for Eddie, as he was living in Calgary, and offered to let him use his cabin on Ghost Lake. This suited Eddie to a T. When he completed the course, he kept working for Bullock Helicopters. When he was in Banff he would run into Jim (who was working for Bert after his return from Europe), and soon they began skiing together again on Victoria Glacier on the weekends.

Jim was always interested in Eddie's flying career and jumped at the chance when Eddie asked him if he would like to come to the Ghost Lake cabin and take a ride in the helicopter. Eddie could see Jim leaning toward a career in flying and felt the experience would give him a real idea of whether or not it was for him. They flew to the eastern slopes of the Rocky Mountains, where Eddie repeatedly landed as high as he could, giving Jim the full measure of the helicopter and what becoming a pilot entailed.

In his quiet way Jim took it all in and thanked Eddie for the experience. Not knowing exactly how Jim felt, Eddie mentioned that Jim could drop by the Calgary airport where a group of mechanics were overhauling a helicopter. The Calgary Flying Club was also sponsoring a day to take people up for a flight in a fixed-wing aircraft.

When Jim came into town, he decided to take Eddie up on his offer. It was a clear day and the club members were indeed taking passengers up on a recruitment blitz to bump up their membership. Jim flew over Calgary and out to the mountains, which were spectacular from the cockpit. It was his first flight in a plane, and Jim was captivated. This was what he wanted to do, and upon landing he immediately signed up to take flying lessons. Everything about flying was thrilling: the freedom of the sky, the beauty of clouds mingling with the land below and the challenge of mastering a machine that required his complete attention. The image of the delicate precision flying he witnessed in Europe had never left him. It took him away from everything going on below and became a world unto itself.

Jim gave his full attention to flying and soon had put in his 35 hours needed to obtain his private flying licence. But he did not want to fly just for his own pleasure. He wanted to get into flying permanently as an occupation. After flying with Eddie in the helicopter, becoming a helicopter pilot became his ultimate objective.

Before he could move on to helicopters, Jim had to get his commercial licence in a fixed-wing aircraft. But once he had his private pilot's licence, Eddie came up with another proposal.

They were at the hangar one afternoon when Jim started talking about getting his commercial licence, which required 200 hours of flying time plus an additional $1,500 to be paid to the flying club. Eddie pointed to a small Piper Super Cub, up for sale for $3,000. Eddie could see the commercial value in partnering with Jim and offered to pay for half the airplane. There was easily enough work around to keep Jim busy. As long as the plane was in the air, they were making money.

This seemed to be a pretty good deal for Jim, as he could earn enough to pay for the licence and get his 200 hours in as well. The north was opening up with the improvements made in airplanes and helicopters, giving geologists much greater access to areas rich in minerals. By 1961, Jim was making regular flights in their plane in northern Saskatchewan around Buffalo Narrows and Lac la Ronge.

Eddie was still flying helicopters for Bullock Wings & Rotors and mentioned to Evan Bullock that Jim would be a good candidate as a helicopter pilot. Jim was happy with this even though he would have to start out as a swamper, slinging drilling mud to drill sites on the confluence of the Peel and Mackenzie rivers at Fort McPherson in the Northwest Territories. Jim was already working hard with Eddie in the Cub, putting in long days where the sun always shone. It paid off. Evan Bullock was impressed with Jim's work ethic and, knowing Jim wanted to fly helicopters, offered him a job for three years, to pay off his training time. It was another fortuitous opportunity that would give Jim a lot of flying time, most of it up North.

×   ×   ×

Jim was still a long way from getting his 200 hours for a commercial fixed-wing licence when he met Hans Gmoser – a man who was to have a big impact on Jim's future as a helicopter pilot.

But there was no way to foresee the opportunity it would bring him when, on a soggy day, Jim drove to the airstrip in Banff and saw a car in the ditch blocking the muddy road. Two men stood by the car, trying to figure their way out of the dilemma. Both men had broken legs and were hobbling around with heavy casts and ineffectual crutches.

The two men were Hans Gmoser and Leo Grillmair.

Jim didn't ask about the broken legs as he helped the two get their car back on the road, but he later observed, "Hans always seemed to have a broken leg." This inauspicious introduction would lead to years of collaboration in the not-yet-founded heli-ski industry.

Hans Gmoser and Leo Grillmair were part of a wave of young men coming from Austria hoping to get a new start after the war in Canada's barely explored mountains. Most of these men who gravitated to the mountains brought with them a high standard in mountaineering and skiing.

In the late 1940s, it was Leo who was the original visionary, seeing nothing but poverty in war-torn Europe, as opposed to the advertised opportunities in Canada. Canada was looking for

Hans Gmoser
(KATHY CALVERT COLLECTION).

good tradesmen and skilled professionals but was rather disorganized in employing them once they arrived.

Leo had already made arrangements to emigrate when he ran into Hans in their hometown of Traun, Austria, near Linz. They were already good friends from school days, and he suggested Hans come too. Hans did just that, a month later. Like Eddie, both wound up in Edmonton, disappointingly nowhere near the mountains. Neither had any money or prospects or spoke any English. Times were tough.

At a particularly low point, the two remembered that an old

Jim and Hans in front of plane
(JIM DAVIES COLLECTION).

friend, Franz Dopf, had an uncle living in Edmonton. They found him through the phone book and were warmly welcomed and treated to food straight from the old country. Uncle Louie became their sponsor. To the pair's delight, both found jobs (Leo as a plumber, Hans as an electrician) and were able to buy some skis, boots and poles. This allowed them to ski at the small hill located above the Saskatchewan River. Leo's joy was so great he could not help showing off to three girls and immediately ran into a tree, becoming the first of the pair to break his leg. It was a very serious break that threatened permanent disability. They had no medical insurance and Hans was barely able to make enough money to see him through his convalescence.

When Leo was well enough, the two moved to Calgary, where they again found employment. But more significantly, they found the mountains. The mountains were close enough to get to in a day and still get back to Calgary at night. But Hans had no reason to stay long in Calgary other than to make money. During the time he was there, he became acquainted with the local climbing clubs and met people who would have a big influence in his life.

Though Leo continued with his plumbing job, Hans made his way to Banff and began making lifelong connections and friends. One of his first friends was Lizzie Rummel ("Baroness of the Rockies"), who hired Hans to work at her small cabin at Assiniboine. Through her he met "Smitty" Gardner, a doctor from Calgary and father of Don Gardner, who would eventually work for Hans at the Alpine Club of Canada's Stanley Mitchell Hut in Yoho National Park. Before long, Hans was working for the Alpine Club[8] and making his mark as a climber on tough new routes in the Canadian Rockies. When Hans needed help, he called on Leo to join him in a partnership that would last the rest of his life.

Hans guided for the Alpine Club of Canada in the summer months, but he was keen on expanding his guiding into winter with ski trips to various ACC huts.[9]

In 1960 Hans decided to undertake the daunting ski traverse of the Great Divide from Lake Louise to Jasper. An earlier attempt in 1954 had failed, and it was becoming a grail to the new breed of climbers and skiers. Most of this country was untouched by mountaineers. Hans asked Jim to fly him over the route to research the problems they faced and where to put food caches for the team. Jim and Hans then dropped the well-packed food parcels, so essential to the success of the trip, from the air.

Jim and Hans practised these air drops on Lake Minnewanka, thinking water might resemble snow-packed icefields. It is interesting that they dropped the load into water, which acts like a solid surface when objects are dropped on it from any height. They had a large pole attached to the well-sealed caches but needed to know what altitude would be optimal for the bundle to land upright, so the flag at the end of the pole would be visible.

Dropping these caches meant Jim would have to fly in mountainous terrain with which he was not familiar, contend with erratic weather and scout out how low he could fly without losing too much power to get out of tight valleys.

Jim's first flight with Hans to scout out the route and find suitable locations for food drops was a survival challenge in itself. They flew the route in February[10] in extremely low temperatures. Both men had to bundle up in sleeping bags just to handle the –30 Celsius in the unheated cockpit. The flight took five hours and Hans could barely stand up once they were on the ground again. The other problem Jim had was how to get the tightly packed supplies out of the plane without losing control. The solution was to attach a bomb rack to the undercarriage of the plane, which they loaded with supplies placed in ammunition boxes.

Jim was learning a lot about mountain flying and would soon be pioneering the skills of landing on snow-covered glaciers where vertical reference was difficult to establish. Landing was especially difficult when encountering unknown snow conditions. Triangulation, using compass and map to pinpoint the drops, was not very precise, and finding a lone flag on a vast, crevasse-strewn glacier was a challenge in itself.

Hans flew with Jim on seven trips to drop food caches (which included liberal amounts of rum), ensuring the pole was visible. One drop was at Fortress Lake, where they had the luxury of landing, but the snow was a lot deeper than it looked from the air and the plane bogged down. In order for them to fly out, Hans was forced to push on the struts to start the plane moving and then run alongside until Jim gave him the nod to jump in.

The expedition to traverse the Great Divide was not a success (which Hans took personally), but Hans had found a talented pilot living virtually next door, who would become a good friend and be invaluable when he went forward with his ski guiding enterprise.

Though Hans was depressed from what he considered a major setback, he typically forced himself back to work – but this time he made it more fun. In the back of his mind, he was looking for ski territory to set up a base camp. He envisioned guests coming in for a week to do daily tours in spectacular country.

The first place he considered was Canoe Glacier in the Cariboo Mountains below Mt. Sir Wilfrid Laurier and its surrounding peaks near Valemount, BC. He enlisted Jim's help again to fly in a group of good friends at the top of their form to a camp set up on the glacier. This was also the first time Hans (in a cast, recovering from a broken leg) geared a trip for filming.[11] Probably against doctor's orders to rest, Hans insisted on hobbling around to do much of the camera work himself. He wrapped the cast in a big mukluk fitted to a short ski.

Jim was eager to fly the group in, as he could indulge in his passions for skiing, flying and exploring the mountains. It took him several flights to get the skiers and camp gear in, but once

McConkey jumping plane
(JIM DAVIES COLLECTION).

everything was established, Jim brought out his own skis and settled down to a week of fine skiing with the other stars of Hans's show. He would be skiing with Nancy Greene, future Olympic champion; her twin sister Elizabeth; Jim McConkey, an iconic ski pioneer; and Nancy Holland from the US national ski team.

Hans took some spectacular shots of the skiers making quick short tracks down the wickedly steep slopes off Sir Wilfrid Laurier, which they had also climbed. Despite this, McConkey decided to liven things up even further by building a long ramp to jump the plane. The cherry on the cake for the film came when Hans captured the famous shot of McConkey sailing over Jim's Piper Super Cub.

× × ×

Jim was always careful to keep any plane he flew in good shape, but he was also flying during a period that had far fewer restrictions,

Piper Super Cub on Wawa Ridge
(JIM DAVIES COLLECTION).

either by Parks Canada or the Department of Transport (DOT). If our present-day paranoia about liability had been in place, the authorities would probably have prosecuted him under the National Parks Act or just thrown him in jail for landing in questionable places. Some of Jim's adventures were probably done on impulse – surprising his fellow passengers.

On one occasion George Capel was caught off guard when Jim decided to land on Wawa Ridge on the boundary of the Sunshine ski area.[12] The weather was good, and the ridge just seemed too enticing not to try a landing there. Unfortunately, Jim had not told the lodge he was flying in and no one had cleared the landing area. Jim lined up the plane and flew in low to make a perfect landing. He came to a sudden stop, however, as the snow was fresh and deep. The plane settled into the snow like a hen on a nest. Jim and George got out and looked over the situation. They wiggled the wings a few times until it became apparent the plane was not going to budge without help.

With a shrug, the two men set down off the ridge in the deep snow to Sunshine Lodge. From there Jim got a ride back to Banff and picked up a more appropriate set of airplane skis. Jim knew the fellow driving Sunshine's snow machine, who was happy to help out. He hauled Jim and George back up to the plane and soon Jim had the plane refitted on skis, though they still had a lot of snow to tramp down to make a runway to ensure liftoff. George recalls, "Jim waved goodbye as he sailed off for Banff, minus one passenger to lighten the load."

Jim liked the challenge of landing in high places. He even managed to touch down on Deception Pass (on the way to Skoki Lodge). It was too precarious to stay long, and after touching down he immediately flew back out again. His only regret was not having had a camera to take a picture of the plane on the pass.

After Hans Gmoser's expedition to Canoe Glacier, the Austrian settled on Little Yoho as a base for his ski touring trips, and Jim flew the supplies in – again dropped from the air. He was gaining recognition as a pilot and soon picked up more business. Being located in Banff was a great advantage as he knew the local people, but more importantly, they did not have to bring in a machine from Calgary, cutting the costs significantly. It was not long before Jim was flying supplies to Mt. Assiniboine for the Stroms,[13] and into Skoki Lodge for Ray Legace. He always found the softest snow to absorb the shock; Leo marvelled that one drop included fresh eggs that never even suffered a crack.

Flying his Piper Super Cub had given Jim a lot of experience in mountain flying, but his heart was set on being a helicopter pilot. With a helicopter, he could land on high, small summits impossible for an airplane. When Evan Bullock said he would train Jim for free if he worked for Bullock Helicopters for three years subsequent to completion of the course, his answer was a resounding, but undemonstrative, yes.

3

Birth of Heli-Skiing in the Bugaboos

By 1961, Jim knew his future would be in flying, either planes or helicopters, and he dropped out of his fine arts studies at SAIT. On November 24, he began his training with Evan Bullock.

Through his own interest in machinery, he was well aware that flying a helicopter was nothing like flying a plane. His experience with fixed-wing aircraft would help him out mainly through what he'd learned about mountain flying. When asked what flying a helicopter entailed, he replied, "Five things." It was like trying to rub your stomach, pat your head and balance three balls in the air at the same time. Just to look at a helicopter in those days made people feel like they were taking to the air with nothing to protect them other than the gossamer exterior of the machine and the skill of the pilot. Any change in the wind or airlift bounced the small craft around, especially dangerous during complicated manoeuvres or when working in tight spaces.

The pilot has five basic movement and steering controls: two hand levers called respectively the Collective and Cyclic Pitch, a throttle, and two foot pedals. Most manoeuvres a pilot executes involve a complex interplay among these disparate controls, which is why flying a helicopter requires such skill and concentration. The helicopter has much greater versatility in function, particularly evident in rescue missions. But this versatility comes at a price: helicopters are mechanically more complex than planes, and thus more prone to failure, demanding constant mainten-ance, and are more expensive to operate.

The first helicopter Jim flew was the Bell 47G2. It had a low-powered piston engine that did not provide the lift future turbine engines would. The instrumentation was also not as well set up as it is on today's modern helicopters, and it took a lot of concentration to determine speed and direction while monitor-ing weight and fuel consumption. The pilot simply adapted to the limitations. As Jim would say, flying the early lightweight, piston-driven helicopters took a lot more skill than is required on modern helicopters.

Jim began his training with Evan Bullock by flying slow move-ments above the ground under the watchful eye of his instructor, to get the feel for ground effects. Once Evan was comfortable with Jim's progress, they moved on to more complex challenges such as hovering turns, auto rotation, takeoffs and landings on tighter, more difficult terrain. By January 16, 1962, Jim records taking his first one-hour solo flight, mostly hovering and fly-ing low to the ground at the airport. As winter approached, Jim tackled even more complicated flying, including approaches to ridges, flying riverbeds and manoeuvring in tight spaces. Evan emphasized perfecting autorotation landings, which enable the pilot to land safely if the engine quits. This manoeuvre requires gaining downward speed to keep the air turning the rotors, and then flaring to maximize control just prior to setting the ma-chine down. It's not unlike pushing a car that won't start until it's going fast enough to pop the clutch to turn the engine over.

Evan was training another man, from Quebec, alongside Jim who may not have taken the training quite to heart. While Jim was flying up north, the Frenchman impulsively decided to visit his girlfriend south of Calgary. She was staying in a motel when he decided to make an impressive landing in front of her unit. Unfortunately, it was a bit too impressive when he misjudged the length of the rotors and hit the building, totalling the helicopter.

Jim was supposed to go to work for Bullock once his training was finished, but the helicopter they'd assigned him had been demolished by the amorous Frenchman. Jim Lipinski from Spartan Helicopters heard Jim was looking for a job, and with a great recommendation from Evan Bullock, Spartan hired him. Jim enjoyed working for Spartan, which he did for a year, before returning to Bullock. Most of the work was in the short summer months in the North, where his first job was flying geologists on forays from a camp near the small town of Tungsten. The camp provided individual cabins and 16 Chinese cooks to prepare food, which Jim particularly enjoyed.

The geologists, of course, were looking for tungsten. Jim was flying a Bell 47G2 with a weight (1065 kg) and altitude limitation (5,000 ft.), over the Selwyn Mountains, which were rugged enough to challenge any pilot. The most promising terrain was up the Flat River that runs into the Nahanni River, north and west of Nahanni Butte. This is rugged, mountainous country with few places to land. Because of the ceiling limitation, their access to the higher mountains near the headwaters of the Flat River was restricted. But the country was spectacular, the food and accommodations well beyond par, and the pay was good.

After flying for Spartan, Jim went back to Bullock Helicopters, with whom he would fly for eight years. Bullock was known for training the best mountain pilots in Canada during the 1960s and 1970s. Though they started out flying geological exploration crews in the North, the company was the first to purchase a turbine-powered helicopter, allowing them to fly deeper into mountainous terrain with greater loads.

×   ×   ×

During his years with Bullock, Jim continued to fly his plane into Assiniboine and huts in the Banff area, the most common job being flying in food drops. His trips to Assiniboine often involved flying in old friends like Ken Jones and Lizzie Rummel, who had a cabin in there. One trip with geologists took him into Drummond Glacier, which he records as his highest fixed-wing plane landing (at that time), at 10,000 ft. These local jobs allowed him to accumulate a lot of hours toward his commercial licence, and on March 22, 1962, he and Eddie Amann purchased a Cessna 180 with skis and wheels.

That year, he flew Erling Strom and his daughter (who had just returned from a lengthy stay in Mexico) to the lodge at Assiniboine. Jim was stunned when he saw Siri Strom approach the plane for the first time. She was one of the most beautiful women he had ever met. The Mexican sun had given her skin a golden glow that enhanced her long dark hair with one silver streak highlighting her face. She had gone to school in Lausanne, Switzerland, and spoke French fluently. She also had a respectable handle on Spanish, and of course her native Norwegian. But Jim was entranced with her vivacious charm, worldliness and spontaneity. She embraced life and set few limits on enjoying the moment.

It wasn't long before Jim and Siri were seeing more and more of each other, despite his erratic flying schedule and her commitment to help her father run Assiniboine Lodge in the summer

Siri Strom formal portrait 1963
(MORGAN DAVIES COLLECTION).

months. Jim got along well with Erling and was always welcome there. The main lodge had a European decorative touch, with a large fireplace and deep chairs that made it feel like home. When guests were not overrunning the place, it could be a sanctuary.

Besides Siri, another rival for Jim's time was Hans Gmoser. Once Jim had his licence to fly helicopters, Hans employed Jim for another trip to the Cariboos, with a group of skiers. They made camp on Canoe Glacier, close to where they had been with the airplane. Jim stayed in camp with Hans, and when the weather cleared, he flew Hans to the broad, flat summit of Mt. Sir Wilfrid Laurier. Skiing from the top of this mountain was challenging, with very steep slopes and open crevasses, making for an exciting film shoot.

Hans used the footage he captured to create a film that focused a lot of attention on using a helicopter able to take skiers to the top of the mountain, eliminating hours used up by climbing to the top of ski runs. Jim wryly remembers that he filmed much of the footage himself as, again, Hans had a broken leg.

Although Hans Gmoser has been given credit for initiating heli-skiing (with Jim's help), he did not originate the idea. The concept actually came from geologist Art Patterson in 1963. Art was an avid skier who spent his summers working in the North. As a geologist, he spent a considerable amount of time looking for rock outcrops and landforms that showed promise of various minerals. His work demanded a lot of flying in helicopters and he had a feel for their versatility (and limitations). Recognizing that many helicopters sat idle in hangars for the winter, burning up money for storage fees, he wondered if they could not be put to use taking people into backcountry areas too difficult to access on touring gear. He realized he knew a lot about helicopters and mountains but little about snow; but he did know Ethan Compton, who ran Premier Cycle and Sports, and who also sold ski and climbing gear. Compton was in touch with the climbing community, so when Art asked who the best guide for this adventure would be, Compton recommended Hans.

When Art talked to Hans about this idea, Hans was puzzled but intrigued. It had never occurred to Hans, who had little helicopter experience, to use them to fly people into a ski area, let alone fly the skiers up the mountain repeatedly, so they could ski down. It went against his principle of being in the mountains, away from all the clutter of the world. It was one thing to be dropped off in a spectacular setting but using this noisy aircraft every day would eliminate that which Hans considered as important as the skiing: the slow, methodical touring up the mountain. The climb was an experience in itself, allowing the skier to get a feel for the snow conditions. He also felt the effort the client made to reach as summit or high col made the run down that much more special.

But Hans's business sense nagged at him. It was actually a brilliant idea if they could pull it off. He met Art for coffee to flesh out the details, conveniently when Associated Helicopters was having a training day and had one helicopter available for a quick tour. Pilot Murray McKenzie agreed to fly them around to look for suitable terrain.

Art originally thought they could locate in the national park in the Sunshine area. This idea was immediately quashed by Parks administration. Parks Canada was not in favour of adding any commercial enterprise beyond what already existed. This meant the location had to be outside of any national park's jurisdiction.

One option they checked out was the Kananaskis area. They actually landed on a shoulder of Mt. Sparrowhawk and put in one run down to Kananaskis Lake, but the snow was terrible and prone to constant wind action. They also found a run below Assiniboine that was only marginally better.

Somewhat discouraged, they nevertheless convinced a group of skiers to try helicopter-supported skiing for a minor fee. They still only had the piston-driven helicopter, which had a limited carrying capacity and was very slow. It took ages to get everyone to the top. Hans skied down with the first group and left the rest to follow their tracks. Though the skiing was poor and the helicopter underpowered and slow, Hans did not give up, and took another group the following spring, this time using Jim piloting his Bell 47G2 in the Cariboos. The prime objective on this trip was to make a film with a number of star skiers.

Hans got a quick reaction from the crowds who came to see his latest film showing the use of the helicopter, but one man, Brooks Dodge, was particularly keen on the idea of helicopter-supported skiing. Brooks was a legendary Olympic skier from the eastern

United States. He had good connections and could round up enough skiers to create an independent group. Initially, Hans felt the best location to take this elite crowd would be Rogers Pass, but again, the skiing was in a national park, where forgiveness is even harder to get than permission. The spring trip with Brooks fell through.

Hans was again on the prowl for a place that had great snow, spectacular scenery and wasn't in a park. In the spring of 1964, he ski toured into the Bugaboos and found what he was looking for. The Bugaboos had everything but good access. Hans used a Nodwell all-terrain vehicle to tow skiers 30 miles up an old logging road behind a machine already overloaded with gear and supplies. It was a messy, cumbersome and time-consuming way to reach the old log sawmill they used as a base camp. By the time they got there, everyone was covered in mud, tired and hungry.

Hans took two trips to the Bugaboos in the spring of 1965 using this base, which consisted of a number of scattered cabins that needed a lot of imagination and stoic reserve to be considered accommodation for the guests. His second group consisted of Brooks Dodge and his group from Boston. Getting them in there was even more arduous with the spring road conditions. Finally, one of the clients wryly stated to Hans that they would all be more than willing to kick in extra money if he would fly them in from the small town of Brisco. The idea made complete sense and broadened Hans's clientele base to include guests who were only too happy to forgo the trip in with the Nodwell.

By 1965, Jim had a respectable number of hours flying both fixed-wing aircraft and helicopters and was becoming more attuned to the vagaries of mountain flying. That year, he began flying regularly for Hans Gmoser in his new foray into heli-skiing. He also married Siri in a small ceremony at his parents' house.

When Jim first saw Hans's Bugaboos base camp, he wondered how much the clients were paying to stay in such rough quarters. Although Hans was stubborn about introducing fancy accommodation, he finally gave in to the idea that they needed a modern lodge if he wished to get the richer (and pampered) guests – and was eventually talked into putting toilets in the guest rooms. He couldn't understand what was wrong with the outhouse, which kept things simple for him.

But Hans had irrevocably opened a door that would take him down the long road of development and new lodges for the elite people who would become his clients. These high-end skiers were more than willing to fly to a lodge with gourmet meals, soft beds and privacy and, above all, a bathroom with toilets and showers. With all this development Hans decided to give his company a new name. He came up with Canadian Mountain Holidays (CMH), which has not changed yet.

When Hans showed Jim where he wanted the first lodge to be located, he pointed to the peaks showing through the clouds and said, "We will have all the skiing here we need." Jim wondered about that, knowing the vast potential of the Selkirk Mountains. He did not think the business would stay small – not for an ambitious man like Hans.

Meanwhile, Jim enjoyed the ambience of the rustic old sawmill. Hans hired Leo Grillmair, Franz Dopf and Lloyd (Kiwi) Gallagher (a new recruit from New Zealand) to work as guides. It was an intimate atmosphere that forged lasting friendships. Jim also liked the clients, who were good to work with. All felt they were at the beginning of something new, but most gave

The sawmill at Bugaboos
(JIM DAVIES COLLECTION).

little thought to how far this business would go. In those first years, the clients were true mountain people and adventurers who thoroughly appreciated the spectacular area in which they were privileged to ski.

Though Jim was an excellent pilot, his second week at the Bugaboos had its problems. Everything was working well until he made a landing at the top of a run called Sauce Alley. The snow was deep and very soft, and the helicopter plunged to a halt when he landed, burying the landing gear in the snow. The disabled helicopter tilted over, catching the rotors in the snow. Everyone got out with no injuries, but the helicopter was still running, and didn't quit until the blades finished beating up the rest of the machine. By then, the helicopter was a total wreck. It shut down all helicopter rides until Jim returned with another helicopter from Golden, BC, to finish out the week.

During those early years at the Bugaboos, everyone was on the steep end of the learning curve, whether it was dealing with eager clients, gauging snow conditions, running the helicopter or predicting avalanches. Both guides and pilots were constantly challenged by the unexpected. A bit of youthful ignorance may have been a good thing, allowing the guides to sleep a bit better, not worrying about how many things could go wrong the next day.

The winters at that time had ideal weather and plenty of snow that developed into stable powder runs on steep terrain. They were so consistent that Hans never really worried about avalanches, which at the time were being intensely studied at Rogers Pass. Another thing he did not give much thought to was Jim's flying, in which he had utmost trust.

But one incident gave Hans a clear insight into what pilots had to deal with all the time. It was a snowy, socked-in day at the sawmill and Hans, whose energy always needed an outlet, got restless and decided it might be a good time to check out the conditions on the slope leading down from Bugaboo Pass. He began bugging Jim about flying him up there so he could ski it solo to learn the terrain. Jim looked out the window into the white wall of snow to see if he could even find the helicopter. He told Hans the visibility was non-existent, making it impossible to establish vertical reference with the ground.

That did not deter Hans. He nagged Jim mercilessly, saying they could fly above the clouds, not thinking about how Jim was going to find his way back through the clouds to the camp. Jim always found it hard to say no to Hans, and before long they were both strapped into the helicopter with packs and skis, Hans eager, Jim concerned. There was enough visibility to find the pass but not enough to establish vertical reference. Hans looked out and said, "This is good. Put me out here."

Jim replied, "I can't land here. I can't see where the ground is."

Hans said if they couldn't land, he didn't mind jumping out with his pack and skis.

Jim looked at him for a minute and said, "Before you jump you might want to throw your pack out."

No problem. Hans manoeuvred his pack onto his lap and shoved it out the door. He said nothing as he watched the colourful pack fall 200 feet to the snowy pass below.

Jim did not relate if much more was said, but he now had vertical reference and was able put Hans down on the pass. As Hans skied off, Jim wondered if his friend was a bit more aware of the consequences of not having well-marked landing sites established – a procedure that would become a priority not long after.

One thing Jim discovered was the behavioural change in people new to helicopters. There is something about a helicopter that makes people want to speed up. It makes them both excited and a bit apprehensive, especially when the rotors whip up snow or dust. He could not watch everyone at the same time and just hoped Hans or Leo Grillmair was doing this for him. When they first started, they could only take a few people at a time, making it easier to watch out for potential accidents.

However, on one occasion, the basket that carried the skis held in place by bungee cords caused a problem. Usually, the weight of the skis helped keep them in place. But on this day, Jim hit a down draft on the way to the drop-off point for the skiers and a pair of Head skis flew into the rotor blades. One of the rotors was damaged but remained sufficiently intact for Jim to land and let the clients off. It held together long enough for Jim to fly back to the lodge. One of the passengers had gone along for the ride, intending to fly back with Jim. Jim did not know if he could make it back and would not take a chance flying with a paying passenger. The poor man, who was left with the skiers, had no idea how to ski (though he had his skis with him). Now he was faced with getting down the steep powdery snow laced with large trees without killing himself. But desperation often brings out the best in people, and though he bashed himself up crashing down the slope he arrived at the bottom intact. Leo was amazed.

The job of getting the helicopter out and replacing it left the skiers touring the slopes for the next week.

On an entirely different occasion a bungee cord almost cost Leo his life. They had landed with a full load of skiers who, as instructed, stepped well away from the helicopter and took refuge from the blowing snow in a sheltered spot. Leo and another guide unloaded the skis, passing them back to the guests. Leo got his own skis out last, holding them down with one hand while he tied up the bungee cords, which had to be locked in place in case they came loose.

In an oversight, Leo missed securing one of the cords. He gave the "all good" sign with his arms and Jim flew off down the slope. Leo turned to the group – with a look of confusion and terror when he suddenly realized he was airborne. A comedy of errors – about to turn tragic – had been set in motion when a poorly secured bungee cord sprang loose and hooked a strap on Leo's boot. The other end was fixed solidly to the ski basket with no hope of release.

Leo, now hanging upside down, wondered if Jim would look back and save him. He doubted if he could get down to the lodge before the cord broke. He was getting fairly high when he saw they were about to pass over the cliff bands they normally skied around. Then, just as abruptly, the cord broke and Leo fell onto the snow slope, just a little too close to the cliff for his liking.

As he scrambled up to the shocked clients, he realized he was in one piece. He was grateful he was unhurt, but it took a moment to realize how close he'd come to being killed. He certainly could not pass this adventure off as a stunt the guides occasionally performed to entertain the guests. The clients all skied down, enjoying the excellent powder – but the image of Leo in the air did not go away quickly. When Jim heard about the near-accident, all he could do was shake his head. The perils of heli-skiing were not restricted to the helicopter alone.

One other event with the helicopter made Jim aware of how vital a good mechanic was for the safety of the helicopter and all on board. Though most crashes are due to pilot error, mechanical failure is a consideration. The remoteness of the Bugaboos made good mechanical servicing difficult, and this would not change until CMH was big enough to support hiring a mechanic to stay on for the ski season.

On this occasion Jim was flying out to Brisco to pick up two snow machines for their operation at the sawmill camp. He was about two-thirds of the way out when he had an engine failure. There was little he could do but autorotate into the forest below. Fortunately, the trees were small due to recent logging and he settled into their cushiony embrace with no damage to the machine or himself. He did not have radio contact, meaning he had to either stay put until someone came looking for him or make his own way out. He knew how difficult it was to spot a downed aircraft in the trees – especially if rescuers didn't know his flight path – so he opted to walk out.

Plunging through the snow over debris left from logging was quite a challenge, but Jim finally succeeded in making it to a small logging road on the north side of Bugaboo Creek. At least the road was easier walking. He was discouraged by the lack of

Helicopter in the trees flying out to Brisco
(JIM DAVIES COLLECTION).

any sign the road was used, but there was nothing to do but plod on.

To his surprise, a truck appeared behind him, driven by two elderly ladies. They stopped but seemed wary of who he was or how he'd got there. They definitely looked as if they'd spent most of their life in the bush – probably in a small cabin farther up the creek. They looked him over when he asked for a ride, and he wondered if they would believe him if he tried to explain the helicopter situation. With great skepticism they told him he could ride in the back with the dog. He had just walked 11 miles through snow and bush and was too tired to do anything but nod gratefully and jump in with the dog. The dog growled at him all the way to Brisco.

Once in Brisco, Jim phoned Eddie Amann in Golden to send in another helicopter for the final week of skiing. They sent an Alouette III that was already in trouble: Jim found metal filings in the oil, indicating a problem with the engine. Eddie replaced it with a Bell 204B Jim kept for the rest of the season.

However, while Jim was finding a different helicopter, Hans had the problem of getting his clients back to the lodge. Clients who were skiing runs that led to the lodge could get back, but a group of 20 were skiing Vowell Glacier, the farthest run from the lodge, with a pickup point in the middle of wilderness, in a valley, miles from any road. Without climbing skins, getting back would be epic, if not impossible, especially for those with no mountain travel experience. The guide was in spotty communication with the lodge, and as night descended his only recourse was to build a fire and tell his clients a lot of stories to keep their minds off where they were. They were filled with relief to see the Alouette III the next day.

×   ×   ×

In the course of flying eight years for Hans Gmoser in the Bugaboos, only one ski accident happened while Jim was there.

As winter metamorphoses into spring, snowpack conditions can change rapidly because of warming days and freezing nights. It's ticklish to determine the best time of day to ski. Leaving too soon risks hitting the sun-shaded lower slopes before they're soft enough to ski and leaving too late can lead to sloppy conditions. With a 3,000-ft. elevation difference and the capacity of the trees to keep the snow cold, there's a very short window to ski a whole run in good powder, particularly if it is long. And sometimes clients can get ahead of the guide, especially if they know the route.

On this day, Leo decided to take a large group of clients down a run called Bay Street before the temperatures got too warm and turned the powder to wet, heavy mush. The skiing up top was excellent and all were good skiers. As they came into a treed gully, they were moving fairly fast, and were caught completely off guard when the surface snow turned to ice. The first person down was a woman who reached the trees before Leo, and when she hit the ice her skis shot out from under her, flipping her on her back. The slope was steep, and with her speed, she plummeted down through the trees, finally stopping when her leg got tangled in a large tree with a deep tree well.[14] It snapped her leg in several places, but at least she'd stopped sliding.

The rest of the group were right behind her, with Leo at the back making sure no one was left behind. When he arrived at the gully, he could see all of them sliding down through the trees. Fortunately, they all stopped before anyone else was hurt. Leo radioed out, alerting the lodge they had a serious accident on their hands.

During his descent to the lower portion of the run after dropping the group at the top, Jim had noticed the change in conditions. When he landed, he had a good view of the slope, but before he could radio the group to take caution in the trees, they were already there. He watched the woman fly down through the gully, hoping she wouldn't hit her head. It was no surprise when Leo radioed for help. Jim grabbed a chainsaw, a first aid kit and a doctor and flew back to the group. He first toed into an open slope close to the accident and let the doctor out to ski over to the injured woman. He then attached the saw and kit to a long line that reached the group when he hovered above them. Leo and the uninjured clients managed to cut down enough trees to allow Jim to toe into the accident site and load the woman in the helicopter. Despite getting to a hospital fairly quickly, she was laid up for some time.

x x x

In 1965, Jim took a contract at Fort Nelson in northeastern BC. Siri had spent some time with him there when she was seven months pregnant, giving them time to adjust to the idea of dealing with a new baby. But by August Siri was home, and close to giving birth to their first child, and Jim wanted to be there, as promised.

But timing is never certain, particularly in the helicopter business, and Jim experienced engine failure on the last day of the job while returning to base with the geologists. Suddenly, he was looking for any open land big enough for a helicopter.

He was fortunate to spot an island in the Wokkpash River that he could reach under autorotation. He and the geologists spent a very cold night out, eating all the survival food. Jim had a single-sideband radio, and the party strung the antenna out over some small bushes. But a single-sideband operates by sending a radio signal up that bounces off the ionosphere and down to a receiver on the same radio band. It is notoriously unreliable, especially when laid out on the ground.

They tried to contact anyone who could relay their predicament but only succeeded in wearing out the battery. Jim pulled the battery from the helicopter and finally got a message to Yellowknife, relaying their coordinates. Another helicopter reached them the following day.

By the time Jim got back to Siri, he found mother and son doing well at the Banff Mineral Springs Hospital. He'd wanted to be there for the birth, but under the circumstances both he and Siri were just glad he was there. He was at least in time to help choose a name for the child. The boy was christened

Siri and Morgan on horses going to Assiniboine
(JIM DAVIES COLLECTION).

Morgan and would grow up to live a life as diverse and exciting as Jim's.

Jim had to return to work up north for the rest of the summer but first made arrangements for Siri and Morgan to stay with his mother until he could get back to look for accommodation for his family in Banff. When he came home, he and Siri set up house in an apartment behind Cougar Street and gave Morgan a relatively stable home, conveniently close to where Jim's parents still lived. Jim spent most of the winter of 1965/66 working out of Banff. Having Jim's parents around as reliable babysitters (and a source of much-needed baby-rearing coaching) gave the new parents an anchor as they settled into domesticity.

Bruce McTrowe, a long-time friend and admirer of Jim's, lived on Cougar Street, close to where Siri and Jim set up housekeeping. Although he was much younger than Jim, he was fascinated by the helicopter and was eager to listen to any stories Jim had of flying. They also got to know each other through their parents.[15] When Jim was working in Banff park, he often landed the helicopter on an empty lot on S Block that Bruce's father owned. It was just a five-minute walk home for Jim and he often regaled the young boys, who were enthralled by the helicopter, with his adventures of the day.

Bruce remembers Jim from those early days as a tall, attractive man, quiet in demeanour but with a wild side that could surprise his friends. He was methodical when working around the helicopter and treated everyone as an equal.

Roy Andersen was another close friend of Jim's from his school and skiing days who saw a lot of Jim during this time. Roy had joined the military after leaving high school, where he put his skiing talents to good use teaching soldiers how to ski. That ended in 1964 when Roy decided to teach skiing at Sunshine Ski School, run by Jerry Johnson.

Jim was only 27 when he became a father, but Roy was impressed with how Jim assumed the responsibility of fatherhood. Jim cared for Morgan when Siri worked with her father at Assiniboine Lodge and thought nothing of bringing the baby everywhere he went. It was common to see Jim changing diapers or feeding the baby, even when visiting the Calgary Flying Club. He drove a white Pontiac that provided lots of room to administer care. Roy remembers those days as "loosey-goosey" when it came to responsibility and was amazed at how easily Jim assumed the tasks of parenthood, which could be time consuming.

When the sun shone long on the first days of spring in 1966, Jim was back in the Bugaboos, but at the end of the ski season he again stayed close to Banff. He records meeting Siri and Morgan in Calgary to give them a ride home to Banff. Jim was particularly pleased to see his son standing up in the back seat of the car. Morgan was growing up quickly.

Jim continued flying for Bullock in the North during the summer months, coming home for breaks between jobs. Siri

Jim and Morgan in helicopter
(JIM DAVIES COLLECTION).

continued to work with her father at Assiniboine and usually brought their one-year-old son in on horseback, holding him securely in front of her on the saddle. It was a busy summer and Jim did not get back to Assiniboine until the first of July. He records having a great time visiting Siri and Morgan, after which they took some time together to visit friends in Golden. The rest of the summer was spent flying throughout the national parks, which gave Jim the opportunity to visit his family in Assiniboine on a more frequent basis.

×　×　×

The summer of 1966 was a busy one for Jim. He flew to all parts of the mountain parks and into BC. Once, he flew Hans into Sir Sandford late in the day and was forced to fly out in the dark to make his next rendezvous in Jasper.

In August, Jim took Cliff Johnson and Bill Fritz into Beauty Creek just north of the Columbia Icefield. Unfortunately, Cliff sustained a severe fall there while climbing. Bill had had to walk out to the Jasper highway to get help, and by the time rescuers reached Cliff he was in shock from serious injuries. He had broken ribs and a ballpoint pen had punctured his chest. He also had substantial leg injuries with exposed broken bones and a great deal of abrasion. Jim flew him to an ambulance waiting at the highway. Cliff probably would not have survived much longer and would've been a poor candidate for a complex ground recovery.

Jim's love of landing in high places never abated, and on a beautiful day he successfully made his highest landing to date on Mt. Robson (12,977 ft.). When he returned to Banff, he was surprised to get a call from the warden service for assistance with a mountain rescue that would be recognized as the first helicopter-assisted rescue by Parks Canada. Little did he know it would come to epitomize his skill as a pilot and dominate the rest of his flying career.

Charlie Locke and Brian Greenwood, both guides, were attempting to establish a new route on the difficult, overhung face of Mt. Babel. They were very near the top of the 2,000 ft. route when Locke, who was leading, fell off and smashed his wrist, making any further progress impossible. Neither could they retreat, as Locke's injury made it impossible for him to rappel down. They were stuck and had to call for help, hoping someone would hear them in the valley below.

When the two climbers failed to return and sign back into the required sign-out sheet, Walter Perren, Banff National Park's alpine rescue specialist, arrived with several wardens to assess the situation. It was clear a lot of manpower would be needed to effect a rescue, even with the aid of a helicopter.

At five o'clock the next morning, Jim found a relatively flat area to land men and equipment below the rescue site, close enough to execute a rapid setup of equipment. Jim records: "It was a beautiful day and the rescue, though dramatic, was successful." Jim immediately left for Jasper to complete his contract there.

×   ×   ×

That fall, Jim's work slowed down and he and Siri took time out to see the latest Hans Gmoser film at the Jubilee Auditorium in Calgary. In November of 1966 Siri took Morgan to Oslo, Norway, where Erling was now living. He had turned 70 and was no longer interested in running the lodge at Assiniboine during the winter months. Jim joined them shortly after, one of the few holidays Jim truly spent away from the pressures of flying and Siri running the lodge. This trip might have been considered a honeymoon, as it was the first time he and Siri were away from the demands of work and could relax and enjoy (for Jim) a whole new culture.

One thing Jim really appreciated on that holiday was skiing from hut to hut in Norway with Erling, who was still very active. Erling had a lot of business details to discuss with Siri, as he only planned to be Siri's assistant with Assiniboine Lodge's summer operation. This meant Siri would eventually be managing the place on her own when Erling left for good in 1975. Erling may

Erling and Siri at Assiniboine
(JIM DAVIES COLLECTION).

have been worried about how she would cope, but he felt that if she carried on with the people he had employed, the business should run smoothly.

During the winter of 1967, Jim recorded another helicopter assist in a ski accident at Sunshine ski area. He quite proudly wrote that the Alouette performed admirably in landing close to a skier with a double compound fracture to her leg. Once she was stabilized on site and put in the helicopter, Jim flew her directly to the General Hospital in Calgary on "the front steps." Better service was never given.

Jim continued flying for Hans Gmoser in the Bugaboos, but in May he also took Hans in to the Fairy Meadow hut with 13 skiers to make yet another film. While there, he had a small problem with the tail rotor of the helicopter when the guard protecting it broke off, but he managed to get back without incident. At the end of May he went to Chicago to pick up an Astazou Alouette and give a demonstration to the police and fire departments of the Windy City. He flew back with two passengers from Mexico with a steady tailwind. By June he was back up north dealing with contracts and helicopters that seemed to need a lot of maintenance.

Canada's Centennial year, 1967, was memorable for Jim, for a number of reasons. First, he was asked to fly for the Alpine Club of Canada (ACC), which was sponsoring a number of Centennial climbs in the Yukon. It was the largest mountaineering expedition ever to be attempted in Canada, taking place over two months and involving hundreds of skilled climbers, in one of the world's most remote and inaccessible mountain ranges. New peaks were named, and dozens were scaled for the first time. It was a massive undertaking that meant a lot of flying in marginal weather and at high altitudes.

For safety reasons, Dave Fisher, the main organizer for the expedition and president of the ACC, insisted two helicopters be used. Jim, along with Derrick Ellis from Golden, were considered the most experienced mountain helicopter pilots at the time and were invited to do the flying. Jim was popular among the climbers because of his quiet demeanour, and was simply thought of as "really cool." Both he and Derrick were happy with the Bell 47G3 B1 helicopters with turbocharger (necessary for the high altitude at which they were flying) they were given to fly.

Jim totally agreed with using another helicopter as backup, particularly after one instance that would terrify any pilot. Most of the work consisted of ferrying people or loads of food and equipment from base camp on Steele Glacier to the high camps for each climb. Jim and Derrick would fly together, one behind the other, in case there was a problem – particularly as the flying was done in what Jim called "hostile terrain." There were few to no opportunities to make a safe landing in the torn and cross-hatched glacial jungle they were constantly crossing. Cool was definitely called for.

On one occasion, having flown most of the way over a very broken glacier, Jim reported to Derrick, "I don't have any oil pressure."

Derrick replied, "I know. The back of your engine is on fire."

And it was. A hot bearing had come loose from the turbo engine and come in contact with the oil, which ignited. Given the terrain, he certainly could not have landed. Jim could have dropped his valuable load of cargo, but he decided against that and carried on, hoping for the best – a calculated risk. With some degree of pride and relief, he says, "And I made it."

He got out, put the fire out, replaced the turbocharger, and topped up the lost oil. Then he returned to his flying mission. With all the excitement in camp, and the dangers many of the climbers were experiencing almost daily, some would probably have been surprised to hear Jim had a problem at all.

Toward the end of the expedition, Secretary of State Judy La-Marsh, whose ministry was responsible for all the Centennial celebrations, came to the camp for a visit, where she met with the camp organizers and guides. Jim flew her to one of the high camps, which had a spectacular view, but one she did not stand around long at to appreciate. Even wearing a thick coat she was freezing cold.

Shortly after, Jim had an opportunity to do what he loved best – landing in the highest place possible in the Centennial Range. He was flying Judy Cook and Hans Gmoser out of one of the camps on a rare day with perfect weather. The good conditions gave them the opportunity to fly at a high altitude where they had a magnificent view of the expansive mountain range. As they flew by Mt. Lucania,[16] Jim said to Hans, "Do you mind if I make a landing?"

This was no problem for Hans. There was not a breath of wind as Jim found a perfectly flat space to land. The three happily got out and took pictures before flying back to base camp. To this day, it is the highest recorded landing for a Bell 47G3 BI helicopter.

On August 14, Jim's Centennial–Steele Glacier contract was over, and he made his way home with a few stops at places now forgotten but steeped in history: Burwash Landing, Watson Lake, Toad River and Fort St. John. From there he went to help a friend stake a claim at Pelly Lake, and finally flew home to Banff via Grande Prairie.

× × ×

The emerging generation of the 1960s embraced the idea of rebellion against the status quo of their parents. As the rapidly changing world unfolded to young people through increasingly ubiquitous communication networks, a nebulous sense of freedom spurred the baby boomers to rise up against the moral constrictions of society. It was contagious, and young people flocked to Banff to escape the restrictions of school and home. With little thought for the hardships of the future, parties never ended. The late 1960s and early 1970s seemed encased in an unbreakable bubble, free from the confines of responsibility. Both Siri and Jim were young when they got married and had no time to adjust to the responsibilities inherent in their new relationship before adding the demands of having a child.

Siri was an independent woman, which appealed to Jim when they first met, but careers demanding that both of them spend most of their time in remote corners of the country did not make for a happy, settled home life. As a result, by the time Jim returned to Banff from the Centennial climbs, his struggling marriage to Siri had reached a point where divorce was the only option.

Roy Andersen, who later became a bush pilot up north (and eventually a helicopter pilot) at Jim's encouragement, noted that the occupation of helicopter pilot was hard on marriages. His own would eventually succumb to the long, absent hours of flying far from home.

After returning from the Centennial climbs, Jim took work up north on Ellesmere Island, but in the fall, he realized his first step when back in Banff must be to file for divorce. His biggest regret in doing so was that he would now see much less of Morgan.

The breakup was hard for Jim, and he needed to get away from Banff. He managed to get in touch with a fellow pilot who was flying in New Zealand and decided to take him up on an offer of work there. As Jim recalls, he flew back from the North, finalized his divorce and went straight to New Zealand. It was summer there, and since the spring skiing in Canada did not start until March, he assured Hans he would be back for the 1968 season.

He landed in the balmy weather of a New Zealand summer and went straight to the South Island, where a camp was set up for the pilots. He was flying for Worldwide Helicopters, who required him to do a test flight to ensure he actually could fly helicopters. The job was focused on shooting and removing deer from the island. New Zealand had seven species of native deer, but the red deer introduced from England[17] in the 1880s had become a pest. Because of a lack of natural predators to keep the population in check, their numbers had exploded with the

Slinging deer in New Zealand
(JIM DAVIES COLLECTION).

abundance of rich flora, particularly in forested areas. Hunting was encouraged, but the small group of hunters had little effect on the growing deer populations. By the 1960s the damage the deer had caused was alarming, including deforestation and consequent erosion. When the helicopter became available, it proved to be an effective tool for culling large populations where devastation was most rampant.

Jim's job was to herd the deer into the open upper valleys, from which they could not escape. The deer were shot from the helicopter by a rifleman, then piled into cargo nets and slung out by the pilot. It was not a pleasant job and Jim hated to see the animals shot. But the riflemen were excellent shots and the job was conducted as humanely as possible. In contrast to the long, drawn-out starvation that inevitably faced overburdened populations, the program was merciful. All of the usable meat from the deer was sold and used to feed those in need.

Girlfriend in helicopter, New Zealand
(JIM DAVIES COLLECTION).

Jim didn't feel he learned much about long lining,[18] but flying around steep, mountainous terrain (as the deer fed mostly around or below tree line) did give him a lot of hours of flying and he learned how to get the most out of his underpowered craft.

Many companies found hiring competent pilots in those early days difficult. The pilots with the most flying time were kamikaze Marines from the Vietnam War who just couldn't seem to resist flying like cowboys with little self-control. Jim didn't stay long enough to see if his work helped reduce the deer population significantly, as he left after four months, but during the time he was there, five crashes occurred due to the inexperience of pilots. Worldwide Helicopters could not afford to keep replacing helicopters and was sad to see a good pilot go.

Jim didn't see a lot of New Zealand while he was there because of his limited days off, but he did spend time in Cromwell, the closest town to camp, where he found time to balance entertaining two girlfriends. Jim enjoyed every minute. If he hadn't made a promise to Hans to be back for skiing that winter, he would have stayed longer.

× × ×

When Jim returned to Canada for the 1968 ski season in the Bugaboos, much had changed. For one thing, Hans's marriage to Marg MacGougan produced their first son, Conrad. Marg had worked as a cook for Hans ever since they'd married, and she continued to do so even with a new baby. Jim was amazed to see that the new lodge, designed by architect and friend Philippe Delesalle, had also been built. Though the lodge had more updated accommodation, it had been costly. Hans needed more clients, which meant finding a more powerful helicopter that was still light enough for tricky alpine flying. Jim felt an Alouette III would work well, with the capacity to fly more people, faster, to the skiing.

One of Jim's priorities was to spend as much time as he could with Morgan. Conrad (Hans's eldest son) was already being cared for at the Bugaboos, so one more didn't make much difference except to add to the workload for the women. Morgan was only three when he made his first trip to the lodge and into the care of Marg and the staff. The following year, Hans's son Robson was born, and all Marg remembers is the blur of endless work, with babies everywhere. The boys were happy, however, playing endlessly in the snow, soaking up the heady, hectic atmosphere of happy clients and the constant sight of the helicopter flying everyone around all day.

The rapid growth of heli-skiing was leading to a demand that one lodge alone could barely handle. Hans seemed driven to promote heli-skiing in Canada but realized he was overrun at the Bugaboos. He and Jim flew deeper into the bush, looking for areas that could be skied with helicopter access. While scouting, they didn't speak much, but just looked, as one or the other would nod to a peak or col. If they both nodded at once, Jim would check out the landing. But this meant getting farther and farther from home base.

Thinking back, Hans remembered the excellent skiing he'd had in the Cariboos. This area already had accommodation in the small town of Valemount and it was not in any national park, where such an operation was prohibited. He was also familiar with these mountains and felt the potential was worth exploring for a second operation under the guidance of a second manager.

Lloyd (Kiwi) Gallagher, one of Hans's former Bugaboo guides, and another guide named Rudi Gertsch, conducted ski tours in Little Yoho and Assiniboine, with bigger mountaineering tours on offer. While Leo Grillmair stayed on as manager of Bugaboo Lodge, Hans approached Kiwi about coming with him to explore the Cariboos. Since Jim was busy flying in the Bugaboos, Hans engaged Jan Elbe to fly them around. Outside of a first harrowing ski down a heavily laden slope, Kiwi felt the place would work well as a second CMH heli-ski area.

Unfortunately, Hans selected this area exactly when Mike Wiegele, one of his best friends, was trying to get a toehold in the heli-ski industry, also in the Cariboo area, essentially becoming his competition. Mike Wiegele had already engaged Gary Forman of Yellowhead Helicopters, based in Valemount, to fly for him. No one could fault Mike for doing this, as he'd seen the success Hans was having and quite rightly thought that, with the thousands of miles of open powder snow slopes dropping away from the peaks to the valleys, there was plenty of room for all. It was a rapidly growing industry and only CMH provided the service. Hans, however, saw it as a betrayal and the once close friends became estranged for life.

Jim went to fly for Hans in the first year at the Cariboos and found the atmosphere strained to the point of being ridiculous. The town of Valemount was very small and both groups were forced to stay in the same accommodation and eat dinner in the same restaurant. It was hard for Jim, who was friends with both pilot Gary Forman and Mike Wiegele. Each group would isolate itself as far as possible in the small dining room, but worst were the mornings. The clients would be hustled out to the two helicopters waiting almost side by side. Confusion sometimes arose when clients did not know which helicopter to head for. If they were on the same run, the lunch stops were subdued as the two competitors glared at one another across a pristine slope. Hans did prevail and soon had a lodge constructed under the watchful eye of Kiwi, who would become the manager for many years. Mike realized the situation was untenable but knew his adversary well. Hans could out-stubborn the best, so Mike looked farther west. In the end he founded Blue River Heli Ski Lodge 90 km south of Valemount. It was another spectacular area in the Cariboo mountain range and Mike's business soon flourished into a very successful enterprise. It was a place he grew to love, shared with his wife, Bonnie, who brought class to the lodge and cabins, making it possibly the most luxurious of all the heli-ski businesses developed. Mike had no desire to go anywhere else.

Hans, however, was just getting started. He would eventually have heli-ski operations in the Bobbie Burns and the Monashees. The expansion of Hans's empire looked as if it would involve a more nomadic life than Jim wanted. He had met Sue Corless by then and wanted to make a life with her that did not entail her becoming a cook for Hans. He was ready to move on, and Parks Canada was the vehicle that would define him as a helicopter pilot.

4

Changes: From Bugaboos to Banff

Jim returned to Canada from New Zealand in February 1968 and was back at work for Bullock on the 8th of that month. After ferrying loads of lumber and equipment to construct the Bow Hut on Bow Glacier for the Alpine Club of Canada, he went to the Bugaboos as promised. He was pleased to see the new Bugaboo Lodge, complete with indoor plumbing.

Indoor toilets had been a bone of contention for Hans, who thought the outhouse was just fine and had a lot fewer of the problems that came with indoor plumbing. He reluctantly gave in but not so far as providing a private bathroom in each room. The compromise was shared bathrooms on the main floor. Hans was not going to usher himself or his guests into the sinkhole of self-indulgence without a fight. As it turned out, he need not have worried, as everyone who came that year was surprised and delighted with the unexpected improvement in accommodation. The good weather and great skiing, with the luxury of their own room to relax in, made for high-spirited company. There was even a large deck built for guests to kick back and enjoy the view.

By 1969, business was in full swing when Hans had an opportunity to really promote heli-skiing in the Bugaboos. Leo had several clients of his own he took climbing in the summer, and by luck one of them happened to be married to Tim Porteous, a speech writer for Prime Minister Pierre Trudeau. Trudeau was a flamboyant man used to taking risks. He enjoyed outdoor sports that gave him a chance to do something out of the eye of the public. He was a hiker, a canoeist and a fine skier, and very fit for a man of 49 years. That summer, Trudeau decided to step up the hiking to mountain climbing.

The client became aware that the prime minister was looking for a guide to climb in the Rockies, and she recommended Leo. Leo was thrilled but realized Trudeau would have to climb the mountain with his bodyguards. It may have been at Trudeau's request, but they settled on Mt. Colin in Jasper as their goal. Colin is a striking peak, not particularly high or difficult to climb, with a low profile in the Colin Range just east of Jasper townsite and south of the Athabasca River. Its relative anonymity may have been the attraction.

Leo knew he would need help and called on public safety specialist Willi Pfisterer and RCMP member Al Moore to accompany them. Willi was an excellent guide and Al Moore had a lot of hard climbs under his belt. The climb was a success, which encouraged the garrulous Leo to extol the wonders of skiing in the Bugaboos. It took little to convince Trudeau to sign up for a trip the following March.

Jim was Trudeau's pilot and liked him for his low-key approach to everything – a man who wanted to be just one of the clients. When Jim first met Trudeau at the Bugaboos, he introduced himself, saying, "Do you remember me?" Trudeau did not recognize the pilot, so Jim reminded him of his trip to Inuvik some years earlier. Jim happened to be flying in the area and attended a ceremony honouring the prime minister's visit when the elders presented him with a dog whip. Trudeau remembered the occasion, but not the shy pilot at the back of the room.

At the Bugaboos, Trudeau left behind any indication of his imposing position. Still, it was hard not to be aware of RCMP officers arriving and leaving each day, one of whom had a brief-case locked to his wrist. Although the prime minister was on a secluded vacation, he could never totally escape affairs of state. In the evenings, after a full day of skiing, he would go through the papers they brought him, sign off on several, then get back to the business of skiing when they left. His casualness and charm worked on everyone and staff soon treated him just like any other client. The relaxed atmosphere and terrific skiing would lead to more trips for Trudeau, one of which included climbing Bugaboo Spire, which was not for the faint of heart. Though the climbing is not as difficult as you might expect, the exposure is extreme and can be very intimidating.

×　×　×

By late spring, Jim was flying up north again, but he came back to Banff, midsummer, to make a short trip to Wyoming with Roy Andersen. The rest of the summer had him flying throughout the North, specifically the Arctic islands. It was on one of these trips he found a Red River cart on Melville Island. The highly unusual object was visible, sitting out in the open on the barren rocks of the tundra, remarkably well preserved. Jim made a quick landing and was amazed to find this primitive mode of transportation so far away from its normal haunts in the southern prairies. It turned out to be a cart Francis McClintock used in his 1857 quest to find the lost Franklin expedition. Jim helped retrieve the cart for the Glenbow Museum in Calgary, along with artifacts found scattered about. Most of these were still-sealed cans of food. Jim

Red River cart on Melville Island
(COURTESY OF BRUCE MCTROWE).

kept a few cans stored in his parents' garage as a reminder of this unusual trip. He failed to mention what they were, however, and to Jim's dismay, his mother threw them out, thinking the mouldy cans were just a health hazard. She was right.[19]

One regret Jim had about flying was that he inevitably seemed to find himself separated from his son, Morgan, for long stretches. He writes during his time at the Panarctic camp: "The annoying thing about this contract is that I will miss Morgan's birthday for the third time."

In the winter of 1969, Jim was flying a new Alouette III as well as a Bell 204 close to his Banff stomping grounds, giving him time to catch up with old friends and attend a few house parties at Banff and Lake Louise. With time off, he didn't worry too much about how long the party lasted. A party (more of which below) at Joe Halstenson's warden house in Lake Louise was a classic for those years and Jim did not miss out. But it was a turning point he never saw coming when he met a very pretty, enchantingly free-spirited lady who would add a whole new depth to Jim's understanding of "relationship."

Banff had a few adventurous women willing to work in the backcountry, where the ratio definitely favoured the women. Sue Corless was a young woman from Ontario who had come west to see the country before she settled down. She'd come to the right place if she was looking for a good time, as the parties never gave out. Sue had met Grace McKinnon prior to coming west when they both worked at the Algonquin Hotel at St. Andrew-by-the-Sea as waitresses.[20] Serendipitously, they both found themselves working at Temple Lodge in Banff National Park the following summer, after Sue worked at the Chateau Lake Louise, where she met Faye and June Mickle. Though she must have had reservations about Bert and his son Don, the civilizing presence of June Mickle must have been reassuring enough for Sue to work for the Mickles at Temple Lodge and Skoki Lodge. It was certainly a guaranteed entry for meeting all the reprobates in the country.

Working in Skoki was quite a change from any outdoor experience Sue had had growing up in Ontario. Although Skoki had all the amenities of a cozy cabin in the wilderness, it was still very isolated, particularly in winter. The Mickles had no radios to contact the outside world for help if a crisis arose. This isolation was made clear when June Mickle's daughter, Faye, became sick with a particularly nasty flu virus. She was too sick to be moved to the hospital, as the trip would entail a long, cold snowmobile ride she would not likely survive. Luckily, constant care and a strong constitution resulted in Faye eventually recovering at the lodge. When Sue became sick, there was no option but to get her to a hospital.

June kept a daily diary recording significant events, with a minimalist writing style even Hemingway might have appreciated. She wrote:

April 11, 1968 – Thursday

Worked all day at Temple. Went to Banff and washed clothes.

Back early

Bob had to bring Sue out of Skoki

Weather – Chilly and snowed a lot

April 12 – Friday

Bob took us early in the morning to Skoki – cooked turkey etc.

Sue had her appendix out

Weather – cold winds – snow flurries

Bob Haney was in Skoki when Sue's appendix became inflamed and undertook her evacuation over Deception Pass to Temple, where a truck was commandeered to take her to Banff. It was a long, cold and painful trip for Sue, but it saved her life. She also impressed Bob with her stamina, and his "chasing her around a bit" stepped up while he was working at Rogers Pass as an avalanche technician. He spent most of his weekends off coming back to Lake Louise in his semi-serious pursuit of her.

Despite Don's reputation as being fairly wild in his younger days, Grace found the softer, more responsible side of him and decided he was worth marrying when he asked. Sue had already met Bob Haney, whom June considered pretty level-headed at the time and who would go on to a successful career as chief park warden in the warden service. An equally successful career in the warden service would develop for Don Mickle, once he settled down with Grace, whose name defined her. Grace was shy but very pretty and probably caught Don's eye because she was so different from most of the girls he chased after. Even Bert said, "I don't know where he finds them" after Don drifted by

Sue Corless graduation picture
(JIM DAVIES COLLECTION).

at some party with two rough-looking girls. To June's delight, Grace brought refinement and stability to Don's life, and Sue was more than happy when they married later that year.

Neither Grace nor Don thought Sue was in Banff for more than a break from university or the east in general, but she stayed. She found the beauty of the mountains and the unfettered almost-innocence of the people refreshingly liberating compared to the more formal, restrictive society of an older, eastern community. One thing that struck Grace was how lively Sue was, recalling a party where Sue commandeered the piano, which kept the party going most of the night. Sue was gifted with the ability to engage anyone in conversation and, with her tall good looks, quickly became the most popular employee at Skoki and Temple lodges.

Working in the backcountry was fun and challenging for Sue, but she wanted to get on with a career for which she was trained:

history and archiving. She had no difficulty getting a job at the Whyte Museum, where she helped Maryalice Stewart with oral history projects.

Sue first met Jim when he came in to donate a muskox skull he had retrieved from the Arctic. Jim had Morgan with him, which may have given Sue the idea he was married. Sue was impressed by the soft-spoken young helicopter pilot, but nothing developed from this brief encounter, as Jim had only a short time off from flying in the Bugaboos.

That season was particularly busy for Hans, who kept Jim occupied from January 25 to April 11 with only two weeks off. But that break led to a pivotal change in Jim's life.

The 1960s and 1970s was a vibrant period in Banff when everyone was young and paid little regard to the social etiquette of the 1950s. Parties were frequent, but one party in particular was memorable for all who attended. Joe Halstenson was a warden living in Lake Louise in a government house provided for employees. He was also a member of Mike Sobey's band, which was quite popular in the Banff area. Most of the band also liked to ski and often stayed with Joe and his wife.

The party in February started with the arrival of the other band members, who'd come to ski but also brought all their instruments. Taking advantage of having a live band for the weekend, Joe decided to throw a house party. Word spread faster than a bush fire and pretty soon people showed up from Banff to Field, BC, and points north on the Banff–Jasper highway. It turned into an epic endurance event of drinking, dancing and socializing that lasted three days.

June and Bert Mickle, and Dale Portman, a young wrangler working for them at the time, were among many in attendance.

June was remonstrating to Dale and Jay Morton that they should be more like Sensible Bob (Haney) – whose normal demeanour was down to earth and practical – when Jay looked up and pointed at Bob, who was swinging from the rafters in the basement in hot pursuit of Sue. The moniker stuck, however, and from that time on Bob became known as "Sensible Bob."

When Jim met Sue at Joe's party everything else for him faded away.

Jim had not seen her since their brief introduction at the Whyte Museum, but now he was getting a good look at the fun side of her nature. Though Roy Andersen was not there, he met them together shortly afterward and it was obvious to him it was love at first sight. All Roy could do was sit back and take in the fact that Jim was "smitten." It seemed obvious to those at the party as well. Even Gord Peyto, another young seasonal warden (who was still sober), remarked that it was hard not to notice the attraction between them. They drifted off as if no one else was at the party, and Sensible Bob decided Sue's chasing days were over. He was right. By late Sunday, the party finally dwindled, but by then Jim was bent on seeing a lot more of the divine Sue.

Sue loved music, and though there was no piano at this party, she added her voice to the songs she knew. Dale Portman remembers seeing Sue at a Mickle party, recalling: "It wasn't long before a chicken dance broke out. There were various forms of the dance, one of which required a volunteer. Bert had learned how to perform the moves from Lawrence W<h>itney of the Sarcee Reserve (now called Tsuut'ina Nation). Bert initiated the dance by leading off with the boys whooping and shuffling behind him in an ever-revolving circle. However, for the dance to be a real success, they needed to replace the chicken with a person (preferably a woman) to dance around. It was crazy and no one (except possibly Bert) knew what it was about – outside of being a lot of fun. Sue never hesitated to get involved. She was a lot of fun to be around."

For Jim and Sue, this was the beginning of a long life together. Leo Grillmair remembers Sue at the Bugaboos, not really there to ski but just to be with Jim and meet his friends there. Jim must have seemed unlike most of the hayseed cowboys she was meeting, as he was initially reserved but polite upon meeting people. His reserve and unusual occupation gave him a mysterious air, but Sue had no problem getting around that with her outgoing personality – and, he was taller than her. If opposites attract, then that magic worked for them, and Jim saw her as often as possible.

Many of Sue's friends noticed that she didn't seem as open to impromptu escapades and toned down her association with the rowdier crowd after meeting Jim. Dale Portman remembers: "I ran across Sue at the warden gymkhana at Hillsdale Meadows in the fall of 1969. I had a bag of ice cubes that needed to be broken up. When I ran into her, I threw the bag at her feet and said, 'Ha, Sue, Chicken dance on this for me.'" She gave him a steely look, lifted her nose and strutted away. He thought her manner suggested that now that she was dating Jim she wasn't the sort of girl who would take part in a chicken dance.

By 1970, the Bugaboo operation was growing so fast that Hans was running at full tilt just to keep up. His ski season was getting longer, and more pilots were hired on. Jim found himself flying skiers throughout the winter<,> and before long Hans even had people in by December. As Jim recalls, it didn't seem to be a particularly happy time for Hans, who looked as though he was carrying the weight of the world on his shoulders. Every increase in time and clientele meant more staff, more bills and every other woe that goes along with a rapidly expanding company. Jim spent some of his time in the Bugaboos that spring checking out new pilot Jim Ritson before flying back to Banff to assist in avalanche stabilization on the Sunshine road for Peter Fuhrmann.

Sue Corless must have known there was risk associated with flying helicopters, but that didn't interfere with their relationship. That summer, Jim worked the Banff area, giving them more time to be together.

One thing Jim and Sue had in common was spontaneity. On a warm day in March they were driving into Calgary when Jim looked at Sue and thought she looked particularly pretty wearing a light summer dress.

She looked back at him, smiling, and said, "Let's get married."

It took Jim no longer than a heartbeat to smile back and say, "Okay."

Jim can't remember what they were going to Calgary for, but it didn't matter. They went to the courthouse for a licence, commandeered two witnesses from the helicopter hangar for $20, found a rather inebriated justice of the peace, and performed the ceremony. Afterward, they all went out for dinner (minus the JP) and returned to Banff as Mr. and Mrs. Davies.

They initially rented an apartment unit on Beaver Street but didn't stay in one place too long during their first years of marriage, moving to the Gourlay house, then to the Odenthals' log house on Grizzly Street. They had a brief sojourn at 347 Muskrat until they bought a house from an ex-RCMP couple where they stayed and settled down.

One thing Sue was happy to do once she was married to Jim

Sue and Jim at Kiwi Gallagher and Fran's wedding
(JIM DAVIES COLLECTION).

was quit working at the archives. Her cheerful ways with people did not seem to rub off on Maryalice, making for a strained relationship at work.

During the early years of their marriage, Jim was still working for Bullock Helicopters (which committed him to more trips up north) as well as for Hans in the Bugaboos. Finally, he delivered on a promised plane-supported honeymoon toward the end of November – a perfect time for a break before good powder skiing started in the Bugaboos. They flew south in a Comanche 250 (more suitable for a long trip) to Mazatlán, then Puerto Vallarta, and as far south as Oaxaca, Mexico, before returning on the 19th of December.

× × ×

Before Jim started flying in the Bugaboos in 1971, he checked out other pilots for their suitability for CMH. Slinging with cargo nets, autorotation and flying in confined areas were critical skills. Jim could never emphasize enough the importance of having vertical reference at all times and setting up well-marked landing sites on all the ski runs. They used pole markers tall enough to last through a few snowfalls, but eventually they even built log rafts that were stable enough to hold the helicopter. This was the first chore of the year, followed up by frequently digging them out after a fresh snowfall.

Many helicopter crashes occurred when the pilot lost his vertical reference point. One of Jim's favourite ways to illustrate the importance of vertical reference was to have pilots fly over a snow-covered body of water and ask them how they could determine how far above the surface they were. When no reference was available in winter conditions, he would throw out a pack and have them land beside that. It brought back memories of Hans Gmoser volunteering to jump out into the snow below to give him a reference.

Another tip Jim gave to pilots he was testing was simple, but ignoring it could prove fatal. Every time Jim landed, he made sure he had enough room to nudge the helicopter ahead by two feet or more, to ensure the skids were on solid ground. The weight of the long tail was sufficient to pull the helicopter over backward if the back of the skids was left hanging in space. This might seem obvious to any casual observer on the ground, but the full length of the skids could not be seen from inside the machine. It was a mistake made by even very experienced pilots and has resulted in fatalities.

Before Jim's 1971 season in the Bugaboos, Peter Fuhrmann called upon him to do some avalanche control work. Jim had met Peter on the Centennial climb in the Yukon before Peter became the alpine specialist for Banff National Park. Doing avalanche control from the helicopter was potentially quite dangerous work. Jim would have to fly as close as possible to the trigger zone near the top of avalanche path and hover, while Peter threw out a bomb. This was not the first time Peter had used a helicopter to access avalanche trigger zones. Earlier he had used Eddie Amann to land safely behind a cornice, then belay Peter as close to the cornice as possible, where he deposited the bomb. They were airborne long before it finally ignited, only to fizzle out, doing little damage to the cornice.

Peter Fuhrmann's success as alpine specialist for Banff Park was due to his achievements in the climbing world combined with an astute political savvy. Both qualities were needed when dealing with park administrators.

Peter's acumen and survival skills were honed through a particularly challenging childhood in Germany, brought on by the rising tide of Nazism leading up to the Second World War. Robert Sandford gives a brief but chilling synopsis of the challenges Peter faced during this period in *The Highest Calling*: "Peter saw the worst of what war can be and was very nearly destroyed by it. Separated from his parents when the tide turned against Germany, Peter fled with his grandparents to Dresden, where they experienced the worst fire bombing of the entire war. After the Russian invasion, Peter spent two and a half years behind the Iron Curtain in a refugee camp. It was here that the Russians killed one of his uncles. Shortly after, his aunt took her own life. Conditions were so desperate that Peter nearly lost a leg to infection. He was so malnourished and sick by the time he was reunited with his parents in Nuremberg in 1947, he was immediately hospitalized."

Peter survived, however, and was able to finish grade school and study commerce for two years before taking a job with the Shell Oil Company in Germany in a management capacity. It

Jim and Peter fuelling up a Bell helicopter
(KATHY CALVERT COLLECTION).

was during this time that his natural athletic abilities and ex-
uberance for life led him into adventurous pursuits of skiing
(compliments of Shell Oil), track and field, bicycling and motor-
cycle racing. The work with Shell gave Peter a polish that would
stand him in good stead over the years, but it was not what he
wanted out of life. He was disillusioned with the highly struc-
tured oil company, ruled by embittered former Nazi officers, and
he jumped at the chance to emigrate to Canada with newfound
friend Heinz Kahl, whom he met in a jazz club in Neuberg.

A promised job with an oil company did not materialize for
Peter in Edmonton, however, and as Heinz was eager to get to
the mountains, they decided to hitchhike to Banff. Peter, who
was never very enthralled with Edmonton, decided to take up
climbing with Heinz, as it was the only sport he could afford.
They bought a small amount of climbing gear from Monod
Sports in Banff.

While on their way to climb Cascade Mountain, Peter and
Heinz were picked up by the personnel manager of Banff National Park's Department of Public Works. He advised them to

come into his office the following day to see what work was available. Peter did not manage to climb Cascade, but he and Heinz got a job working for Parks as surveyors.

Living in Banff and learning the art of rock climbing with Heinz introduced Peter to the local climbing community.[21] When Heinz announced he had earned his guide's licence from Walter Perren, Peter reasoned that this achievment should be within his scope as well. He continued to climb diligently until he felt he was ready for his exam, and made an appointment with Walter to take the test. By fall, Peter had his guide's licence and could hang out his shingle as a Canadian Alpine Guide.

Peter began to guide for the Alpine Club, where he met up again with Hans Schwartz, who later settled in Jasper. They had become friends on an expedition to Peru to climb Huascaran and eventually guided together on the Yukon Centennial Expedition, where he also was reaquainted with Jim Davies.

Although Peter continued with his day job with the Department of Public Works, he also took as many guiding jobs as he could fit in. At the time, he was working in Calgary only one floor above the Parks Canada office, run by director general Don Coombs. But Peter didn't meet Coombs until Coombs attended a VIP trip to the Columbia Icefield with Ottawa brass, which Peter guided. When Walter Perren became ill and passed away from leukemia in 1967, Coombs asked Peter over for coffee to discuss the future of the public safety program; Coombs suggested Peter apply to run it, when the competition came up. A number of people applied, but the ones with the most experience were Peter, Willi Pfisterer and Fred Schleiss.

Peter was quite forward during his interview as he worked to convince the board he was the man for the job. When asked by one of the interviewers what the difference was between a vertical and a ring piton, he ignored the the question and immediately launched into what he felt they should be looking for rather than the uses of pitons. He astutely outlined that increasing tourism would be the future problem with regard to rescue work and pointed out the tremendous need for a "top-notch international rescue system." The idea that accidents were bound to increase was not startlingly new to the board, but the idea of an international calibre rescue team probably was. Peter relates, "I gave them a big spiel about what I thought the needs were and how it should be done. They all agreed and we had a good session after that."

Willi Pfisterer was also a contender for Walter's job. Willi got his foot in the door with the park service when he was hired as an avalanche observer in Glacier National Park in the winter of 1965. He was happy to get steady work and moved his family up to Mt. Fidelity for the season. Willi spent three seasons in Rogers Pass learning the technical aspects of avalanche forecasting and data collection, which helped enormously with his role later as an alpine specialist in Jasper National Park.

Willi was an independent man, and his boss, Fred Schleiss, found him difficult to deal with.[22] But Willi recognized the value of what he was learning in the art of avalanche prediction. He recalls, "I grew up in an avalanche area. We had all kinds of troubles and accidents. Being out in the field, I had a real gut feeling for the whole thing, as a guide, you know. I am still sitting here after 50 years of it. But, scientifically, I knew nothing. So at Rogers Pass, I was there for three years and learned all that. You cannot phone down to the forecaster and say, 'I have a bad feeling – you should close the road.' You have to come up with some facts, and that I learned at Rogers Pass."

One thing Willi appreciated about his position was the opportunity to travel to other avalanche control centres in both the
United States and Europe. Along on the trip were Peter Fuhrmann and Fred Schleiss, and they visited Jackson Hole, Wyoming, and Alta, Utah, as well as some ski venues in the Reno
area. Observing avalanche forecasting in different locations gave
those involved in the Canadian avalanche industry access to the
most up-to-date techniques in the world. It also gave Canada the
opportunity to become a leader in the avalanche control business.
Pfisterer noted, "Rogers Pass Avalanche Control really had their
act together. This was the biggest avalanche control centre in the
world. We went to Switzerland and to America to the ski hills to
look at what everybody was doing. We took the best of them all
and applied it at Rogers Pass."

Willi, with his guide's licence and experience at Rogers Pass,
felt he would be a shoo-in for head of public safety for the parks,
but in fact, Peter got the position. That surprised Peter also, and
he had to think hard about what it meant. The territory was huge
and his snow craft was a bit lacking. Upon futher discussion,
Parks Canada decided to hire both Peter and Willi, which led to
one of the best collaborations ever seen in the park system.

By the end of January 1971, maintaining avalanche stabilization
along the Trans-Canada Highway and the Banff–Jasper highway to the north was becoming a point of concern for Parks.
It fell to Peter and Willi to find the best solution for their re-
spective park responsibilities. Willi did not have much highway
to protect and concentrated most of the avalanche control on
the Marmot Basin ski hill. Peter, however, had major slide paths
threatening the Trans-Canada Highway, as well as the Sunshine
ski area to protect, including the access road. But he was actually

away in Mexico in January and February when the snowpack began to reach record depths. The steady cold temperatures did not result in any natural releases, and when Peter returned, the snow loads on the avalanche slopes that potentially affected the Trans-Canada were ominous. In 1970–71 there was still much to be learned about the ability of a large slab to propagate the release of huge quantities of snow from recessed gullies. Peter had had only two winters to establish a control program, and his data to date gave very little indication of what he would be dealing with in the unpredictable winter of 1971. He was not alone, however, as these conditions caught everyone off guard.

This author writes in *Guardians of the Peaks*:

> In those two years, Peter began experimenting with helicopter bombing, bypassing DOT regulations against taking primed high explosives into an aircraft by using Nitrone, a blasting agent not classified as "high explosive," which was used in seismographic well exploration. Peter came across this little item over yet another lunch with the president of Canadian Industries Limited (CIL), who had to get rid of the material, which was out of date. He was systematically blowing it up at considerable cost and was more than happy to give Peter two tonnes of the stuff to throw at all the mountains he wanted. Peter noted: "It wasn't normal parks procedure, especially when delivered over lunch hour," but it did give him a "free" supply of explosives for several winters to come.

Peter had already done some helicopter bombing with Jim the previous year and Jim had no reason to question the validity of this practice. It was clear some of the avalanche paths they bombed had never been stabilized before, and Parks Canada was not set up to launch artillery from the highway, so Jim was quite willing to see how effective the helicopter could be. It was not possible to use artillery from the Sunshine road, and the mortars they tried proved to be inaccurate.

Peter started his campaign against the heavy snows of the "Year Cycle" at the Sunshine ski area parking lot. These slopes were of great concern, because if the buildup of snow above the parking lot and the road released naturally, there would be no way to ensure the safety of anyone in the area. If Peter had any hesitation about bombing avalanches, a dramatic change in the weather tipped the scales in favour of taking action when a sudden warming trend made the release of natural slides ominously likely. The biggest threat from uncontrolled slides is the inability to predict when they will release, making it impossible to protect the highway or railroad tracks.

Peter recalls: "We closed the parking lot and didn't let anyone come down from [the ski hill at] Sunshine. We stopped everything. Then we flew up and threw a bomb into the Goat's Eye slide path." The avalanche that came down was massive, and indicative of things to come. When the white dust cleared, Peter saw nothing but "utter chaos." The avalanche had buried 32 cars, pushed two buses over and sent big fuel supply tanks shooting through the air "like torpedoes." Snow hit the Brewster information building and ticket booth, creating a pressure chamber effect that blew the whole roof off. But nobody was killed or injured. Peter remembers: "We were aghast. The parking lot was destroyed."

Subsequent bombing along the paths above the road left slide deposits 20–30 ft. deep, requiring a major cleanup just to reopen the resort. Any skiers caught up at the hill had to hoof it out over the snow and timber debris of the now very wide slide paths. There were no immediate repercussions, even though assistant superintendent Guy Myers, who was new to the mountains, was a bit unstrung about whether the correct action had been taken or not. It was new to everyone else as well.

But it's hard to argue with saving lives and very difficult to second-guess whether leaving a slide to nature would not have resulted in loss of life, so the program continued. The next concern was the Banff–Windermere highway. Fortunately, this road saw little traffic in those days, so no one complained about the massive slides released by Peter's Nitrone bombs, nor the several days it took to clean them up.

Mount Bosworth in Yoho was a different story. Although Peter had not included the snow collection basins on Mt. Bosworth above the Trans-Canada Highway at Wapta Lodge in his control program, he had eyed them nervously from the beginning of his tenure as alpine specialist. He had "advised the superintendent a number of times" that Mt. Bosworth posed a critical threat to the highway and the railroad. Under the existing conditions Peter was convinced a slide there was a disaster waiting to happen.

All hesitation at bombing this slide path evaporated when a small avalanche scudded across the highway while it was open to traffic. A driver observed the snow dust released in the slide obscure a car ahead of him – it simply disappeared in a white cloud. The driver immediately turned around and reported the incident. Although later investigation revealed the first car had scooted through safely without realizing an avalanche had come down, no one knew this at the time, and the report led to a tense search of the debris that night.

Peter has no trouble recalling the conditions the day they closed the highway to traffic and flew up to stabilize the slope: "It was drizzling on the summit of Mt. Bosworth – terrible, high-hazard conditions. I threw the bomb out of the helicopter and the moment it hit the snow, the slide started. The explosion hadn't even happened yet. I could have thrown a rock into the slide and it would have accomplished the same thing."

As he and Jim flared away in the helicopter, they could see a fracture line of deep instability snake through the surface of the thick slab, spreading across the slope in both directions, releasing tonnes of dense snow. The mass began to move slowly down, growing larger as it descended. When the bomb went off, the awesome inertia of potential energy was released. The impact of the explosion was incidental to the destructive power of the solid blocks of snow hurtling downward, ripping out huge, hundred-year-old stands of timber, in their rush to the highway and the CPR tracks below.

Neither man had ever seen anything like this despite the amount of control work they had done in the past. Frozen earth mingled with the snow turned the avalanche black.

Nor had Andy Anderson, then chief park warden in Yoho National Park, who was somewhat knowledgeable about avalanches himself. Andy had worked in ski areas in the avalanche control program with Walter Perren and knew quite a bit about explosives and avalanches – but this scared the pants off him, and for good reason. He was part of the observation team below and, through the fogged-up windows of his warden truck, could not see whether he was clear of the slide. He threw the truck into reverse, hurtling backward to avoid the oncoming avalanche.

From the relatively safe position of the helicopter, Jim and

Peter watched the massive slide roar across the road, over Wapta Lake and on up to the CPR tracks on the far side of the lake. Chunks of timber flew into the air like thin black sticks flung from a cloud of snow and debris. The slide took everything out, right to the ground. It also widened the narrow, previously unconnected upper chutes into one huge slide path.

If there had been no immediate repercussions over the Sunshine parking lot slide (except for impending lawsuits), that was not the case this time. Much of the complaint had to do with a freight train on the track when the slide happened. Although it was not hit, the impact of the snow on the rail line, and the damage done to it, resulted in a panicked call to Anderson from Banff Park superintendent Harley Webb to stop all bombing immediately. Still in alarm mode, Harley then called Jim Raby, regional director of parks in Calgary, who contacted assistant superintendent Guy Myers in Banff, to sort it out.

Myers sorted it out by shutting Peter's program down altogether. The situation was only temporary, though, as Raby supported Peter's initial decision to bomb the slope and instructed him to "get back and do what was best." Undoubtedly there was some fallout over not having notified the CPR of the control actions, but no one thought the slide would go that far.

×   ×   ×

Jim Davies's 1966 involvement with the evacuation of an injured man from Beauty Creek and the support he gave on the Babel Tower rescue indicated that people were beginning to see a greater role for the helicopter in evacuation of lost or injured people.

One other noteworthy rescue (which also took place in 1966 but did not involve Jim Davies) was significant for being successful under dramatic circumstances; it was also one of the last in which Walter Perren would participate. The accident occurred in Rogers Pass in late summer when two Americans decided to climb the ridge route on Mt. Sir Donald. They ran into problems on the descent when bad weather caused them to get off route.

Fred Schleiss, the chief avalanche forecaster in Rogers Pass, was the most experienced climber in the area, so when the call for help came in, he jumped into action, hauling two wardens with him. Unfortunately, the rescue party ran into trouble. On the steep approach, one of the wardens slipped, badly injuring one arm. Fred suddenly had his own rescue to contend with, and it was all he could do to get the man safely down. Knowing he needed help to do anything for the Americans, Fred called his brother Walter Schleiss to come up and help Perren.

Perren too realized he needed expertise beyond that available within the warden ranks and brought in Don Vockeroth, then working at Lake O'Hara as a park patrolman. Don was well into establishing his own climbing career and was more than capable of assisting. But even with his experience, Don found the conditions, when the pilot flew them up the mountain, to be quite tricky. He recalls: "We got out there and the rescue was in progress but was getting more complicated and the weather was just a blizzard. It was very bad weather. So, we were flying up to the Uto/Sir Donald col in bad weather and the helicopter goes up the west side and the updraft sent the winds ripping over the col.... [The pilot] has to tip the blade and hold it just to stay there."

Walter and Fred felt they could speed up the approach by

jumping out at the col. But getting out of the gyrating helicopter was much trickier than they thought. Don remembers, "There is actually a little slope, not flat but about 15 or 20 degrees and only about eight square feet or something ... and Walter says, 'okay you get out.'" The "little slope," however, that hung innocently above the looming void below, was covered in ice. Don was a bit shaken at this prospect, wondering how to make the transition from the helicopter to the ice with no protection. He laughs: "I had to put a crampon on. Then I was sitting on the skid.... Walter is hanging on to me and the machine is just bucking. After I get that [crampon] on, I got onto the verglas, which was about one inch of ice. Then I drove in a piton. It felt good!"

From that point, Don was able to help both Fred and Walter out of the helicopter and retrieve enough gear and food for the stranded climbers. The Americans were actually working their way down the ridge when the team reached them, despite one fellow being injured and barely able to climb.

The hot food improved the climbers' outlook, but the hardest part of the rescue was still ahead. They now had to get the injured climber onto a stretcher and lower him to a location that was helicopter accessible. Don is quick to point out that this was the early days of helicopter assistance in rescues, before standards were set. He remembers, "You're just learning how far you can push it.... You don't consider the risk factors. There was no 'risk management.'"

Despite the difficulties, the party was brought to a spot where they could be flown out. It was a major rescue accomplished by personnel working together from different parks and aided significantly by a brave pilot willing to take a chance. Don was hugely impressed by the young pilot's ability but added, sadly, that he died only a few years later when his helicopter ran out of fuel.

Using helicopters to evacuate people or get rescue personnel in close to an accident site was not new in 1966. The first recorded rescue by a helicopter occurred in Long Island Sound, New York, on November 29, 1945. The rescue came about more by happenstance than planning. The east coast was under barrage from a hurricane-force storm wreaking havoc all along the coast. A barge had broken up in the sound and the crew sent up flares for help. The sea was far too rough to send in boats, and people on shore stood helplessly by, knowing the men would be washed overboard. However, a policeman remembered the nearby Sikorsky helicopter base where, earlier, the public had been invited to a demonstration of a helicopter lifting loads using an external rescue hoist. The winch had just recently been installed on the new army YR-5A that was used for the rescue.

The police got in touch with Jimmy Viner, a helicopter test pilot and somewhat of a legend. He agreed to try the winch system to retrieve the stranded men. Though conditions were perilous, they had no choice if they were to get the men out. It was a bona fide rescue, using a simple loop as a harness, that could only be accomplished by a helicopter. The rescue was a success.

The helicopter industry had entered a new area of service. A Bell 30 was used that same year to rescue two ice fishermen on Lake Erie. The helicopter was proving its versatility, but it would not be used distinctly in mountain rescue until the Swiss adapted the use of the winch to their own helicopters in late 1969/70.

Before the Swiss introduced the winch lowering system, helicopters had only been used to pick up injured parties if they were in a spot where the helicopter could land, and steep mountain terrain was a serious constraint. In Canada the first documented use of a helicopter extracting a victim from steep mountain terrain did not even happen in a national park. Walter Perren, who always had an open mind about rescue aids that could save the victim without putting the wardens in danger, got a call from provincial ranger M. Verhaege, stationed at Canmore, on August 27, 1961, at eight in the morning. Dieter Raubach, who was climbing Mt. Blane with Gordon Crocker, a fellow member of the newly formed Calgary Mountain Club, first reported the accident. From his information, it was apparent that Crocker was lying injured with a broken ankle and possible internal trauma at an elevation of 9400 ft.

Walter's first concern was to reach the climber with supplies before nightfall. But the evacuation would need a high camp and would probably take two days if the helicopter could be used. With some nervous anticipation, he requested a helicopter from Foothills Aviation in Calgary. When Raubach described the terrain the accident had occurred on, Walter also realized he would need the assistance of experienced climbers. Accordingly, he contacted fellow guide Hans Gmoser, as well as Klaus Hahn from the Calgary Mountain Club. Walter understood that, once the high camp was established, the helicopter could only be used if a substantial platform was built on the steep hillside to support the weight of the machine for both loading and unloading supplies and men. He was able to commandeer the use of inmates from a local detention centre to build the structure, which was a feat in itself. He writes (of the need to bring supplies to the injured climber): "This was achieved [on foot] by D. Raubach and myself at 6:15 pm. August 27th Mr. Raubach was left with the injured man and I climbed back down to the high camp, elevation,

6,800, which had been established by the rest of the party with the help of the helicopter."

The following morning (August 28), Walter returned with a small rescue party to the men above, reaching them at noon to begin the arduous process of securing and lowering the injured climber, hoping to get to the helicopter pad that day. Walter writes:

> We transported and lowered the injured climber down the mountain with help of a Gramminger seat carrier, to an elevation of 8,000 feet, arriving at 6:30 p.m. Climbing in the dark was considered too hazardous on account of loose rock and it was decided to break up the operation. Warden Carlton bivouacked with the injured climber; the rest of the party climbed down to high camp, arriving at 8:00 p.m.

The following day the same rescue party, without Gmoser or Hahn, climbed back to the bivouacked party to effect the rest of the lowering using a rescue basket. The operation was concluded at 4:00 p.m. Walter also concluded that "the portable radios and helicopter were of extreme value."

× × ×

Another interesting rescue using helicopter support occurred on Mt. Cleveland in Glacier National Park in Montana, in 1969. Peter Fuhrmann and Willi Pfisterer (Parks Canada alpine specialists) attempted to employ a US Air Force Huey helicopter on a massive search. However, the machine was late in arriving and was immediately grounded by poor weather. When the skies did clear, the helicopter was cumbersome, and the pilot was not willing to fly close to the mountain. Clearly, the United States had not pursued the use of helicopters in rescue situations in the mountains.

But the Swiss did pioneer the true measure of the helicopter's capabilities. The Swiss Air Rescue began in 1943 when a group of helicopter pilots were called upon to help evacuate people from a flood. They continued to extend themselves with evacuation assistance in more and more mountainous regions and at higher altitudes. They had bigger machines than those Jim piloted in Banff, with big turbojet engines, which helped access the higher mountains, and more importantly, enabled them to carry extra weight.

On September 24–27, 1970, the Swiss had a chance to demonstrate the use of a winch to access steep faces during the Swiss Air Rescue's Second International Helicopter Symposium, held on the Kleine Scheidegg, a pass between the Jungfrau's Eiger north face and the Lauberhorn. For the first time in the history of air rescue, mountain guides and paramedics were suspended on the end of a hoist cable beneath a hovering helicopter. They did this at five different sites on the north face of the Eiger, followed by a successful operation winching an injured climber, again off the north face of the Eiger.

Peter Fuhrmann, head of public safety for Banff National Park in Canada, saw the article on the rescue in a German magazine and knew he had a solution that would change mountain rescue in Canada forever.

5

Permission or Forgiveness

When Jim was flying for Bullock Helicopters, the idea of using the helicopter in life-saving situations was not given much thought, other than applying the machine's obvious ability to evacuate stranded or injured people by landing, then loading them into the aircraft. Bush pilots had already been doing this for years in the North, but accidents in the mountains usually occurred in places inaccessible to aircraft for landing.

Jim had done some pioneering of inaccessible landings with his fixed-wing plane when he landed at Assiniboine, Sunshine and, momentarily, on Deception Pass. He also practised landing on lakes and glaciers when he flew airdrops for Hans Gmoser before the guide's ill-fated Jasper–Lake Louise ski-tour trip. His attraction to landing on the highest peak around, when conditions were favourable, continued when he started flying helicopters.

Jim was a careful pilot, but he loved a challenge. Peter probably detected this willingness to take calculated risks when Jim agreed to dynamite avalanche paths from the helicopter. He felt Jim was the best mountain pilot around and did not hesitate to corner him with the idea of using Swiss Air Rescue's method of employing a winch and long line to get people off mountains.

Although Peter (and Willi Pfisterer) were developing the work of mountain rescue in the parks, Peter was particularly frustrated by the number of deaths that occurred while transporting victims out from remote locations or over technically difficult terrain. In 1971, emergency evacuation required many people to haul the injured out over cliffs, across rivers, through dense bush or crevassed glaciers to get them to medical aid. If the distance was too far or too rough, or the weather was unforgiving, the consequences were grim for the injured.

With enhanced interest in alpine sports into the 1970s, the number of people running into difficulty was dramatically increasing. It was with considerable interest, then, that Peter read the article – handed to him over the fence by good friend and neighbour Bruno Engler – about rescuers in the Alps using helicopters with a winch cable and load hook to reach stranded climbers. It was an article in the Bergwacht (mountain watch) magazine. The instant Peter read the article, he knew he had the answer to the rescue dilemma in the Rockies.

The idea was so radical that Peter felt he had to learn more about what European air rescue was doing and how, before he dared bring it to the attention of the Parks bureaucracy, lest he end up sounding like a fool. Instead, he took a holiday later that fall to Germany and met Ludwig "Wiggerl" Gramminger at the Hofbrauhaus in Munich for a beer. Wiggerl invented the Gramminger seat used in cable rescue, and the Jenny Bag. They had a fine time, and both Wiggerl and his wife, Paula (who sewed the rescue harness) became his good friends in the process.

When Ludwig brought Peter to see the helicopter setup in operation, Peter (who knew the helicopters used in the mountain parks) was discouraged to see the Germans were using large military machines like the Huey while the Swiss were using Alouette III "sand Lamas" with rope or cable winches attached to the side. He did not think that getting the military involved back in Canada was a viable option. He did learn, however, that the early rescues used a knotted rope attached to the body of the helicopter (even on the more powerful Alouette III), which could be used by lighter, smaller helicopters like the Alouette II. He returned home with the directions to make a similar knotted rope. They dared not attach it to the cargo hook or the skids, which caused the machine to become unbalanced with a swinging load. This was solved initially by using a cable passed through the body of the machine, which worked fairly well.

The system worked for the Swiss, but they played in a much bigger ballpark. Rega (Swiss Air Rescue) was, and continues to be, a private, non-profit, air rescue service that provides emergency medical assistance in Switzerland and Liechtenstein through an insurance plan. It was started by Dr. Rudolf Bucher in 1952. Later, through generous donations, it could afford the extra personnel it took to run a winch system. Because the machine was so big, it could not get in close to the mountain and often worked with very long cables. Rega also dealt with far more rescues than occurred in Canada within any working year.

It was evident that a winch system was out of the question for Canada with its limited staff and small helicopters. But Peter was not one to throw the baby out with the bathwater, and he knocked a few ideas around with the pilots and Gramminger, wondering how a simple, lightweight sling could be adapted to the smaller, single-engine helicopters used at home. They came up with the idea of using a shorter, fixed sling using 60 and 100 ft. lengths that would allow a smaller helicopter to work in closer to the mountain, getting into small places previously thought inaccessible.

Peter was still excited when he got home, but he needed to know from an expert what would work. He felt he could convince Jim of the viability of using a sling rope attached to the underbelly of the helicopter, though convincing the Department of Transport would be another matter.

Jim did not want to commit to this obviously risky work until they had seen the system in Europe for themselves and talked to the pilots about logistics and problems. Peter talked Willi Pfisterer into joining him and Jim on a trip to Switzerland to attend an ICAR (International Commission for Alpine Rescue) meeting. It was attended by 16 alpine nations and involved 25 different helicopter models. ICAR was formed in 1948 and its mission is to provide "a platform for mountain rescue and related organizations to disseminate knowledge with the prime goal of improving mountain rescue services and their safety" around the globe.

Such an innovation would have to apply to all the mountain national parks. Peter probably expected more resistance from Willi, but surprisingly he was prepared to entertain the idea. In the spring of 1971, all three boarded a plane for Switzerland.

Though what they saw was impressive, it was clear a military helicopter was not feasible in the Canadian parks system. As Peter had observed, the operational budget would be prohibitive and the helicopters too big to fly in close to the mountain. The Canadian helicopters did not require as big a payload as those used in Switzerland and the operating altitude was much lower in the Rockies, making the smaller helicopter feasible in Canada. But they could not go back to Parks Canada unless they had a plan that incorporated the Bell 206B JetRanger helicopter, the mainstay for most of the flying in the mountain parks. Before that developed, however, Jim was flying the Alouette II with a turboshaft engine and could handle the initial training and rescue missions.

Jim contemplated taking on the dicey job of rescuing people with a fixed-sling rope, but there was a lot to consider. First, he had never performed a sling evacuation with rescuer and victim.

Second was the commitment to his flying time, and whether the additional hours would be acceptable to Bullock. If he agreed to fly rescues for the park, he would have to be on permanent call, or train another pilot to fill in for him when he was gone. With all the work Bullock did up north, Jim could not see the company agreeing to promise both a helicopter and a pilot to be used exclusively in the park.

Third, this type of helicopter work carried with it increased risk. Risk was also expensive to insure, especially if Parks didn't have approval from DOT.

On the other hand, Jim was getting hooked on the idea of using the helicopter for mountain rescue. The mountains had become a playground for a multitude of baby boomers who now had access to cars. They came in droves looking for a wilderness experience for which they were poorly equipped. The growing frequency of rescues suggested the work would keep Jim busy all summer and employed closer to home.

In addition to the number of search-and-rescues rocketing skyward, the number of bear problems was multiplying as well. With the influx of tourists crowding the towns and campgrounds, garbage was everywhere. None of the landfills had been properly secured from bears, and back then garbage receptacles were far from bear-proof. Whereas in the past the bear-savvy local residents often just chased the bears off and knew enough to take their garbage to the landfill, this was not a solution for tourists. In fact, landfills had become a target for tourists who were almost guaranteed a bear sighting, with a good chance of seeing a grizzly. The interaction between bears competing for food always livened things up, giving the crowd a real show.[23] As a result, Jim was being called out to remove a growing number of problem bears.

Other work Jim could rely on, if he decided to stay in the Banff area, was being employed to fight fires, either with water bombing (monsoon bucket) or shuffling crews and equipment around.

It was also 25 years since the end of the Second World War and both the United States and Canada were entering a time of prosperity. Money was available to build roads, cabins, campgrounds and trails in the backcountry. Despite constant conflict with Parks Canada over environmental assessments, the ski areas also continued to expand. All of this meant a lot of helicopter time on construction projects.

Jim thought long and hard about becoming involved in search and rescue, with its multifaceted problems of logistics, weather, topography and all the unforeseen snags inherent in bringing someone back alive. He had been happy working for Bullock, but much of the work was repetitive, ferrying people and equipment in the North.

And of course, another – very significant – reason to fly for the mountain national parks was the location. His principal agreement would be with Banff National Park, but Jim would also cover Yoho and Kootenay national parks. Jasper would have its own pilot (Gary Forman) doing much the same work as Jim. One thing Jim had learned: his relationship with Sue was much more fulfilling when he was around on a regular basis. Working out of Banff meant living at home year round.

But perhaps the deciding factor for Jim was the challenge of heli-rescue.

×   ×   ×

Integrating helicopters into mountain rescue already had some precedents. Jim had picked up injured people from remote parts of the park. He had even used a sling rope to recover a body from a crevasse.

A few years earlier, quite by accident, Jim became involved in pulling a man out of a crevasse on Victoria Glacier. He was flying by when he spotted Paul Peyto, a Banff local, with a small group of people gathered around an open crevasse, looking as if they'd lost something (or someone). Jim found a flat place to land and joined them. It turned out the group had been heading up the glacier when one of their number fell in the crevasse. Paul told Jim the man was really stuck, and they couldn't get him out. They could reach his foot, sticking out of a pinch point, well down the crevasse, but that was all. They were pretty sure the man was dead.

Jim suggested, "How about I tie a rope to the cargo hook, and you climb down and tie it around his foot? Then I'll try to lift him out." It was better than anything else they had come up with.

Jim secured a good length of rope to the hook under the helicopter and then hovered over to the crevasse. Paul caught the end of the rope and, with a bit of slack, was able to climb into the crevasse and tie the rope to the man's foot.

Jim began to lift slowly. Abruptly, the man's body swung free above the group. It was a rather macabre sight, seeing their friend dangling from the rope upside down in the air. Jim laid him out on the snow, the hikers loaded his body into the craft, and Jim flew him back to Banff. It was evident this solution was far preferable to organizing a big rescue party to pull the man out and carry him manually to the trailhead, from where an ambulance could take him to Banff.

The big challenge in 1971, however, was to fly injured climbers off mountains – much more inaccessible than glaciers – eliminating the need to send a rescue team in by foot, which put more people in danger. Peter knew the leap from landing safely and putting people into the helicopter, to slinging them on a fixed line, would be difficult to pass by the Department of Transport. Peter would have a limited opportunity to get approval from both Parks Canada and DOT. To succeed, he would need a solid argument and a reliable helicopter and pilot.

The first big problem was how to attach a rope to the helicopter so it would not throw the helicopter off balance, once in the air. A swinging object attached to a skid was not doable, and fastening the rope to the cargo hook was not acceptable, as it would be too easy to hit the eject button and release the load, both the rescuers and the victim. Eventually the problem was solved by bolting two permanent flanges to the bottom of the helicopter that secured the rope with heavy duty, screw-gated carabiners. Peter devised the rescue line out of two strands of climbing rope knotted at four-foot intervals to keep it together in the air. The first line was 60 ft. long but eventually he made shorter ones that could be attached to the longer rope if extra length was needed.

Finally, on a windless day at the Banff airfield in the early summer of 1971, Peter explained the system to a crew of skeptical

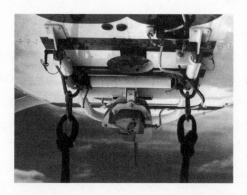

Sling hookup under the helicopter
(KATHY CALVERT COLLECTION).

wardens. Peter recalls: "I said to Jim, 'Look, why don't I sit in this marvellous seat and hook on with the knotted rope as per the diagram – and you take off ten feet and put me back down.' And that's the first lift-off we had." From there, it was magic. Jim lifted the wardens,[24] who were alternately terrified or thrilled as they swung through space like Superman above the valley below.

But if Jim had to fly the unweighted sling rope without a person on the end, the possibility of it getting sucked up into the rotors created a source of danger. Jay Morton, one of the wardens, recalls, "Someone made a phone call to the garage and immediately somebody came roaring out with some bolts and plates from a guardrail and they screwed them on to the end of the rope." Jay still has a picture of himself flying over the Banff highway traffic circle with "these goddamned guardrail weights hanging above my head.... That's how primitive it was."

That first demonstration had the young wardens looking at each other in disbelief. Scott Ward, another warden, recalls, "I was there at the Banff airport in '71 when Fuhrmann first tested the heli-sling rescue with Jim and we all watched in amazement and the general consensus was 'No way are we doing that. That's crazy!'" These exercises (and the first rescues using the sling) were actually done before the system was approved, but Peter and Jim believed enough in the method to take the chance. They used Cascade Mountain ledges to practise on, depositing and picking up a number of nervous wardens.

×   ×   ×

Peter hoped the wardens would see the advantage of this form of rescue, but getting it accepted by both the park administration and the Department of Transport was the first step. If Peter didn't clear that hurdle, none of the wardens would have to consider it again. The federal Department of Transport (now Transport Canada), which controlled flight regulations in Canada, were a conservative lot, not given to strange new inventions that might jeopardize safety. Though slinging objects under helicopters was not new, flying human cargo on a non-releasable attachment was.

But first the proposal had to be accepted by Parks Canada. It did not help when Jim flew a slightly alarmed Jay Morton down the main street of Banff past the superintendent's office. As they flew by, Jay waved at his ultimate boss, Banff park superintendent Steve Kun, who was at that moment discussing why the airport should be shut down because of a perceived threat to wildlife.[25] Just then, one attentive administrator observed, "And there goes one of them now!" Kun spun around in time to see a smiling Jay zoom by the window and disappear into the sunny skies.

The next day Peter was called in to account for this unexplained phenomenon.

Steve Kun was not opposed to the idea of rescuing people by

helicopter with this unorthodox method, but he needed much more documentation before presenting the program to the minister in Ottawa. It was a Catch-22 conundrum. Authorization could not be given till the system was proven, and the system could not be proven without authorization to use it. But Peter was a bold man and was willing to take risks for something he believed in. The axiom "forgiveness is easier to get than permission" applied.

Peter followed up the Banff demonstration with one in Jasper. Dale Portman remembers it well. "The first thing they did was have the pilot from Hinton, Alberta, fly a 45-gallon fuel barrel around at the end of the sling rope. On a couple of occasions, he banged it into the guardrail near the airport." So, when the time came to use human guinea pigs, "many of us wardens that day had a dry mouth and puckered sphincters as we reached for the end of the sling rope to be lifted off from terra firma."

As Peter was driving toward the Jasper–Banff boundary after the demonstration, he heard, over his radio, of a rescue in progress. He realized the operation was at Pinto Lake, very close to where he was. Because he'd just come from the Jasper heli-slinging demonstration, he had all the equipment he needed in the back of his car. He proceeded to the staging area on the highway to see what was happening.

A young man had slipped on a steep ice slope and fallen onto the rocks below. His injuries were serious, and all the rescue team could do was fly rescuers to the pass, where they made their way carefully down to the injured man. The incident happened on the Pinto Lake side of the pass, which was thick with old-growth trees. The trees were too tall to allow the helicopter to get near the man, and it seemed likely they would have to build a platform for the helicopter to land on. It was getting dark quickly, meaning they would have to wait until the next day to build a platform that would hold the weight of the helicopter.

Warden Jay Morton, who was familiar with the recently intro-duced sling rescue, was at the staging area set up at the highway and was surprised when Peter drove up out of the blue. Peter was glad to see Jay, as he was familiar with the rescue procedure, hav-ing been introduced to it in Banff. He would make an excellent supervisor to organize the ground crew. Peter had monitored their progress on his radio and knew the only way to get the man out before dark was to sling him out on the rescue stretcher. Again, to Jay's surprise, Peter had all the rescue sling gear in his car. They managed to talk the new young pilot into passing the rescue rope through the body of the helicopter and then lift off so that Peter could attach it to the end of the sling line with the stretcher. The pilot had never seen anything like it but was quick to follow Peter's instructions. Peter radioed to the rescuers on site to clear enough trees to get himself and the stretcher in. This reduced their work considerably and they were soon ready to bring Peter in.

Once the helicopter lifted off, Peter sat comfortably in the res-cue harness with the attached empty stretcher in front of him at chest level. Flying up to the injured man was quick and they loaded him onto the stretcher without a problem. They hauled the stretcher out to the middle of the rock slope for greater tree clearance and brought the helicopter back with the long line. While the helicopter hovered overhead, Peter clipped himself and the loaded stretcher to the dangling line and gave the signal to lift them off. It was fortunate that the helicopter could fly straight down, gaining much-needed air speed for lift. Even with this manoeuvre, the rescuers had to bodily lift the basket into the air to get it off the ground. The risks were enormous, as neither man was sure if the machine had enough power to get them over the pass and down to the highway. Suddenly, the unit was clear of the trees and Peter, clipped to the stretcher, experienced a rushing downward plunge toward Pinto Lake. This downward dive provided the air speed and lift they needed to support the weight of the two men and stretcher. They were lucky in having a skilled pilot who was familiar with the weight limitations of the machine. In order to get back over the pass, the pilot had to circle above the lake, slowly gaining altitude until he was able to clear the pass and drop down to the highway below.

But minutes after becoming airborne, the pilot told Peter, through the cumbersome portable radio, that he was going to have a problem when they reached the staging area, as the helicopter he was flying did not have the power to hover to lower the them to the ground. He had to maintain forward air speed to avoid stalling and crashing.

Frantically, Peter radioed down to Jay to get everyone possible around the landing site. His plan was to have the pilot come in with enough speed not to stall while the ground crew grabbed the stretcher and ran like mad, giving one person a chance to release the carabiner attached to the stretcher. It was a desperate manoeuvre that could have dire consequences for the lives of pilot, rescuer and victim, not to mention the future of the heli-rescue program. Despite the improbability of executing this spontaneous coordination between the helicopter and the ground crew, it worked.

Though a long line had been used by the helicopter at Pinto Lake to bring an injured man out, it was so dicey and uncontrolled that Peter preferred not to use the case as an example of the new mountain rescue program. This rescue also spotlighted one of the problems associated with using piston-driven helicopters.[26]

Jim knew the limitations of the piston-driven machines. He had been using the more powerful Bell 204 (alternately with the Alouette III) in the Bugaboos, where the turbo-powered helicopters could now carry as many as 12 skiers in one flight. The Bell 206B was a giant step forward in helicopter design, being one of the first to be powered by a turboshaft. The turboshaft engine radically improved the practicality of the helicopter due to its high power-to-weight ratio. It also used less fuel and had lower maintenance and operating costs. The Bell turboshaft rapidly became the most successful helicopter at that time.

×　×　×

The next rescue gave Peter solid evidence of how useful the helicopter could be in steep-angle rescue situations, using the vertical sling rope the way it was intended.

Jim was flying an Alouette II helicopter in June at a warden heli-slinging training day when a call came for a rescue on Mt. Edith. The terrain was such that, if the victim were to be evacuated with a ground team, reaching the accident site would be too time consuming. The use of a helicopter could mean the difference between life and death. Peter made the decision to use the helicopter.

A reader would not know the real importance of this rescue from looking at Jim's log book. Jim wrote: "Pickup at compound. Rescue of injured climber on Mt. Edith 7,400' using vertical sling

Wounded cadet on Mt. Edith
(JIM DAVIES COLLECTION).

from Mt. Edith to hospital lawn, injured man and Peter." In fact, it was a dazzling success, as they flew right over Banff townsite and the warden compound, directly to the hospital.

The rescue was not quite as simple as Jim's terse writing implied. A corporal in the Canadian Army was hit on the head by rockfall while participating in a training climb on the east face of Mt. Edith, just north of Banff townsite. The flimsy helmet liner the man wore was insufficient to prevent a serious indentation in his skull, leaving him unconscious but alive. The leader climbed down and alerted the RCMP by radio, giving them the details of the accident, which they immediately passed on to Peter. When Peter was given the information, he called on Jim Davies to sling him into the site.

When Jim approached the location, he realized he would have to do some fancy flying to get Peter on site. The steepness of the ground did not allow Jim to get close to the injured man for fear of hitting the rotor blades on the cliff face. To get Peter to the stranded party, Jim was forced to rock the machine, setting up a pendulum motion on the long line that enabled him to swing

Peter close to the face. After a couple of tries, one of the army members sitting with the victim pulled him in and attached him to the anchor they had set up.

It may have been at this moment that Jim became aware of the implicit trust he would have to have in the men he would work with. For a short time Peter was simultaneously clipped to the belly of the helicopter and the mountain when he secured himself to the piton anchor.

Unlike slinging an inert load that could be released, this situation meant Jim had no control over this phase of the rescue. He was helpless to abandon the site – no matter what eventuality arose – until the rescuer released him from the line. At that moment, a long thin line of trust quivered in the air, establishing a silent dialogue between rescuer and pilot.

Once Peter was on the mountain, he felt he would have enough room to bring in the rescue stretcher that Jim brought up next. With some difficulty Peter could reach the stretcher and detach it from the sling line. With careful manoeuvring they loaded the corporal and signalled Jim to come back. As the ring of the rescue line swung in to them, Peter quickly clicked himself and the stretcher to the sling line. After unhooking the victim from the anchor, some of the men helped lift the load (Peter and the injured party) off the cliff. Once they were free of the mountain, Jim nosed the machine into a steep dive to pick up the air speed needed to transport Peter and the cadet to the lawn in front of the hospital, where a stretcher was waiting.

No one could miss the odd site of Peter hanging from the sling, clutching a stretcher, as they flew back to Banff – particularly superintendent Steve Kun.

The next day, Peter was again called up to defend the use of the helicopter in spite of having no authorization from Parks Canada or DOT to take such action.

Peter was ready for this. He had a letter from the doctor who treated the patient, saying the soldier would have died without immediate attention. Scott Ward, one of Peter's heli-sling-trained wardens, was there to unload the basket from the helicopter and bring the injured man into the hospital. He remembers: "I was also on the receiving end of the stretcher at the Banff Hospital when Peter and Jim slung in with the first victim from Pinto Lake rescued by heli-sling. It started to sink in then that maybe there was something to this after all." Kun agreed that the use of the helicopter was important in saving the man's life.

After the rescue was over, Peter and Jim had a better idea of the details that needed to be nailed down in the proposal to Parks Canada. It was evident to Jim that the rapid evolution of helicopter performance could now allow the use of helicopters in mountain rescue to grow. Although Peter's experience in trying to use a helicopter for evacuating injured people was frustrating,[27] he could see the potential of the program with the right helicopter, the right pilot and the right warden training program. He needed someone like Jim, who knew the mountains better than anyone, to be committed to the program if it was to be successful. Jim told Peter that if the program could get approval, he would be available in Banff on a 15-minute call-out basis. Peter finally had substantial data with which to approach Parks Canada and DOT for formal approval. The wardens involved in the public safety program were much more receptive, knowing Jim would be the pilot to whom they were entrusting their lives.

Steve Kun conceded that the park rescue service needed the helicopter, particularly with the alarming rate of accidents happening almost daily (often more on weekends). He gave his support to Peter but cautioned that the program still had to be approved at the regional level and the federal level in Ottawa, and by the Department of Transport.

But Peter had a strong ally in Regional Office. Jim Sime – former chief park warden now working in Regional Office for the warden service – was able to cut through a lot of red tape and mediate between Parks Canada and DOT. Sime had come up through the ranks of the warden service and never stopped considering himself a warden at heart. He was also one of the more enlightened men in the Calgary office. He still needed Peter to come with him to Ottawa, where he could deliver his "bucket of blood" approach to opening the eyes of bureaucrats who knew little about their western national parks.

When dealing with Ottawa's administration (Parks Canada or DOT), Jim Sime was the right man for the job. The warden service never had a better friend with more personal interest in the well-being of the service than Sime. Peter and Willi Pfisterer both worked directly for him, which suited them eminently. Sime also controlled the purse strings for the newly developing rescue service and was generous when expenditures were justified. And with helicopter rescue, expenses were necessary.

The door was cracking open for Peter with Parks Canada, but he was well aware he had been lucky on both rescues in having reasonable conditions to allow the helicopter to operate. But such rescues were still dangerous if the helicopter was underpowered. They needed better equipment, trained pilots, effective liaisons with the ambulance service, and trained rescue wardens.

Peter was shocked by the amount of persuasion required to

convince Parks Canada in Ottawa that heli-slinging was a life-saving tool that should not be ignored.

First, he encountered the entrenched idea that people undertaking dangerous sports should be left to save themselves. The administration in Ottawa saw no reason to risk employees' lives (or money) to rescue these people. Peter pointed out that leaving cadavers hanging over popular climbing routes or dangling above well-used hiking trails might not be the best image for Parks Canada. Also, Ottawa was willing to spend millions of dollars to save pilots irresponsible enough to fly single-engine planes without filing a flight plan – so how was mountain rescue different?

Next, Peter argued that using the helicopter saved money. Slinging men into a rescue scene was cost effective when compared to the expense of sending in a large ground party over several days to do the same job.

Third, if Ottawa was concerned about risking people's lives to save climbers, Peter noted, the helicopter substantially reduced that risk by not exposing large numbers of rescuers to the hazards of the rescue.

Fourth was accountability. The climbing era had arrived in the Canadian Rockies. Regardless of Parks management's attitude, ground teams simply could not save lives as effectively as the helicopter could. Eliminating the use of the helicopter would mean people would die needlessly, and it would lie at Parks Canada's door if that were to happen.

The arguments were compelling. Peter gained Parks Canada's support.

It was probably just as well Peter had to go to the lengths he did to convince Parks that helicopter sling rescue was necessary to bring Canada into the modern age of alpine rescue, because he had a much tougher sell with the Department of Transport. The success of his meetings with Parks Canada forced him to have his argument well thought out and practised before tackling this formidable arm of the government. Jim Sime was actually the principal negotiator with both Ottawa and the Department of Transport, and he recalls it took several months of delicate campaigning to elicit a positive response from this department.

The stumbling block with DOT was the attachment of the sling to the aircraft. Swiss Air Rescue's work notwithstanding, what was being proposed in Canada had not been done before. No one else in the world had attempted a sling rescue using one rope solidly attached to a light, manoeuvrable helicopter. Nothing like this had ever been approved by the Department of Transport, mainly because of the danger to the helicopter and pilot. If the line could not be released, any entanglement with earthbound objects (such as trees, wires etc.) jeopardized the survival of both machine and pilot.

The rescuers, on the other hand, felt much safer knowing they could not be jettisoned, either by accident or by design. Both Jim Davies and the wardens he would be working with felt it was necessary to come together as a team and accept joint risk.

After much negotiation, the parties finally settled on issuing a waiver for the new rescue technique that mollified but did not eradicate DOT's unease. The first stipulation was acceptable: DOT stated that, because of the life-saving scope of the sling rescue, Parks Canada could continue to use it, but it would be restricted to their use alone. No other agency or private company would be given permission to sling human cargo in such a manner. The second stipulation limited the rescue operation to areas that were not contaminated by overhead wires or other obstructions that could tangle the sling line. Since most rescues occurred in open spaces, this was doable, but staging areas had to be carefully selected to avoid entanglement with trees. For a pilot this was obvious. With these restrictions, permission to go ahead was granted.

Chief park warden Bert Pittaway in Banff formally signed off on the final acceptance of this system.

Jim was glad to have this red tape out of the way and be given permission to fly rescue missions with the sling rope. He was offered a single-source contract to fly regular work hours with the stipulation he commit to a 15-minute call-out for any emergency rescue. On this basis, he went ahead and purchased the Bell 206B JetRanger and formed his own company, which he named Inter Mountain Helicopters in memory of Al Gates, a well-known former pilot in Banff.

In Jasper, Willi Pfisterer recruited Gary Forman, who also agreed to be on standby as their rescue pilot. Jim knew Gary through Bow Helicopters, for whom they had both worked. Jim checked him out on his slinging ability and other necessary skills like autorotation and flying in tight conditions, to ensure he had the skills for the job. He was pleased to note Gary was a consistent and careful pilot who was well aware of maintaining good vertical reference. To his credit, he carried out this role in Jasper for many years with no mishaps. As Gary grew older, the role eventually went to Todd McCready, who became an excellent rescue pilot and was honoured with the Robert E. Trimble Memorial Award for distinguished performance on a rescue operation.

Aug. 5--1971 Mt Edith Rescue

Peter slinging cadet with mine basket to Banff hospital
(JIM DAVIES COLLECTION).

6

Development of the Public Safety Program

The early 1970s saw a significant change in the type of person hired on to the warden service as older wardens retired. In the early years, many wardens were similar to Jim's dad, veterans from the Second World War, with a background of farming or ranching. They gravitated to the warden service, where the back-country work was a way of life. They lived in their remote districts year round and loved it.

When the districts were no longer manned year round, many of these wardens were relocated to town, a very unpopular move for most. Many of them either retired or found other work, convinced they'd seen the best days of the warden service. Parks Canada was still accepting young men with outdoor experience but was gravitating more and more to those with university degrees. They were also hiring those who showed an aptitude for climbing. Parks also had to comply with a new set of qualifications for hiring personnel. Affirmative action was a result of pressure to make hiring open to women and Indigenous people.

In the meantime, rescue work carried on. Of the men trained by Walter Perren, Bill Vroom was considered the most experienced, with his natural climbing ability and capacity to handle exposed situations. Peter relied heavily on him in the first years of the heli-sling program.

In 1972, after helicopter sling rescues had been approved on a limited basis by DOT, Bill's ability to move comfortably on steep, dangerous ground was seriously tested on the 3/3.5 Couloir, a very demanding new ice route in the Valley of the Ten Peaks at Moraine Lake near Lake Louise.

Two experienced climbers from Salt Lake City, Utah, had set off early in the morning of August 13th to climb the route, giving it the respect it demanded. Despite the early start to avoid rockfall,[28] the leader was hit on the head by a rock when the team reached one of the steepest parts of the climb. His partner pulled the seriously concussed man off to the side, under the protection of a large rock that was frozen into the ice, and covered him with a light sleeping bag. It was only ten o'clock in the morning, but the climbing was severe enough that, once he'd stabilized his friend, the second man was slow descending and did not get help until six o'clock that night.

Despite the lateness of the day, Bill Vroom flew in with Jim Davies and the surviving climber to locate the victim and assess the difficulty of the terrain. It was not hard to find him, but the man was resting in a forbidding place, so steep Jim was concerned about hitting the snow chute with the rotor blades. Finally, Bill saw better cover, not far from the injured man, that provided some sort of stance to get in an ice anchor.

Bill's backup partner on this occasion was warden Monty Rose, who had little experience in high-angle rescue. Before they went in, Bill had to show him how to attach to the sling line and to the Jenny Bag.[29] Then, with some trepidation, Bill went in solo to set up the anchor for Monty and the rescue gear.

It was midsummer, with calm, warm conditions and good flying weather, which meant the rockfall hazard remained high. The tricky part for both of the rescuers was the time it took to set up the anchor. Bill needed the security of being attached to the helicopter sling line while he put in the ice screws, as a second rockfall could easily take him off the mountain.

Bill's curt description describes the balancing act he and Jim had to maintain at this point: "Jim slung me in until I touched the ice, then with some of the expert flying we have come to expect as routine performance from this pilot, he held me almost perfectly still while I sank the toe spikes of my crampons into the ice to steady myself."

The helicopter was also in jeopardy from rockfall while Bill completed this manoeuvre. With great relief, Bill detached himself from the helicopter and signalled Jim to bring in Monty and the rest of the rescue gear. With both men now established on the couloir, they made their way to the climber and the shelter of the overhanging rocks.

Monty found the exposure on this mountain face a little less steep than it appeared from the air, but not by much. The stark verticality of the couloir was emphasized by dark-blue ice runnels in the chute. As the men worked, rocks zinged out from the skyline far above. On top of this, a storm was coming in. Any thought of getting the man off under the rushed conditions of high winds, rain and coming darkness soon faded. Bill realized they would have to spend the night out. He radioed Jim to see if he could sneak in some bivouac[30] gear before the storm hit. He wrote: "Jim came up very quickly with a pack slung on the helicopter rope. When he approached the ice chute he had his landing light on and light rain was falling. He slung the pack to Monty, who was anchored out in the ice chute." The full force of the storm hit just as Monty reached their protected stance, and Bill knew he'd made the right decision.

The one item they had not been able to bring to the shelter was the rescue basket left out in the ice chute, tied to ice screws. Bill wrote vividly about watching the basket being pummelled by rockfall in the illumination of the brilliant flashes of lightning that cut through the dark, heavy rain. As he watched the basket swaying on its lone ice anchor, Bill thought the victim would be far more comfortable if they could retrieve it and have him lie prone on the comfort of the foam pads lining the bottom. Though it was risky, Bill decided to chance it and, with considerable effort and risk, was able to retrieve the basket. He settled the climber in the stretcher under the cliff, hanging from the ice screws.

When daylight came at six o'clock in the morning, Bill and Monty manoeuvred the victim and stretcher with some difficulty over to the rock outcrop in the chute. The continuous rockfall made any action in the open exceedingly hazardous. But when Bill finally had the victim and stretcher secured to the anchor, Jim was overhead to retrieve the load. Again, there was the short, dangerous point of transferring the weight of the basket to the sling line while still hanging on to the ice anchors.

Bill wrote: "Jim lifted the helicopter slightly and took the weight of the basket on the sling rope…. I then quickly took out my knife and cut the two sling ropes that the basket was hung to the fixed line by. The basket swung clear from the mountain on the helicopter sling rope and Jim swung the helicopter out from the mountain and proceeded directly to Moraine Lake Road."

Monty was next to go, with a load of gear, but Bill remembers that just before lifting off, two large rocks went sailing by, barely missing him. Then Jim was back to pick up Bill and conclude this demanding rescue.

Bill Vroom slinging off from 3/3.5 Col
(KATHY CALVERT COLLECTION).

x x x

Both alpine specialists, Willi Pfisterer and Peter Fuhrmann, of the Banff and Jasper parks' rescue services knew it was imperative to train wardens to an increasingly demanding standard if both parks were to safely conduct rescues.

It was always the objective to have the wardens in charge of all mountain rescues, and for each park to have its own individual team.[31] The role of the alpine specialists was not to run the rescues or even be involved; their job was to train the wardens to be able to do the job themselves. The responsibility for this training was interesting. Peter was in charge of the warden training for Banff, Yoho and Kootenay national parks. Willi was responsible for Jasper, Waterton and Glacier national parks. This worked quite favourably for Peter, as he had Jim, whom he trusted implicitly, for his rescue pilot. Willi had Gary Forman, also a skilled heli-sling rescue pilot, to fly for him in Jasper, but at first, he had no good candidates for Waterton or Glacier.

In these early days, there was no test to determine if a pilot could do this work, and the alpine specialist just got hold of whatever helicopter pilot was in the area and asked if he could sling the wardens up onto a mountain. If the pilot agreed, then the school went forward. On Willi's first school in Glacier, he commandeered Fred Baird from Golden, who had some long-lining experience,[32] and asked him to fly the wardens around, just to show them how it was done.

Fred did not have the proper flange attachments, so they passed the rope through the belly of the helicopter. Gord Peyto, a veteran warden from Glacier, had much the same reaction as Scott Ward in Banff and Dale Portman in Jasper, but "if Willi told you to do something, you did it." He was rattled, despite many assurances of safety, and clutched the sling rope like a drowning man finding a lifeline. Willi yelled at him to let go, which led to the harness slipping down around his legs, giving him another "Oh, no!" moment. Once he settled in place, he finally became comfortable.

Peter and Willi also monitored each park to ensure they had all the right equipment and personnel to execute a rescue on their own. They would drop in unannounced to inspect the various park rescue rooms. Each park was expected to have all the rescue gear neatly organized and up to date. This was sometimes hard for a small park like Yoho with a limited budget. It took persistence, but both Peter and Willi were good at applying pressure to those park superintendents who would not loosen the purse strings. It was important when time was of the essence during a rescue (and especially if wardens from other parks came to assist) that all rescue wardens work with the same gear with which they were familiar.

× × ×

The first person hired by parks with serious climbing skills was Tim Auger from Vancouver, who had put up some serious routes on Squamish Chief on the coast and was making a name for himself down in Yosemite National Park – the home of the huge blank granite faces. Aside from his climbing prowess, Auger was a typical university student (a literature major at university who had no real ambitions outside of climbing) looking for a summer job when he got hired on in a trail crew position at Lake O'Hara in Yoho National Park. But the beauty of O'Hara took him by surprise, and he knew he would never leave the Canadian Rockies.

Tim was just leaving for another big summer in Yosemite when he got an offer of a seasonal warden position in Lake O'Hara. Though he found the decision difficult, in the end, Lake O'Hara and the soaring peaks of the Great Divide[33] won out and he took the position. During his first summer as a warden he decided to take fellow warden Sid Marty on a small but classic climb on Grassi Ridge. It was literally at his doorstep, a short hike to the base of the rock from the warden cabin. It also turned into Tim's first mountain rescue.

Two parties ahead of them were having problems with the route. At one point, the upper party, slower and less experienced, knocked a large rock down. A man in the second group, Peter Spear,[34] was injured on the leg. When Tim and Sid got to him it was apparent Spear and his party could not carry on.

Tim remembers, "We had the ingredients [to evacuate the casualty] because I had heard about the split-coil carry …. A coil of rope is split in a certain way so you can put the patient's legs through the loops and basically pick them up like a pack and piggyback them down." Sid Marty was a large, strong man, and Tim was confident he could carry Peter down a gully system that led straight to the road, even if Sid was not so sure. It was a great accomplishment of improvised rescue and command that did not leave Tim. Whether he thought so at the time, he had just made his first contribution to building an extraordinary mountain rescue unit that still excels today.

The other warden who would play a considerable role in the expanding function of public safety was Clair Israelson. Though all the national parks in the mountains were experiencing an increase in backcountry and climbing accidents, it was Banff that took the brunt of the growing problem. Jim Sime, a former warden who had come up through the ranks and was now head of resource conservation for Western Region, was acutely aware that most of the current wardens were aging and would not be able to bridge the demand for rescues while waiting for a younger, more enthusiastic crew to replace them.

Clair was already interested in the mountains and had taken some steps toward learning skills in skiing and outdoor activity when he heard that Parks Canada was looking to a younger generation to join the warden service. The job sounded great to him and he applied successfully for it. He spent his first summer as a warden in Waterton National Park and loved it. What he couldn't believe was being sent on all the climbing and training schools and being paid to do it. It was not long before he got a full-time position in Lake Louise, where he filled the public safety role.

The young wardens coming along would form a rescue team that Jim would work with throughout the 1970s and 1980s. As climbers, they pushed their limits. A lot of recreational climbers were coming to the parks from Britain, Europe and the United States, where many new routes and mountains had been climbed. They were turning to the remote Canadian Rockies, looking for fresh conquests in the spectacular peaks along the Great Divide. They also set a high standard in rock climbing and mountain-eering, taking them into difficult, dangerous terrain. In 1971, the climbing expertise of the warden service was not in this league at all. Clair realized this when he mentioned at a warden meeting that he planned to climb the infamous Greenwood route on Mt. Babel. Everyone thought he wanted to die young. From that point on, Clair made it his mission to raise these climbing standards with those who wanted to work in public safety.

Tim Auger was trying to do the same thing in Yoho, but the park was just too small to have a select team. This was true of all the small parks, meaning that every warden had to have public safety training. Tim, like Clair, also realized the warden climbing standards were rapidly falling behind the increasing difficulty of new routes being tackled on some very big mountains. Tim was also pushing his own limits. He knew his future was in climbing, and he was the first warden to obtain his full guide's licence in 1974. Whether his future would be with the warden service was becoming a source of frustration for Parks Canada. They were aware they needed good people in this field, but Tim repeatedly turned down offers of full-time employment. He was having fun climbing in his work-free winters and returning home to his beloved cabin at Lake O'Hara in the summers.

Jim Davies was happy to be based in Banff, where he knew

most of the wardens' capabilities in public safety. There was nothing more unsettling than watching poorly trained wardens fumble with their gear or the hookup system. He did not worry about them when they were in the air, as he had all the control; it was landing and extracting them safely in steep or difficult terrain that could prove tricky.

Though 1972 was really the beginning of heli-sling rescue programs in Canada, it took most of the year to work out many of the glitches in the system and for Jim and the wardens to become familiar with each other and their abilities. By 1973 much of this was coming together in both Banff and Jasper. Kootenay National Park had warden Hans Fuhrer, who was an excellent climber and made sure the wardens who wanted to excel in this field had every training opportunity available. Yoho had Gord Rutherford in this role, and Tim Auger was there to respond to any technical rescues. While Tim was there, he kept the rescue room in top condition and went climbing with anyone who would go with him. Waterton, of course, had Clair Israelson until he was transferred to Lake Louise. Two competent wardens in Waterton who took up the slack were Max Winkler (chief park warden) and Derek Tilson. Derek did not come to the warden service as a climber or skier, but he took it up eagerly and found that he had a natural aptitude that he developed quickly in the schools.

But wardens wear many hats, and with promotions, transfers to other functions (for example, fire) or other parks, or policy decisions[35] a stable public safety team could not be guaranteed. On the plus side, if a well-trained individual moved to another park, there would be added strength in that park. By training as many individuals as possible, Peter and Willi hoped there would always be enough capable personnel to handle basic rescues, but they also considered setting up a team of well-trained public safety wardens that could handle more-technical rescues in any park.

×   ×   ×

In 1972, Jim had other concerns on his mind, too. Both of his parents had smoked heavily most of their lives, with foreseeable consequences. His dad, Bert, was only 66 when he developed lung cancer. None of the present-day advances in medicine were available to patients and the prognosis was dire. Bert was hospitalized and Jim's mom, Lila, stayed with him as much as she could. Siri and Lila had always had a good rapport and Siri offered what support she could when she was not working in Assiniboine. The disease progressed rapidly, and Bert passed away that year.

Siri had been staying at Bert and Lila's the winter after Morgan was born. She worked at Norquay as a ski instructor each winter and had Morgan on skis as soon as he could walk. Morgan remembers a temporary move to Vancouver, when he attended kindergarten and Siri taught skiing at Grouse Mountain. Life for Morgan had always involved moving from one location to another, depending on the season and the parent. He stayed in Banff with Jim and Sue for his elementary schooling, which gave Siri a break to head back to Mexico for part of the winter. Siri always returned to Assiniboine in the summer to help her father, Erling, manage the lodge, and she was, in effect, managing the place when her parents moved to Stowe, Vermont, in 1970. In 1975 she became the sole manager. Morgan spent all his summers at Assiniboine and became familiar with the horses

Morgan jingling horses at Assiniboine
(JIM DAVIES COLLECTION).

brought in for the guests. By the time he was ten, he was a proficient wrangler.

Jim was wholly engrossed in the rescue program and was happy to be settled full time in Banff when Morgan came to live with him and Sue. Morgan enjoyed Sue's flair for parties – particularly his birthday parties. When he was ten, Morgan spent more time with Jim and Sue, as Siri decided to go to Africa for a last trip with her father in 1975.

When Siri returned, she picked up Morgan, saying she'd found a wonderful place to live in Vancouver. Actually, what she had found was a piece of land north of the city in a place called Deep Cove. She purchased the land for $25,000, likely getting a good deal because the land was high up on the side of a mountain and the only access was by foot. It was a good climb of 47 stairs to reach the bench on which her cabin would eventually sit. It was the highest piece of granite solid enough to build on, with a million-dollar view.[36] From there, she could look all the way up Burrard Inlet to the Fraser River Valley. It was quite a challenge to build a small Pan Abode cabin in such a remote location, so far from roads it seemed more like a backcountry cabin.

Morgan thought they could never find a better place. Now he had the mountains at his back to play in, but he also discovered the joys of mountain biking and kayaking. Reflecting back, he didn't think a kid could have had a better environment in which to grow up.

× × ×

By 1975 the explosion of public safety incidents was beginning to overwhelm the warden service. It was rapidly becoming apparent the part-time approach wasn't sufficient to keep on top of the rescue demands. Wardens hired in past years for their backcountry skills were getting older and had little interest in getting killed on a rescue mission. However, the bringing in of young people had been thwarted by a hiring freeze, and parks now found themselves desperately short-handed in all the functions requiring experience and skill. When the federal government was forced to lift the freeze, it added an affirmative action clause, saying a minimum number of new hirees had to be First Nations, and a minimum number, women.

Tim Auger looked at this obligation and wondered how he could find recruits who met the new requirements and who had a climbing background. He didn't know any Indigenous climbers; he associated First Nations people with horses and flat ground. But he did know a few women climbers.

Kathy Calvert got a call from Tim one day that would change the course of her life. Tim asked her to apply to the warden service, saying, "If we have to hire women, I would sure like to see them hire some who can climb." She was currently embroiled in a frustrating master's program in insect physiology and had selected "of all things" the Rocky Mountain spotted tick for her research. At that point her research ambitions exceeded the technology available to produce meaningful results, and the future of her project looked bleak. Any other work seemed preferable to what was beginning to look like a lifetime of working with ticks. She agreed, went for the interview and was hired.

In Lake Louise in 1975, Clair found himself now heading up the public safety program full time under Jack Woledge, the area manager. Jack was focused on being a dog handler at the same time, and was happy to let Clair run the public safety shop. With almost carte blanche go-ahead, Clair revamped the rescue room, updated the equipment, set up training schedules for the warden staff and, in general, took command. Clair had some serious training ahead of him to bring himself up to the level of climbers setting new routes – in fact, to the standards of the Association of Canadian Mountain Guides. It was not long before he accomplished this.

Things changed in Banff that year as well, when Tim Auger married his fiancée, Cheri, and accepted the full-time position in charge of public safety. Jim Sime, who was still working in Calgary's Regional Office,[37] was concerned about Tim's philosophy of creating a specialist team. Jim had come up through the warden service and did not want to see the wardens assigned to only one aspect of the job. He strongly felt all wardens should be competent in every area. Sime suspected putting Tim in charge of public safety would lead to specialization in this field. He was right.

Sime had had this discussion with Rick Kunelius, a good friend of Tim's and a fellow warden from Yoho, back in 1973. The next year, Rick moved to Banff from Yoho to work in public safety. A harrowing rescue experience on Mt. Cascade left Rick convinced the park needed much more experienced climbers in this job, and he shared this opinion with Andy Anderson, Banff's chief park warden. Rick, too, had noticed accidents were occurring on steeper and more exposed places well beyond the climbing ability of most of the wardens in Banff, none of whom were great rock climbers willing to tackle the outer limits of extreme climbing. In fact, they were getting scared. Peter Fuhrmann had been organizing the rescues, but his job was to train the wardens rather than do the job himself.

Andy Anderson could see most wardens were attracted to the job because of the backcountry, but that left a big hole in acquiring people with climbing experience. It simply wasn't part of the warden image. But as chief park warden, Andy had considerable pull in getting the people he wanted, and Banff did acquire a number of wardens who had skill and a desire to work in the mountain rescue field.

Lance Cooper arrived in Banff in 1973 after joining the warden service in Kootenay National Park in 1972. He saw better opportunities in Banff with public safety and was happy to bring his creative mind to early equipment development. Two other wardens critical to establishing a core rescue team were Peter Whyte and Keith Everts. Peter, an unlikely-looking warden, moved to Banff from Yoho in 1973. He did not fall into the lean and wiry category so typical of the mountaineer, being heavy-set and not physically inclined to the work. But he was brilliant at administration and had an uncanny bent for facilitating awkward meetings or strained relationships. Keith had worked with

Peter Schaerer, learning as much as he could about avalanches in Rogers Pass.

Keith, who was influential with Andy, wanted to maintain the strength inherent in a non-specialized warden service (which he favoured). Nevertheless, he could see the need for a dedicated public safety team, and he backed Tim Auger.

The decision was made, and the small group of Tim, Lance, Peter, Keith and Rick Kunelius organized themselves in the dingy rescue room in the basement of the Banff Park warden office. Tim was in heaven. The rescue service finally matched his idea of "what a serious mountain rescue place was really like." By then, the visitor recreational use had exploded in every sport going and rescues, minor or major, were piling up like dominoes, sometimes up to three or four a day, and leaving the wardens swimming in work.

Through all of this reorganization, Jim and Sue Davies were enjoying their time together in Banff, and it was a nice change for Jim to come home to a well-cooked meal and the same bed to sleep in. And if Morgan showed up, it made life even better. Most of the kinks in the heli-sling rescue system had been worked out and Jim and the wardens he worked with were becoming more efficient.

Perhaps the most important part of establishing a core mountain rescue team was the establishment of a protocol to be used throughout the mountain parks. Tim Auger introduced a new hierarchy of response to rescues. This change did not necessarily sit well with the older wardens. Tim did not want to play the role of hero, but the specialized nature of the evolving public safety job made it difficult, if not impossible, to keep a certain level of elitism from creeping in. Peter

Whyte's role on the public safety team, as almost a liaison officer with whom most wardens felt comfortable, recognized this, and he often stepped in to smooth misunderstandings and mediate grievances.

One item Tim felt was important to change was the organization and hierarchy of involvement, from field level to rescue leader. Protocol was important to determine leadership and responsibility. Although, under Walter Perren, the mechanics of the rescue operation were quite functional, clarification of lines of authority was needed. Peter Whyte was meticulous about using plans, a trait he'd picked up from working with the Alberta Forest Service.[38] At first, the protocol was established through trial and error, followed by a critique or debriefing after every event. As the wardens started to have a number of rescues under their belt, they learned what worked best and continually advised Peter with additions or changes that would lead to a finished directive. With the inevitable changes in personnel over the years, this became a Bible which has been followed to this day.

As the rescue team's pilot, Jim was the first line of consultant when assessing how the rescues would play out, and had the final say on how the helicopter would be used – or if it could be used. It was important to have this established in the protocol in case Jim was away and another pilot was flying. But most important of all was the need to work smoothly as a team. Peter Whyte states, "You had to work as a team, or you wouldn't last. The guys had to depend on each other.... It was so cliquish ... but it had to be, to survive."

Jim found working with Tim came easy, and he appreciated Tim's laid-back humour and the calm he exuded when working in a dangerous situation. Communication between them seemed to flow without words. Jim remembers one rescue, shortly after Tim arrived in Banff, that epitomized these qualities.

A small plane had left Calgary with three people on board, headed for Golden, BC. When it did not show up as scheduled, the RCMP were alerted. The RCMP knew their limitations in the mountains but did drive up the Trans-Alta gravel road servicing the overflow dam on the Ghost River. From there, they could see a red dot farther up the South Ghost River and surmised the pilot had mistaken the South Ghost valley for the Lake Minnewanka Valley that leads to Banff.

The RCMP called the Banff warden office for help. Tim notified Jim, saying nothing more than "let's go," and soon they were flying over the crash site. Closer reconnaissance showed the plane on its side with the right wing in the trees and the tail in the air, on fire. Again, not saying much, Tim pointed to a flat spot where Jim could land, about 1,000 ft. from the plane.

The plane had crashed the day before, forcing the survivors to spend the night out. When the plane had come to rest, its occupants were hanging upside down in their safety belts. The pilot and the two men had freed themselves, but the woman (the wife of the third man) was overweight and had to be cut loose. When the strap was free she fell several feet to the ground, breaking her femur. The night must have been a horror for her. Fortunately, her husband was a paramedic and had stabilized the fracture.

When Tim got there, he found three people. The pilot, whose face was badly smashed, had opted to walk out. Because of the woman with the fractured femur, what could have been a simple evacuation required extra help to get her to the clearing where

Tim with the survivors of the plane crash on Ghost River
(JIM DAVIES COLLECTION).

Jim's helicopter had landed. Jim laconically adds, "We picked up the pilot on the way out." It was incredible that there were any survivors at all.

This was one of the first involved rescues Jim and Tim did together, and it would lead to years of flying missions made easier by a common rapport.

One thing Tim considered important was establishing where individual responsibility lay when accidents occurred. Though Banff National Park had well-defined boundaries, this meant little when agencies outside the park needed help. Although technically, helicopter rescues were restricted to using the sling only in the national parks, they did not turn down calls for help from outside the boundary. Kananaskis, which was not a park at the time, would enlist Parks's help if evacuating injured people was beyond the capability of the provincial forest rangers. Mount Yamnuska was a place where many people got into trouble and park wardens always responded. It was done with little publicity and none of the managers complained as long as they were saving lives. Peter Fuhrmann remembers one such rescue where

Jim's helicopter skid was used as an anchor for a cable rescue off the face.

It was also not clear where the line of responsibility between Lake Louise and Banff was drawn. As Tim admits, "There was Clair, who was a really strong personality out at Lake Louise, and no doubt there was a certain amount of territorialism," but they did all train together and mostly assisted each other if the workload got heavy or something major was under way. With the escalation of serious rescues, Clair did not hesitate to call on the Banff team for support when the terrain became difficult or dangerous. But there was no question they were working in his piece of the park and he was the rescue leader.

It wasn't long after Tim's arrival in Banff when Clair asked for assistance on an accident on Victoria Glacier. The request validated Peter's vision of different teams working together.

A young woman had broken a leg while descending the steep ice slope below Abbot Pass. The accident was reported late in the evening, ruling out the use of the helicopter before the following morning. Her companions had left her at the bottom of the "Rat Trap" (more frequently called the "Death Trap") near a large open crevasse, in an area heavily prone to avalanches, and it was paramount to move her to a safer location. A ground crew went in that night with gear and hot food to stabilize her. One interesting aspect of this rescue was the use of horses. Clair had spent time in the backcountry and knew the value of these animals. He was able to save time and energy by arranging a horse party to take men and equipment as far as the Plain of Six Glaciers Teahouse. Still, Tim reflects that it took most of the night under dangerous conditions to locate the woman and set up a camp. Clair's plan worked well, but ironically the victim was only in the tent ten minutes before Jim arrived with the helicopter in the wee hours of the morning to fly her out.

Teamwork and the role of the helicopter were dramatically highlighted on a serious rescue in August 1975. The rescue, on the Super Couloir on the north face of Mt. Deltaform, was of a decidedly different nature. This was a steep, nasty place that became "very ugly" when the weather turned bad.

Jerry Rogan and Jim Elzinga were attempting the second ascent of this route, which was considered at the time to be "one of the most extreme climbs yet done in the Rockies." When they set out, the weather was superb, so there was no initial concern as they were very experienced mountaineers. But, whether through oversight or the promise of the brilliant blue sky, they failed to get a weather forecast. Forecasts in the mountains, particularly as you get close to the Divide, can be notoriously wrong, so the forecast might not have been very accurate even if they had heard it.

The first indication that all was not right (besides the black clouds obscuring the mountain) came the next morning. Jerry Rogan's wife called the warden service at nine o'clock to say her husband and his partner had not returned from their climb the night before. Fearing the worst, Clair called for Jim to be on standby, but the weather had turned bad overnight, and Jim could not fly that day at all. It was not until noon the next day that the skies cleared enough for Clair and warden Traf Taylor to check the lower half of the mountain. They located the expected tracks in the couloir leading to the steep part of the climb but found no one on any of the possible descent routes (other than another injured climber they picked up on the 3/4 Couloir). Jerry and Jim's tent was found in the meadow, strongly indicating that the two climbers were still somewhere on the face. The men had now been on the mountain for 48 hours.

If Clair had nightmares of impossible rescue scenarios, this was one. He needed backup. Tim and Peter Fuhrmann came from Banff with all the gear they could cram into Peter's station wagon. Tim ruefully recalled that surviving Peter's driving was the scariest part of the rescue. "It was pouring rain when we were driving and ... he drove like a maniac. It was a driving rainstorm on the Trans-Canada Highway, but his windshield wipers were so bad that they basically didn't clear the water off the windshield. All you could see were the shimmering headlights of the vehicles that were getting wider and wider apart as he would pass.... He had this red cherry light on, and he would pass when it was invisible. I was terrified." That was nothing compared to getting up Moraine Lake Road. "He still had his foot to the metal, and he went over a bump and landed so hard that the shocks ground out and both the front hub caps let go at the same time and were rolling beside us before peeling off into the woods. I remember Peter just bearing down and driving on saying 'remember this place!' like we are going to come back and find the hub caps on that featureless road."

As he wobbled out onto the parking lot at Moraine Lake wondering how to avoid the return drive, Tim could see the seriousness of the rescue situation. But more than that, he was dismayed to learn the missing climbers were his own close friends. Despite the pall of clouds clinging to the mountain and obscuring the upper face, Tim, Peter and Jim flew another aerial reconnaissance. They saw nothing. In frustration, they set down below the face and called up with a loud hailer. Faintly, from high in the mist, two indistinct voices could be heard, confirming that the two were somewhere on that vast freezing face and still alive. But little more could be done except to prepare a survival pack for Jim to sling in to the party if the weather cleared. Jim's years of flying in the mountains meant that he knew his limitations with the helicopter and did not equivocate when asked if he could get close enough to drop the pack. But getting anywhere near where they suspected the climbers were was just not feasible that day. Jim flew back to Banff knowing he might have some tough flying if there was the least break in the weather. It was especially hard to give Tim any bad news, knowing he was very committed to saving his friends.

Tim reluctantly drove home with Peter to get some sleep before tackling the problem early the next morning, now two days after the missing men had set out for their climb.

Clair spent a second anxious night debating the wisest course of action. Uncharacteristically, he revealed rare uncertainty in his decision making and asked Peter Fuhrmann what he would do. He recalls Peter's disconcerting response: "It's your territory and your rescue. It's up to you."

The weight of leadership settled on him like a shroud.

By morning, however, Clair was calm and prepared for the day. One thing he was convinced of was that he was responsible for the rescue team. He would not jeopardize anyone's safety. Tim had no notion of making dangerous decisions either, but as the bad weather persisted, he suggested putting a ground team up as high as possible to see if they could establish contact. But Clair had no idea where the two men were, or if one or both were injured. A lone climber could be hidden in any of the deep gullies or overhangs riddling the face. So, the waiting game, hardest of all, began as the anxious team stood by for a break in the weather.

To keep the tension down, Clair kept everyone busy preparing gear for "all possible eventualities," which included setting up a base camp at the bottom of the climb. From this location, voices were heard again at noon of the third day. The weather then closed in with a vengeance and nothing further could be done until the clouds scudded briefly away in the afternoon, allowing Jim to slip in a short flight. Jim found no trace of them.

As the day wore on, pressure mounted on Clair to send a ground team up the regular route. The climbers would not survive a third night out. Still, Clair held out. Finally, as night approached, the weather cleared enough for Jim to fly. He searched the face to the top, then tipped over the back side of the mountain.

He spotted the men.

They were struggling down the snow-plastered south slopes, soaked to the skin in below-freezing temperatures. They had decided to climb on, and not wait for a rescue. Jim was able to pick them up, which was fortunate, for the climbers still would not have lived had Jim Davies not been able to fly in. They had mistaken the direction of the Deltaform/Neptuak Col, which was the only possible way down, and were headed for the cliffs that ring the back of the mountain.

×   ×   ×

These were early days of heli-sling rescue. But soon Peter Whyte, along with Tim Auger and Peter Fuhrmann, had a working protocol to ensure the safety of the team while saving (or recovering) accident victims. This approach to rescue work congealed in 1975 and was proven successful during the summer of that year on some of the team's most challenging rescues. Each rescue was debriefed as soon as possible at the end of each mission. Jim did not go to these sessions, but for each rescue he would assess the conditions and tell the rescue leader what he needed the crew to do to ensure their safety as well as his own. If he noticed a warden doing something on a rescue that made him uneasy, Jim did not hesitate to tell him.

Cliff White remembers very clearly Jim warning him about the carabiner attaching his sling harness to the rescue line O-ring. The carabiner was large and equipped with a protection sleeve that could be screwed down over the open end of the gate. He had been told not to screw down the protection sleeve while slinging on a rescue, but on this occasion, Cliff noticed the gate on the carabiner was open, leaving the carabiner no safer than a metal hook. This made Cliff uneasy, so he decided to screw down the sleeve just enough to keep it from opening.

When they landed, Jim saw Cliff struggling to release the carabiner. He finally got it off, only to see Jim approaching him, fuming. Jim did not like having to hover in one spot where the winds could be unpredictable, making it dangerous to stay those extra minutes. Cliff acknowledged this, but the next time he had to sling under the helicopter he did it again, thinking they were going to a safe place to land and the extra minutes would not matter so much. Again, he struggled to release the bound sleeve, and again he saw Jim heading in his direction. All Jim did was look at Cliff and say, "That's twice." Cliff was cured, unwilling to find out what his fate would be for a third offence. He decided to take his chances with the carabiner rather than with Jim.[39]

When Jim bought his helicopter and formed his own company in 1971, Sue fully supported him. She jumped at the chance to leave the museum and work as the secretary for Inter Mountain

Helicopters. This change gave her freedom to work her own hours, as long as work was done on time. As the volume of rescues grew, Inter Mountain Helicopters was ready and on standby. By then the working relationship between Jim and the public safety team was on solid ground.

Jim Murphy's experience on a rescue on Wenkchemna Peak brought home to him just how important the bond between pilot and rescuer really was.

Two climbers had set out to climb Wenkchemna Peak near Lake Louise but were badly off route and wound up in an ice gully in a terrifying tangle of hanging ice seracs.[40] They climbed up one spindly serac and were trying to surmount a second. The second serac was seriously overhung, preventing them from reaching its top. Realizing they were not going to make it, one climber, a dentist, opted to jump back down to the serac from which he had just escaped. In the process, he hooked his crampon strap on his pant leg and fell onto the top of the serac they had just abandoned. Only now he had a broken ankle and was stuck on top of an icy spire that was vertical on all sides and little over a metre and a half in diameter.

His partner was able to find a way down and scuttled back for help. But it was late in the afternoon, and Jim Murphy and Cliff White were just leaving work for the day. Murphy and Cliff flew in with Jim Davies under rain-soaked skies to see what could be done, just as it was getting dark. They found the man huddled on the pinpoint of ice.[41] All Murphy and Cliff could do was sling in and try to set a belay[42] while hanging from the sling rope.

Cliff slung in first. He set up the anchor while Jim Davies returned for a stretcher. Cliff established the anchors on the higher serac to belay the injured climber from above, giving himself room to work, but Davies recalled, "It was very crowded on the top of this serac." It was now getting quite dark, and with the threatening weather Jim was not sure if he could fly back in. The situation would have been pretty precarious if Murphy, Cliff and the injured man had to spend the night on the tiny ice pinnacle. Knowing this, Jim decided to try.

With huge relief, the two wardens and the victim heard the familiar whop of the rotor blades as the precious sling descended from the barely visible belly of the helicopter. Now was the crux of the rescue. The wardens had to attach the stretcher and Murphy to the sling while freeing the well-bundled captured victim from the anchor. This dicey transfer required quick work and delicate flying. If one anchor was left in place, the machine would crash when Jim tried to fly off. Everything went smoothly, however, and Jim was able to get back for Cliff, who was now feeling very alone on the lofty perch. It was rescues like these that cemented the trust between pilot and rescuer.

×   ×   ×

In the same summer of 1975, Clair was having mixed success with several rescues on Mt. Temple. The East Ridge and the Greenwood–Locke Route on Mt. Temple were proving quite popular but were definitely challenging when it came to rescues. One climber impressed Clair in particular with her fortitude and climbing ability when her partner suffered a fall in the Black Towers on the East Ridge. The Black Towers are easily the crux of this climb if the individuals try to climb through them rather than skirt around their base. These towers are crumbling and steep, requiring tedious belaying and delicate climbing.

Clair was passing by on a reconnaissance flight with Jim when he spotted a single climber frantically waving and apparently in trouble. They could not get in immediately because of bad winds but were able to get close enough to drop a bag with a radio to establish communication. It was a Japanese party, and its members did not speak English. This presented a challenge, but Clair enlisted the aid of Greg Yavorski, a Cadet Camp instructor, who was able to translate for them. In this way, Clair learned the female climber's partner had fallen while trying to lead through the towers and had been seriously hurt. Hoping to get help, the young woman climbed on through "difficult and extremely exposed rock, unroped, to reach the summit icefield." The winds abated enough for Jim to sling wardens John Flaa and John Steele in to prepare the woman to be slung down to the staging area.

Getting her partner out was another matter. This would be a much more technical rescue, so Clair enlisted the aid of Gord Irwin and Tim Auger. When the woman left her partner with her spare clothing, he was alive, and because of this, Clair took the unusual course of recruiting Dr. J. Boyd, who was not only a medical doctor[43] but also a good climber. Involving a citizen to go in as a rescuer defied protocol and would not be possible in the current age of litigation fears, but these situations were much more lax in the early 1970s

On a fly-by, Clair spotted the victim hanging from a rope but could not tell if he was alive or dead. Jim slung the rescuers onto the precarious towers above the victim. Once the station was established, Dr. Boyd rappelled down to the man but there was nothing he could do. The climber was dead. The rescue team slung him out to the staging area on an extended line.

Although they were not in time to save the man, the rescue stood out for the success of operating in such difficult terrain and the pluck of the young girl who survived. Clair was always impressed by the malevolent nature of the aptly named Black Towers.

× × ×

By the end of that busy summer, Jim had been flying helicopters for 14 years, testing the limits of the aircraft in new applications such as heli-skiing and mountain rescue. The innovations in heli-sling work did not go unnoticed by pilots from the United States and Europe.

Jim also set a precedent for high alpine flying and landings – mostly because he liked to land on the highest thing around. And he had done all this with no accidents resulting in death or injury. In addition, he was violation free.

For these accomplishments, in 1976, Jim received his first and most prestigious award, the Robert E. Trimble Memorial Award, which states: "The Robert E. Trimble Award honours a qualified pilot who is especially distinguished in mountain flying. The award was established in 1961 to focus attention on a pilot who has displayed exceptional ability and good judgement in high altitude flying, provided outstanding service to others, contributed to high standards of safety, and brought credit and recognition to the international helicopter community."

Jim was proud of the Trimble award, in part because it recognized Canada's significant role in mountain rescue, particularly the use of the fixed sling in helicopter rescues, which accounted for the majority of rescues. In the following years Jim would more than justify this award as the number of rescues continued to grow dramatically in all the mountain parks.

The award ceremony was held in Dallas, Texas. This honour seemed like an excellent opportunity for Jim to get away and enjoy being feted by his peers, and to thank the people who had recognized his work. But the idea of being in the spotlight terrified him. Jim had no intention of going down there to make a speech in front of a huge crowd. He politely accepted the award, saying his commitments in the park would not allow him to attend.

Jim's arrangement with the park specified that he be available on 15-minutes' notice; however, it was unrealistic to expect a pilot to be available every day of the year. Peter and Tim accepted this. Both Jim and the team were fortunate in having a qualified rescue pilot by the name of Don McTighe, in Golden, BC. Don was working for Okanagan Helicopters and was trained in mountain flying and heli-sling rescue. Because of his location it took longer for him to reach the eastern slopes of Banff, but this time lag was not significant. Don was an excellent rescue pilot for Glacier National Park, but they had so few accidents that he was usually free to fill in for Banff, Kootenay and Yoho. He was also not that far from the Columbia Icefield and Jasper and could be called on if Yellowhead Helicopters could not send a pilot.

× × ×

Yoho National Park shared a boundary with Banff, defined by the Great Divide. Yoho did not get near the visitation Banff did, but it encompassed some of the highest mountains in the Rockies. It also had some wonderful climbing areas like Lake O'Hara and Little Yoho. It was in Little Yoho that Jim flew one of his more memorable missions. Dale Portman was the rescue leader of what he later dubbed "The Family Rescue."

On Thanksgiving weekend in 1977, a group of Alpine Club of Canada (ACC) members took their annual cleanup trip in to the Stanley Mitchell Hut, in the Yoho Valley. Don Forest, Kathy Calvert's father and Dale Portman's future father-in-law, was part of the group, along with Kathy's youngest sister, Sylvia. Most of the group set out to climb Mount President, while a few stayed back to prepare a turkey dinner for the evening celebration.

Among the climbers were three young lads from Calgary hoping to gain some leadership skills and get some route finding experience behind them. They were to take turns breaking trail and selecting the route up the glacier. The three fellows were travelling together on one rope while Sylvia was just behind, leading the second rope of three, which included her father, Don. The first three had skirted around the lower side of a crevasse.

As the leader of the first rope ascended above the crevasse, anchored by the remaining two, a small avalanche broke above them. The volume of snow the avalanche contained would not have been enough to bury a person on an open slope, but the debris knocked the leader off his feet and carried him into the crevasse, which absorbed most of the avalanche deposit. It had been a soft powder avalanche, and a cloud of snow settled around the group, obscuring the other two rope-mates, but once it cleared, the remaining climbers saw that two lads were safe but the leader of the group was gone.

Everyone was galvanized into action. They followed the rope into the snow-choked crevasse and started digging with their hands and ice axes, hoping he was just under the surface. What shocked the group almost as much as the accident was that no one had brought a shovel with them. It was mid-October so they had not anticipated avalanche activity.

It was quickly apparent that the boy was deeply buried and the team's tools were inadequate. Help was needed. One of the surviving boys was deemed the fastest and fittest and the best candidate to be sent out for help. Two of the party accompanied him to the valley bottom to ensure his safety.

He headed for the warden cabin located in the same meadow as the ACC hut, but this was only a patrol cabin and infrequently occupied. No one was there. Unfortunately, he did not know this and decided to wait for the warden to return. After some time passed, he realized no one was coming, leaving the messenger no choice but to hike out to Takakkaw Falls trailhead and drive to the main office in Field. By early afternoon, the climbers digging out the boy were making only slow progress toward the victim and were desperate for assistance. They wondered why they had not heard the sound of an approaching helicopter.

Dale Portman received the report at one o'clock in the afternoon and called the rescue helicopter in from Banff. He headed for the rescue room with Gordon Rutherford to gear up, taking several shovels along with personal gear, the avalanche rescue pack and the slinging gear.

Ironically, Kathy Calvert and warden Randy Robertson were doing a horse patrol near Twin Falls, in the same valley as the accident, when they saw the helicopter headed for Mt. President. They suspected something was up and rode down to the trailhead, where they got on the radio for an update. Hearing about the call-out, they loaded their horses and drove back to the warden office to gear up, if needed, for the rescue.

Once they arrived back at the office, things got hectic. The survivor ran up to Kathy, saying, "Don't worry, your dad's all right."

But before she could clarify what he was talking about, a call came in to dispatch reporting that a two-ton truck had careened off the Trans-Canada Highway on the Field Hill and the ambulance was needed.

Meanwhile, Jim had managed, by setting down on one skid, to land Gordon and Dale near the crevasse. They tossed the rescue gear to the waiting climbers and jumped from the helicopter. Those waiting their turn to dig apprised the wardens of the situation. Dale knew some of the people there but was surprised when he heard a female voice say, "Hi, Dale," which was followed by a male voice, "Hi, Dale." Sylvia popped out of the hole, followed by her father, Don. Don had a laceration between his eyes from an excavation accident but was oblivious to the blood and had a faint smile on his face as he greeted his son-in-law. The slice in his forehead had come from Sylvia, who had walloped Don with her ice axe in a spurt of digging frenzy.

It was apparent to Dale that the shovels were not going to be enough and he ordered pails sent on the next flight. Dale took a turn shovelling. It was slow going, as there was room for only one person to dig at a time and each digger needed to be roped up and belayed in case the snow below him collapsed in the crevasse.

Jim Davies, on returning from the first flight, spotted Kathy and her partner in the warden office, and told them to get their gear together to fly in. Randy couldn't go, as he was needed to drive the ambulance to the truck accident, so warden Eric Langshaw was enlisted in his place.

Kathy was slinging in under the helicopter with pails dangling from her hips, above a bunch of small figures looking up at her, when suddenly a person popped out of the crowd with blood running down his face.

"Dad!" she cried, "What are you doing here?"

Before he could answer, Sylvia joined him with an ice axe in hand. She cried out, "Kathy, what are you doing here?!" It was a family reunion on a tragic long weekend.

By this time the tunnel was ten feet deep, but the excavators followed the rope down another ten feet before reaching the climber's body. He had been hanging from his harness with the entire weight of the snow on top of him, and it's doubtful he lasted long.

In Kathy's biography of her father, *Don Forest: Quest for the Summits*, Sylvia talks about the moment when the victim was brought to the surface. She remembers how quietly the body was brought up in the darkening afternoon and solemnly slung out to his family waiting below in the town of Field. She related to her sister, Kathy, later: "I watched in morbid fascination as the wardens wrestled with him, trying to get him packaged into the body bag. He had stiffened in an awkward position and when one leg was being forced into the bag, the other leg shot out and kicked me. I was devastated."

Slowly people became aware of their own safety as night came on. About half the group had left for the ACC hut shortly before the body was found. Now the remaining few, including Don and Sylvia, gathered their gear in the encroaching gloom. Sylvia retained an indelible memory of "looking back up the glacier at Kathy and Dale amid all their equipment, standing alone on the snow, waiting for the helicopter to come." Sylvia was only 16 at the time.

As Kathy put it, "Darkness was coming on fast and so was an impending storm. We anxiously waited for Jim to return as the wind whipped around us and the cold settled in. Suddenly, Jim was on the radio. He announced: 'It's getting dark, there's a storm coming in and I'm running out of fuel. I can make only one pass and if you are on the line I'll get you out. Otherwise you're on your own.'" Kathy recalled "a swirl of wind and snow, as a red ring swung toward us. Dale reached up to click on his rescue carabiner, then I clicked on, then both of us being jerked violently forward. The bulky gear attached to the sides of our harnesses prevented us from flying backward as is normally the case, so we flew face forward, rushing headlong toward the valley so fast that tears spilled from my eyes."

Dale remembers, "One minute we were standing there with all this gear hanging from our harnesses and the next, we found ourselves sailing face first, swooping across a crosshatch of crevasses below. Within minutes the meadow was below us and we touched down. We unclipped while the helicopter landed 30 metres away. The clouds had closed in, obscuring our view of the President Glacier. We quickly sorted out the equipment, unhooked the slinging gear attached to the undercarriage of the machine and turned down an offer to stay [in the ACC hut] for supper. In fading light, we made our way in [the body of] the helicopter back to Field and the compound."

Sylvia added a poignant memory: "Thanksgiving dinner that night seemed unnecessarily gleeful to me. People were laughing and smiling and telling stories. How could people be happy when someone had just died? Maybe that was the difference between being an adult and just a teenager. I crawled upstairs to the sleeping area and cried."

For climbers, death can sometimes be just around the corner. Maybe the group was reacting to the fact that it could have been them. Most were seasoned veterans and later, in a quieter moment, each reflected on the mishap and the need for a shovel. But in that situation even several shovels would not have changed the outcome, as the boy was buried so deep.

The next day, Kathy and Dale drove to Calgary and got on a plane destined for Europe and a much-needed break from work.

× × ×

Not only was the helicopter business constant work, but many of the days were long, starting at sunrise and lasting until the final job was squeezed in before sunset. The work was outgrowing the capacity of a one-man company, and with Sue's encouragement, in 1977 Jim sold his business to Okanagan, with whom he had good relations, staying on as manager. His department did, however, retain the title of Inter Mountain Helicopters.

With the increase in the number of rescues, pilot fatigue was becoming a recognized issue. In the 1970s, pilots were not restricted by the Department of Transport to a maximum number of hours of flying time. Burnout was not mentioned by anyone in public safety, though it did occur. By 1978, though, the names of other pilots began to pop up in the Inter Mountain Helicopters logbook, names such as Gordon Jeffery, Jim Becker, John Bell and Keith Ostertag. These pilots covered the standard flying jobs and did not get involved with the rescues, leaving the tricky work to Jim. Interestingly, Jim had a fire pole installed in his house so he could get from the main floor to the basement quickly.

It was not until Kananaskis Country was created, with Lloyd

Gallagher as head of their public safety program, that the problem of burnout was addressed. For Jim, the problem never really arose, since he was getting significant breaks with the additional pilots flying routine jobs.

7

Eclectic Use of the Helicopter

Though Jim had been awarded an exclusive agreement to fly for Banff National Park because they needed a pilot who could execute rescues using the fixed-sling rope, most of his daily work was diverse – and sometimes it was even more dangerous than executing a rescue. The variety of work appealed to Jim and he rarely had a boring or repetitive day. Jim was called upon to fight fires, transport bears, bomb avalanches, fly food and equipment as needed, transport people working for Parks Canada, and all manner of jobs around construction. He also continued to fly supplies for Assiniboine Lodge, Skoki Lodge, the Stanley Mitchell Hut and Fran Drummond at Twin Falls Tea House.

The most dangerous of Jim's jobs, aside from mountain rescue, was relocating bears. In the past, Banff National Park had had difficulty finding pilots, and when they did, the pilots often did not have the necessary skill with long-lining, nor did they know Banff's backcountry very well. In some cases, they either did not show up or went to the wrong location.

Moving bears into the backcountry was not new when Jim joined the park, but without the helicopter, wardens were limited to areas a truck and bear trap could be driven to. When the Bell 206B helicopter became available with its greater carrying capacity, it was possible to sling the bears in the cargo net into much more remote country. The bears, however, varied greatly in weight, anywhere from 300 lbs. to almost 800 lbs. This limited the number of assistants who could accompany Jim in the helicopter if the bear was particularly heavy.

During the early 1970s bears were becoming a bigger and bigger problem. One thing managers could not ignore was the casual way tourists behaved in the park. Visitors often did not recognize any of the obvious dangers around them. It was common to say, "Tourists leave their brain at the park gate when they pick up their park pass." The national parks had to adjust to the increase in visitors by revising policy, rescue services, signage and infrastructure, including waste disposal.

One of the biggest and costliest problems was providing adequate storage for the garbage that was attracting bears to townsites and campgrounds. All the national parks at that time still had open, unfenced dumps, which enticed both bears and tourists. When people asked where they could see a bear, they were told to go to the dump in the evening. This led to unfortunate bear–human interactions and an increasing number of bears being moved to the backcountry.

As the relocation of bears became routine, biologists had an opportunity to monitor their movements and behaviour. They also tried out various drugs to see which was the most effective sedative and how long it lasted until the bear recovered. Because this practice was not well documented, tranquilizing a bear with drugs that were still experimental made the procedure a bit of a gamble. In order to understand drug effects better, the biologist would accompany Jim when he slung the bear out for relocation. They could then monitor how long the bear was asleep and its behaviour on waking up.

On September 25, 1973, the wardens trapped a large, garbage-habituated grizzly that had become used to people and had already been moved twice before. On this day the bear was tranquilized with a light dose of Sernalyn (often referred to as angel dust on the street) to allow the bear to recover quickly so it could be filmed. This drug was dangerous to people for its mind-altering effects, which could induce hallucinations and violent behaviour.[44]

On one occasion, Wilf Etherington[45] was the wildlife biologist working with the bear, accompanied by Bill Schmaltz, an award-winning film producer and wildlife photographer who often worked for the National Film Board. Wilf was heavily into studying bears, and once they were tranquilized, took their vital measurements, assessed their health and age and, if needed, gave the bear an ear tag. This meant the bear was subjected to a lot of physical handling. Wilf had already studied this particular grizzly on the two previous occasions it was moved, but he had used Anectine[46] rather than Sernalyn. This choice of drugs was to prove critical.

Jim planned to fly the grizzly to an alpine meadow in upper Tokumm Creek, northwest of Banff, about as far away as they could get from Banff townsite without passing the problem on to Jasper. Jim's big concern was how long the bear would stay tranquilized after all the manhandling it had in Banff. The last thing Jim wanted was for the bear to wake up in the net while being flown, though at least it was on the cargo hook and could be released if it became a problem.

The bear was still groggy when the helicopter landed, and both Wilf and Bill got out of the aircraft to free the bear from the net. Jim watched them nervously when they started filming the bear as the drug wore off. Eventually, it lumbered off to some low bushes, but both men followed to continue filming. Jim, who had extensive experience with relocating bears, began to worry about how long they were taking.

Eventually he got out of the helicopter, concerned the bear would soon be fully active and not too happy. He walked down to Bill, who was still filming, to say they'd been there too long and to get back to the helicopter before the bear fully recovered. Wilf was standing on the slope just above Jim and Bill. Suddenly, faster than a lightning strike, the bear looked up the hill and charged. It went right by Jim and Bill47 and straight for Wilf. Wilf ran for his life but didn't get far. The bear flattened him, flipped him over on his back, and bit his face off.

The minute the bear attacked, Jim and Bill sprinted for the helicopter. Jim had not shut down the aircraft and the two of them were in the air in seconds. Jim did not carry out a long debate in his mind as to what to do, but immediately tried to distract the bear from Wilf, actually setting one skid on the bear's back to drive him off. It worked to the extent that the bear tried to swat the helicopter out of the air. At one point it ran back downhill into the bush to escape the machine.

The grizzly was gone long enough for Bill to try and drag Wilf into the helicopter, but he could not do it alone. While the bear was distracted, Jim saw Wilf sit up, then fall to the side, immobile. At that point Jim knew he was dead.

As soon as Bill tried to pull Wilf into the helicopter, the bear returned to grab its prey. It was beyond being afraid of the helicopter, and for a moment Jim thought the bear might climb in. Jim yelled: "Let him go, let him go! He's dead!" Blood now smeared both the outside and the inside of the helicopter. Jim lifted off while Bill managed to close the door. Both men were badly shaken.

Jim immediately tried to contact someone on the radio. He managed to reach Rick Langshaw, seasonal warden at Saskatchewan River Crossing, sending a broken message to bring a gun and meet him where Tokumm Creek emerged from under the Banff–Jasper highway. Jim also managed to get the Banff warden office and have Monty Rose drive out with his rifle. Monty was an expert shot who could be relied on to shoot the bear.

Rick showed up with a rifle and what bullets he could find, not sure they were meant for that gun. He had just arrived that spring as a fresh new warden and had not yet had basic gun training. Jim picked him up and dropped him above the body where he could crawl onto a large rock they deemed safe from the bear. Then Jim returned for Monty, at Tokumm Creek, and brought him to the mauling site. The bear had not left the area where Wilf's body lay, but continued to beat the bushes, yowling the whole time.

By the time Jim and Monty returned (Bill had remained with the warden trucks), Rick had sorted out his bullets and decided to try out a few rounds to see if he had the correct calibre bullets. Jim didn't know what he was doing but became alarmed when the shots began to pass under the helicopter. Could this day get any worse? He managed to get Rick to stop shooting, before locating the bear, who was still taking his revenge out on the willows. Jim got close enough to hover over the bear, giving Monty a chance to deliver the killing shot.

They were now free to wrap up Wilf's body and fly it down to the warden trucks waiting at Tokumm Creek. Though Rick had never seen Jim so shaken, by the time they reached the highway, he was calm enough to fly to Fay Glacier, where a team of geologists was waiting for a pickup. Jim must have had some explaining to do, to get them into the bloody helicopter.

Although flying bears was still fairly new for Jim, he had flown a few before with no problem, but this scenario made Parks reassess and restructure its approach to dealing with bears.

×   ×   ×

In the meetings that followed, Jim declared he wanted one very skilled warden with a gun on board as backup when flying bears. He felt that once the bear was on the ground the animal should be free to explore its new home without further distractions from the biologist.

Another thing that came to light in the analysis of this particularly tragic event was the fact that the bear went past two men to get to Wilf. It was Wilf who had done most of the work with the bear and his scent was firmly imprinted in the bear's memory. Previously, under Anectine, the bear would have been able to see, hear, feel and smell everything being done to him, and was aware that Wilf was his tormentor.

The Canadian Wildlife Service shop began to look for another, safer drug that would knock the bears out without leaving them traumatized by the handling. Most veterinarians had not worked with bears, but they did recommend Ketamine, an anaesthetic with milder side effects.

From that point on, a warden was assigned to be present with a gun on all relocations.[48] Wardens also brought bear spray with them when the product came on the market.

The bear relocation Jim remembers most vividly also happened in the early years of the program. This time, a small grizzly bear was getting too familiar with easy pickings at campgrounds. It did not hassle people but learned that when it approached them they ran off, leaving the lunch. The bear had three strikes against it when the warden service decided to move it to a new home. Jim had Bill Vroom and Monty Rose (with the gun) fly in with him.

The location to which they flew the bear was a high meadow at the head of Roaring Creek, which runs into the Red Deer River. It was early June, and the meadow was laced with old snowdrifts. A small snow-covered creek draining the meadow ran close to where the bear was released. When Jim deposited the bear on the ground, Bill and Monty rolled him out of the net and then hopped back in the helicopter, waiting for the animal to wake up.

The bear slowly woke but lay there for about ten minutes, which was normal. When the bear tried groggily to move, the helicopter was behind it. The only escape lay ahead across the creek, where it could reach the cover of stunted spruce trees on the other side. The bear ambled in that direction, but while crossing the creek, its substantial weight broke the ice. As it was still drugged, it did not have the strength or coordination to fight the current and it dropped into the water, completely submerged.

Jim looked at his companions, wondering if they realized the bear was going to drown without help. Neither of the men did anything to help the animal. Finally, Jim jumped out, ran over to the bear and hauled its head out of water. The creek was surprisingly deep, but Jim was able to hold its head up until the bear became mobile.

Once the bear could breathe it bolted for the far bank and lay

The bear Jim rescued from the creek
(JIM DAVIES COLLECTION).

down, crossing its paws in front of it to support its head, and looked straight at Jim.

Jim watched the bear rise and walk slowly to the trees, glancing back once at Jim. It may be anthropomorphic, but Jim swears the bear was saying thank you. Just before Jim got into the helicopter, the bear once again lay down, looking up at Jim. This time, Jim swore it was saying "thanks."

There were a few words exchanged in the helicopter; Jim couldn't understand why neither of the two wardens had come to help. Jim had his camera with him and photographed the bear from the air to capture the moment, noting that at no time did the bear become aggressive. It was one of the most rewarding rescues Jim had in all his years of flying.

× × ×

Another, more comical incident involving a bear occurred east of the park. The Gap, as it is called, refers to the entrance to the mountains from the east where the Trans-Canada Highway goes toward Banff from Calgary. The area is known for having high winds, but that was where Mickey Bailey decided to locate his game farm. All the animals there were tame, most having come to the enclosure as orphans. All had become used to being handled by humans at a young age.

One spring, the wind brought down a large tree. It fell across the fence where Mickey's bear was kept. The bear, being no fool, took this opening of the enclosure as an opportunity to visit the outside world. Warden Ed Carlton, who became involved with the effort to return the bear intact to the farm, told this story best. He sent the following letter to the editor of the *Banff Newsletter*:

I evidently touched a tender nerve with my remark on the "garbage" content in the Newsletter produced by he/she Editor, so please accept this sincere disclaimer of any intention to wound or hurt the feelings of any person. To remedy this shocking state of affairs I would like to relate a recent episode which involved our Wardens, Jack and Perry.... On Monday a distress call came through to the Wardens in the compound from Mickey Bailey, game farmer entrepreneur, to borrow some Sernalyn, a serum used in immobilizing wildlife, evidently knowing our reputation for expertise in this field! Unfortunately we are not considered adult enough to have this potentially dangerous drug on hand, so our two Wardens raced the clock to Kootenay Park, met their Warden Terry Gibbon on the Vermillion Pass and took over custody in a laborious handing over ceremony, (Terry wanted to hear all the news from the big Park.) before torpedoing back to the heliport, leaping into "Hawkeye" Jim Davies' helicopter and ferrying out to the Bow River below the game farm.

The reason for this mad dash – a day earlier "Mucho," a 750lb.

Kodiak bear, of ponderous geniality, had escaped through the wire to freedom ... wandered east to the timbered slopes of Mount Yamnuska, encountering two elderly maiden ladies, who, after a slight pause to exchange amenities, he promptly treed! News of this disaster put Bailey and his helpers hot on the trail and they coaxed "Mucho" back toward the preserve using an apple as a decoy. Once again fate played her hand and just as he reached the wire, a motorist, to exercise his four dogs released them from his car – "Mucho" split the scene right now! ...

Toward dusk, two anglers, intent on their task of catching the fishy denizens below them in the Bow River, when one, threading his line through the eyelets, felt a strong tug on the lure and swung around in horror at a huge brown bear. A wild screaming look and two fishermen, like Eliza, never touched water as they crossed the wide Bow River ...

Again, Bailey used the old apple trick while "Mucho" ambled along toward home until it reached the railroad track ... , a locomotive whistled around the bend ... and the Kodiak was out, out and away! This big brown bear at large was shot with 10 cc of Sernalyn (more than enough for a fatal dose in his native habitat), but it kept him down for seven minutes. His huge inert form was manpowered out of the brush, into the open helicopter cargo net, and then up, up and away, with the spotlight beaming ahead into the darkness, and then "Mucho" ended up in the waiting maw of his pen within the wire. Mission accomplished, and with the spotlight peering ahead, on a starlit night, the helicopter and our dauntless Wardens returned to Banff. And I must admit, with such literary genius as the above, I can understand why the aforementioned regarding the Newsletter content was made. I feel the only solution is to bow

out and will fold my tent and silently steal away. AND THAT'S
THE LAST WORD!

E.C.

Jim was also involved with the Black Grizzly of Whiskey
Creek,[49] now infamous for the number of people it killed and
mistakes the park people made before catching it.

Whiskey Creek runs between the town of Banff and the
Trans-Canada Highway. The creek courses through heavy bush,
clogged with willows and bog, perfect for concealing a bear. As
the creek runs slowly, meandering through dark pools creating
excellent habitat for fish, it is popular with residents who like to
fish close to their backyard.

In 1980, Banff still had not cleaned up its garbage problem, and
the residents and restaurants[50] disposed of their trash in light
aluminum cans that were far from bear-proof. The initial attract-
ant for the bear in this case, however, was a large cache of meat
stolen from the Rexplex recreation facility near the northwest
edge of town and stashed in the bush.[51] When the bear discovered this incredible supply of food, it claimed all the territory
along the creek, moving in permanently to dine out on garbage
in the evenings and hole up in the dense cover during the day.
It may have been there for some time, becoming territorial and
fiercely protective of its food supply. With no clue that such a
menace lurked in the thick bush so close to town, it wasn't long
before a tourist became the bear's first victim.

By the summer of 1980, bears seemed to be rebelling against
the dramatic increase in humans monopolizing their territory. A
new bear encounter arose almost every week and wardens were

Tame bear from Bailey's wildlife zoo
(JIM DAVIES COLLECTION).

kept hopping, moving bears to the backcountry. It was a thankless job when the bears made it back to town almost before the wardens did. A cynical comment came from one warden who observed, "They always beat us back – they just want another fix to get them through the week." This bear, however, had the makings of something out of a Stephen King novel.

Tom Barrett was a newly hired reporter for the *Edmonton Journal* when this story came to light. He wrote:

> The first attack occurred on August 24th when two Calgary businessmen enjoying a weekend in Whiskey Creek were suddenly charged by a massive bear while walking through the bush. Bob Muskett tried to run but fell down. The grizzly stood over him menacingly, but then attacked his friend Ernest Cohoe, who had fallen but drew the bear's attention when he got to his feet. Cohoe was horribly mauled with his face virtually removed by a ferocious bite. He was rushed to a Calgary hospital in critical condition and experienced a long string of surgeries,

but one night he pulled out his life support tubes in an apparent
– and successful – suicide attempt. He may have finished the job,
but it was the bear that killed him.

Jim Davies took the unlucky Cohoe to Calgary and was not surprised to hear of the man's death. He'd seen the damage the bear had done while loading him for evacuation and knew no amount of surgery would ever put him back together. Jim was surprised when he got back to Banff and learned the wardens had shot a large black bear and reopened the area. When asked if he thought they had found the right bear, he was adamant that they should be looking for a large grizzly and keeping the area closed. It is amazing the wardens even found a black bear in the vicinity, as black bears tend to give a grizzly a wide berth.

Tom's article continued:

> The second attack followed on September 1st, just a few days after Parks Canada officials killed a large black bear they believed had mauled Cohoe.
>
> In this case the victims were two men, who assumed that the bear scare was over. Like Muskett and Cohoe they were strolling through the Whiskey Creek wetlands not sensing any threat when a giant grizzly suddenly charged them from the bushes, much as the earlier pair was attacked without warning. Andreas Leuthold started running then dove to the ground and played dead as the bear sank its teeth into his left shoulder and clawed his back. The grizzly then went after his friend Remy Tobler and badly mauled him, leaving his scalp hanging by a thread and one eye out of its socket, plus many other very serious injuries, before moving away. Despite his fear of the bear,

Leuthold raced for help and his friend was evacuated quickly [by Jim] to a local hospital for emergency surgery. It was increasingly clear that the attacker was not just a grizzly bear, but also a highly aggressive and outsized one.

After the second attack, the warden service was out in force and very jittery about it. Wardens combed the thick bush, armed with shotguns loaded with lead slugs. Jim flew from early morning to late in the day, hoping the bear would move into a large enough clearing to be identified. The noise and the presence of that many people merely drove the bear deeper into the bush.

Everyone was astounded when a third man staggered out to the Norquay Road after running into the bear.

How the man got into this area was, at first, a mystery, with all the closure signs and the area ringed with armed wardens. It turned out that the young man had been spotted by the RCMP while trying to steal a vehicle. They gave chase, and the thief sped away on a bicycle, but realizing the bike was not too useful in his escape plan, he then ran into the bush, ignoring the closure signs.[52] He may have thought the closed area would be a deterrent to the police. It was.

Not long after he crossed the creek, the thief ran into the bear. Fortunately for him, he was not nearly as badly mauled as the other victims and was able to stagger out to the road for help. The RCMP felt he had been punished enough and dropped all charges.

In the end, the bear was caught in one of the many baited snares set for him and was finally disposed of. Jim slung the bear to the warden compound, and, after examination, flew him to the park compound for disposal.

Black Bear of Whiskey Creek being flown out by Jim
(JIM DAVIES COLLECTION).

Tom Barrett, the reporter, was told to go to the compound to get final pictures to record the end of this tale of mayhem and terror. He was surprised at what he saw, writing, "The bear was attached to a helicopter by a steel wire around his neck and another around one hind leg. The sight of the massive grizzly bear approaching from just above the trees with magnificent snow-capped mountains in the background, dangling from the bottom of the big chopper with a hind leg pulled waist high as if in a dance, and his massive head facing upwards like he was looking for a way out was like a scene out of a Fellini film."

Needless to say, Parks Canada very quickly started cleaning up the garbage problem with proper, bear-proof bins and fencing the dumps. If the park had any reservations about the expense, they could add the $100,000 paid out to Tobler when he sued the government for negligence. The park's preventive work in reducing tragic human–bear interactions marked a significant slowdown for Jim in slinging bears into the backcountry. When the human food supply dried up, most bears withdrew to their normal habitat in the bush, where they fell back on their native food supplies

× × ×

Jim's encounters with animals were not restricted to bears. While Jim Sime was fighting for the heli-sling operation, the regional parks director also realized the value of having a search and rescue dog available in the parks. As with helicopters that did not show up, or got lost if they came from Calgary, Jim Sime had learned that calling the RCMP for a search dog was equally frustrating. Although RCMP dogs were trained to find lost people, they also had attack training, and unfortunately often the dog's response to finding a missing person was to attack. This was not suitable for Parks purposes, where missing people were usually children or lost hikers. Being mauled after enduring being lost, cold and scared would probably result in a lawsuit.

The first rescue dog Jim worked with[53], in 1971, was Ginger, and his handler, Alfie Burstrom. Ginger was wonderfully gentle and ideal for the work. The same could not be said for the psycho dog Faro, partnered with handler Earl Skjonsberg. Faro, assigned to the Banff park, was notorious for biting anyone he came near, without the least provocation. Ski lift operators were terrified of him. No one wanted to quarry[54] for him, as he never stopped biting. The mild-mannered Earl seemed to have his hands full just keeping him away from bystanders during dog handling demonstrations or during actual rescues.

So, when it came time to put Faro in the helicopter to be taken to a search, Jim was adamant that Earl have the dog under control. Earl had a struggle but managed to keep Faro from attacking Jim. What Jim did have to put up with was a highly agitated dog whining and barking non-stop. Whenever he could, Jim would sling Faro and Earl into a search area; there was little the dog could do once it was hanging from a harness at the end of a sling rope. Fortunately for Jim, most search and rescue dogs did not pose significant control problems, though a dog in the cab was never a comfortable situation.

Dale Portman, a Parks Canada dog handler and park warden, tells this story (that did not involve Jim):

> I was in the helicopter with my dog and we had dropped off two wardens to try and pursue and hopefully grab a poacher. We left them and flew up to a meadow that the outfitter and his pack string would probably appear in. We were the backup. As soon as we landed I had to run up quickly and apprehend the outfitter, leaving my dog in the cab with Ron Elan, the pilot. When I returned to the helicopter afterward, [Ron] chewed me out pretty good. I guess when I left, Sam put his muzzle up to the back of Ron's head for all the time I was gone, emitted a deep non-soothing growl until I returned. Ron didn't even dare blink while construing all the nasty names he hoped he could yell at me. I can chuckle about it now, but Ron's probably still pissed off.

One incident caught Jim completely by surprise. He was called in to fly a cougar to a movie location south of Canmore, with the cougar's handler. Jim had some assurance the animal was

Bailey's tame cougar

tame and fully trained, but he remained skeptical. Arriving at Seebe game preserve, where the cougar was being kept, Jim was introduced to the animal by its trainer. The cougar, indeed, seemed quiet and obedient. With reassurance from the trainer, Jim agreed to take them to the movie set.

Once Jim was in the helicopter, his two passengers climbed into the back. However, only the trainer was able to buckle up his seat belt. The cougar was lying down looking nervous but otherwise quiet. When Jim revved the rotors to move forward, the cat suddenly had a change of mind. It went crazy, tearing into the back seat and trying desperately to get past Jim in the front. The trainer, not expecting this, finally used the choke chain to manhandle the cat into the back seat. One thing for certain was that the cougar was not defanged.

Jim managed to get down and eject his passengers before more damage was done to the helicopter. Jim never tried to fly with odd animals again; only warden police service dogs were permitted in the cab.

× × ×

Though danger could come from unpredictable sources with the helicopter, certain jobs definitely had more risk attached. Rescuing people on mountains and relocating bears were easily the top of the list, but other jobs had their own inherent dangers.

Jim had been introduced to fighting fires using water and retardant drops when he flew fixed-wing aircraft, and to some extent with the helicopter. Although many wildfires in the national parks were left to burn naturally, in the 1970s Cliff White increased the parks' role in fire prevention and control by using the heli-sling method to get a light crew quickly into sites where a fire was still small and containable. Flying was much faster than land transportation, and the helicopter could get fairly heavy equipment in as well, to put fires out before they became too big to fight with a limited crew.

Normally each park looked after its own problems and only asked for help if the concern seemed to be beyond the resources of the park. But in the hot summer of 1976, Kootenay National Park was having a hard time keeping control of the numerous spot fires cropping up. The Kootenay fire service contacted Banff, asking their fire crew to drive over and see if they could help.

Cliff White responded by flying over with Jim so he could get a good look at the amount of fire activity in the park. Just over the boundary, they spotted a small wisp of smoke rising from the far side of a valley, about 800 ft. up the slope from two other fires closer to the road. Cliff was sure Kootenay would not get the fires out before they grew out of control if they had to drag a lot of people and equipment there on foot. But Jim could sling a crew in if a rescue sling was available.

However, Hans Fuhrer had Kootenay's rescue gear under lock and key and the sling could not be used except with his okay. There was a certain amount of territorial marking among the various national parks; some parks did not want to have a rescue or fire poached from them. Calling Hans did not result in getting the rescue rope.

But this was a situation that needed handling immediately, so Jim suggested he and Cliff get out whatever gear was available in the helicopter and call out some firefighters from Banff. They found some climbing ropes in the cargo hatch and retied the line with the equalized knots, adding a rescue carabiner to the end and attaching a bag of rocks to keep the line weighted. When the first firefighter slung out, there was a sudden yell of pain. The rocks in the pack were tied too low on the line and kept hitting him on the head. Cliff shrugged and decided they had to put up with it if they wanted to put out the fire.

Just before the first contingent took off, a young seasonal warden from Kootenay's head office drove up and asked what they were doing. When told they were slinging some firefighters in to the upper fire, the young man tried to tell them they could not do so without Hans's permission. Cliff said it was not up to him and directed the warden to place his concerns with Jim, now inside the helicopter and revving up. As the young man pounded on the Plexiglas window Jim pointed to his headset and revved the engine even more. The warden finally stood to the side as the first load of firefighters and equipment flew in. They had the spot fires out in no time and flew home. Though there must have been some discussion over this at another level, Cliff was quite sure Kootenay firefighters never walked to a fire again.

The helicopter was also used to sling buckets of water onto a fire if a water source was a reasonable distance from the fire. Because the helicopter could hover and lower the bucket, smaller sources of water could be used. In addition, should the pilot get snagged in the water or branches on shore, the bucket could be released from the cargo hook. The big fixed-wing water bombers required large bodies of water to scoop the water and a long field clear of any objects at the end of the lake for a gradual ascent when fully loaded. This greatly restricted their use in mountainous country, making the helicopter particularly valuable in fighting spot fires.

Generally speaking, slinging water buckets[55] to a fire was pretty straightforward, but early in his career Jim saved the life of a fellow pilot who lost control of his helicopter when he started to raise his bucket out of the Hay River. Both were flying for Bullock out of Fort Nelson in northeastern BC when they were called in to put out a small spot fire.

Jim was filling his bucket and did not fully see what happened, but he did see the helicopter get pulled into the huge river with its strong current. Suddenly pilot and machine were gone. Jim released the water in his bucket and landed on shore, wondering if he could wade out and find the man. Before he had time to think things through, a hand rose up from the brown water of the river. The pilot had somehow freed himself from his machine and was more than thankful he hadn't drowned.

Within minutes, Jim was in the air, flying the empty bucket as close as he could get to the floundering pilot. Thankfully, the other pilot was mobile enough to crawl into the bucket despite a large gash on his forehead. Once on shore, the man was taken to the hospital in Fort Nelson.

Jim wasn't sure exactly what happened but later learned that the line from the helicopter to the bucket managed to get caught on the tail of the machine. There must have been too much slack, momentarily, in the line. The laden bucket then acted like a sea anchor, pulling the machine under the water, which was quite deep there. The helicopter was smashed by rocks and current, making it difficult for the pilot to claw his way out of the machine, bouncing with every toss of the river. The sharp edges of the helicopter's shattered sides gashed the man's forehead, and it was amazing he got out at all.

×   ×   ×

Many of Jim's entries in his flight log recorded the regular jobs most pilots would fly, but what made Jim's log unique was the variety of missions he often carried out in one day. It was not uncommon for him to accomplish three to four jobs in one 24-hour period, often criss-crossing the park. Cliff White reflected on this and concluded Jim's head must have been doing cartwheels to keep everything straight. Jim never forgot where he placed fuel dumps or how much fuel was there, or where he had dropped people off and what they were doing.

A grateful surveyor told of one particularly harrowing incident. Matt Weir was a surveyor for the federal government in the early 1960s when he was told to refine his surveys from a benchmark high up on Cascade Mountain. There was a good landing spot for the helicopter just below the benchmark, about 50 ft. from the summit. Matt settled in, with the arrangement he would be picked up the following afternoon.

All was well until a violent thunderstorm hit the mountain during the night. Lightning was striking everywhere, alarming Matt, as he had little shelter and was a prominent target. After a few hours of howling winds, lightning and soul-chilling rain, he was sure it was his last night on earth. Suddenly – unbelievably – he heard the sound of an approaching helicopter through the claps of thunder. His hair was now standing on end from all the static electricity in the air.

He watched as Jim landed the helicopter on the small patch of level ground. As Matt reached for the door, sparks of lightning came from his hand. He could not believe Jim had risked his life to come and get him.

Jim's time flying for rescues was less than the time he spent on public training schools for the wardens. Some of these training exercises wound up being an evacuation when things got dicey and the weather turned the exercise into a retreat in bad conditions.

Kathy Calvert remembers a typical "Fuhrmann Sanction"[56] on Mt. Louie. Peter's trips, and his warden schools, often started later in the day, increasing the chance of not getting down before dark or running into bad weather. This practice was so common that his schools started to be referred to as a "sanction."

On this particular school, Kathy was climbing with Hans Fuhrer, who wasn't much taller than she was. Since the majority of the climb was in a tight chimney,[57] Peter sent them up as the first party.

Kathy recalls:

I always liked climbing with Hans, as we faced the same problems and advantages of having limited reach. Small size was an advantage in a chimney, however, where a smaller person could wiggle more easily between the confining walls of rock. On Mt. Louie the regular route is in the bowels of a grotty chimney. Jim flew us onto a fairly roomy ledge at the bottom of the chimney, which eliminated the long, tedious scramble over rock-covered slabs. Because it was already getting into the afternoon, this gave us a head start on the weather. Hans and I set off, enjoying much of the climbing. Hans never lost his happy grin, which lightened up everything.

About halfway up, we noticed no one was behind us. We waited a bit until we could see a helmet, but it was a long way down. There was a lot of grunting and clattering so we carried on to the summit. As soon as we popped out of the chimney we were blasted with snow. We set up a small bivouac and huddled together to wait for the rest of the party to show up. I believe there were about eight of us in all.

By the time the others arrived, the whole mountain was plastered in snow, which turned to ice underfoot, making things dicey as we clambered down to the start of the rappel route on the back side of the mountain. Peter worked out a system to lower two climbers together, which meant tying a knot to join two ropes. This sped things up but on one rappel the knot got caught in a crack and it was necessary to climb up and free it.

The last rappel off Louie is probably one of the airiest and most dramatic on any climb. By now everything was getting wet, including the ropes, making them soggy and heavy, adding to the time to set up each rappel. I was one of the last to go down and found out why we lost sight of each person the minute they went down. After a few feet of descent there is a large overhang and most of the 150 ft. rappel was completely free from the rock face.

I was glad to be off the mountain, as twilight was fading fast and the storm was not letting up. The seven-mile walk out seemed like a long way, but I rationalized that at least I would warm up. I looked over at Peter talking on the radio to Banff dispatch. He was trying to get Jim before it got too dark to fly in. Jim was there in an astonishingly short period of time and I have never been so happy to see a helicopter. We were in the Banff warden office in minutes, alive, dry and tired, but happy.

Jim was also giving of his time when it came to friends. When he first started with Parks Canada his workload was highly variable and, on some days, very demanding. He was the only pilot flying and could pretty much go where he wanted without anyone raising an eyebrow. Requests for work largely came from Banff National Park, but he did maintain his service to Assiniboine, located outside the park.[58] So, when Jim had free time, he could devote some of it to friends. His wedding present to Bruce and Cheryl McTrowe was a wedding ceremony in a beautiful high alpine meadow behind Mt. Aylmer. It was very special to Bruce to have a small wedding party flown up along with the justice of the peace to conduct the ceremony.

In 1972, Tenzing Norgay came to Canada on a goodwill tour sponsored by the Alpine Club of Canada. The Calgary Section of the ACC put on a banquet for him attended not only by climbers but a wealthy crowd of politicians and lawyers.

After climbing Mt. Everest, Sir Edmund Hillary was appalled

Bruce and Cheryl's marriage on a mountain
(JIM DAVIES COLLECTION).

by the poverty he saw in Nepalese villages and vowed he would return to do what he could to alleviate their plight. He devoted himself to assisting the Sherpa people of Nepal by establishing the Himalayan Trust in 1960, the goal of which was the construction of schools and hospitals for people, in even the remotest of regions of the country. Tenzing Norgay, his Sherpa guide on Everest, was visiting as an ambassador for that endeavour.

Tenzing also really wanted to visit the Rockies. The club contacted Jim and asked if he would fly Tenzing into Assiniboine. On one of the more brilliant days of the year, Jim flew him to the lodge,[59] where he met Lizzie Rummel. Lizzie was thrilled to meet a kindred spirit from mountains halfway around the world and three times as high. The trivial matter of altitude meant little to Tenzing, who loved mountains just for their beauty. He was quite taken with Mt. Assiniboine, graciously saying it was the most spectacular mountain he had ever seen.[60]

Mount Assiniboine is spectacular and is often compared to the Matterhorn in Switzerland. Its beauty is enhanced by its

Tenzing Norgay with Siri, Mt. Assiniboine
(JIM DAVIES COLLECTION).

isolation from the much lower surrounding peaks that fade away, leaving it to gleam like a jewel on bright blue-sky days. It seems pristine compared to other comparable mountains because it is on the edge of a vast Canadian wilderness not found in places like Europe. Either way, Tenzing was impressed and had a very enjoyable day hiking with Lizzie. The yard-wide smile on Lizzie's face indicates this was one of the highlights of her stay in the Assiniboine valley.

On another occasion in more recent years, Jim gave Marg Gmoser a flight to remember. She had been developing problems in both knees that got so bad she was forced to use crutches just to get around. Any hiking or skiing was not possible, and her activities were put on hold until she could have knee replacement surgery, which is notorious for taking years to get.

She was at a particularly low point when Jim phoned her up and asked if she wanted to go for a ride. He explained he had some maintenance work to do on Mt. Cathedral in Yoho.

Sometime during the last ice age the small glacier near the summit of Mt. Cathedral began collecting meltwater between the rock and the ice, creating a subglacial lake and a jökulhlaup – an Icelandic term for a type of glacial outburst causing a flood. When the volume of water became too great to be contained by the ice, it overflowed down the mountain. By the time the gushing water reached the lower half of the mountain it had picked up enough rock and debris to turn it into a viscous, relentlessly moving sea of mud, not unlike a lava flow. On a few occasions, the torrent took out the highway and train tracks below. By the time the sludge stopped, the cleanup was massive, and the highway and rail lines were blocked for several days.

Engineers and geologists needed to study this unusual occurrence (more common in Iceland) and set up stations to monitor the rate of water accumulation. The objective was to drain the water before it erupted into a major flood again. It was Jim's job to fly in periodically to check the equipment to make sure it was still intact. In the Cordillera Blanca of Peru, where they had the same problem, Peter Fuhrmann had observed they used large industrial pumps to drain the water. He mentioned it to Parks Canada, who adopted the method and whose pumps are working to this day.

Marg was thrilled with the offer to join him. Just to get out and see the mountains meant everything to her and this particular day was warm and cloudless. The flight took them over the most spectacular scenery the Rockies had to offer, and Jim had time enough to make it a tour she would never forget. Her spirits rose as she realized how much she missed being in the heart of the mountains. When Marg finally got both knees operated on and regained her independence, she never took lightly how lucky she

was to have a second chance to once again walk in alpine meadows and take in all they had to offer.

×   ×   ×

The scope of Jim's work for the mountain national parks was
wide and varied. Toward the end of the 1970s and well into the
1980s, Parks Canada was flush with money, and they spent it.
Anything the helicopter could be used for was put on the itin-
erary. It was the peak of Parks Canada's achievement under the
Department of the Environment and it had considerable powers
of enforcement. Maintenance of park facilities was a priority and
even backcountry trails and campgrounds received full attention.
Parks was operating with a full staff and the variety of work increased whenever someone thought a job could be more easily
done with a helicopter.

8

The Contract

By 1980 the government was sparing no expense for national parks, though much of that went to Banff, Canada's most famous park. Banff National Park certainly had a lot to offer and was close to Calgary, but accidents can happen anywhere, and the smaller parks limped along with more austere budgets. If Tim or Clair needed the helicopter for a rescue or training schools, it was sent without question. When Dale Portman was looking after public safety in Yoho, asking for a helicopter required a lot of justification even if it was needed for a rescue. The rule was: if you could get the victim out without using the helicopter, so much the better.

Warden Kathy Calvert remembers a winter rescue at the bottom of Laughing Falls, where an inexperienced skier coming from the Little Yoho Valley had hurt himself on the way down the steep, heavily treed hill. One of the injured man's companions skied down to the Takakkaw Falls warden cabin where Kathy was stationed. The young man was adamant that a helicopter be sent to pick up his buddy, who could not walk. He went on about how the man must be evacuated before nightfall, throwing in a few concerns like hypothermia and severe frostbite

Kathy radioed the request to Dale Portman in Yoho. Dale realized he would have to get permission from the chief park warden, Hal Sheppard, and told her to go assess the situation for herself.

When she reached the ski party, they had already built a big fire to keep warm. They were quite put out, seeing one lone female warden with no helicopter. Just as Kathy was beginning to explain why she was alone, the injured man jumped up and ran to the other side of the fire to escape the smoke. In Kathy's opinion, he appeared able to make it on his own. Nevertheless, to placate the group, she radioed in and arranged for a snowmobile to come in with a toboggan.

Help finally arrived and the injured skier was duly trussed up and dragged behind the snowmobile on the toboggan. When the wardens came to a very steep hill (Hollinger's Hill) they were concerned the toboggan would overrun the machine, as it had no brakes. It seemed safer to lower the toboggan with ropes on a brake system. The wardens asked if the man could step out of the sled while they rerigged it for the lower.

The man looked at the hill, then at the wardens breaking out coils of rope. Without a word he grabbed his ski poles and walked down, muttering about the lack of helicopter support. He left the impression he wasn't going to let this backward rescue outfit negotiate lowering him down the hill in the toboggan and putting him at further risk. The ride in the toboggan was anything but pleasant, but most of all, he seemed miffed at not getting his helicopter ride, an attitude that made some of the wardens present secretly glad the helicopter was not employed.

Although the decision was made not to use the helicopter, the financial saving was likely not that great. Jim could have had the man out to the highway in less than an hour. As it was, the park had to foot the bill for overtime pay for seven people on a rescue that took over five hours to complete. The hourly rate for the helicopter was certainly less than the pay in overtime.

This was the last time a helicopter was turned down in favour of manpower.

By the 1980s the tendency to specialize in a particular function was increasing, especially in public safety where the climbing standard and sophistication of gear were developing rapidly.[61] Keeping pace with the leading climbers of the day suddenly went in a new direction with the development of winter ice climbing. With big winter routes still unclimbed, it was an open challenge to climbers who were pioneering this field to make some significant first ascents. The wardens could not ignore this new challenge aided by innovations in lightweight gear and fearsome ice tools. The new gear made it possible to make these ascents, and the unclimbed north faces of high, remote mountains became a magnet for world-class climbers.

Ice climbing was embraced in Canada by the Calgary Mountain Club, which pioneered several climbs in the parks. But it would be the Americans, many with notable Himalayan ascents to their credit, who were the first to take a serious look at the unclimbed beauties clustered around the Columbia Icefield. These spectacularly soaring peaks, with their ice-clogged summits, were awesome to look at from the comfortable safety of the Icefields Chalet. But up close and personal they were intimidating, dangerous and ugly. Chic Scott described them as "cold and wet, and raked by rock fall ... enough to frighten the bravest climbers."

The attraction of these potential routes was not lost on the parks' public safety teams, and they decided to get a close look at what they might face if they had to evacuate an injured (or dead) climber from one of these peaks. Though most of these mountains were in Jasper National Park, all the wardens on the public safety team were sent on ice climbing schools. After assessing the difficulty of executing a successful rescue in these places, they concluded it would require the joint effort of the more skilled wardens, regardless of which park they worked in.

Jim Davies and Gary Forman, Parks's helicopter pilot from Valemount, soon had a taste of the challenges involved on a multi-park rescue.

The Banff Cadet Camp phoned the Banff warden office late in the day (who passed the message on to Lake Louise) to report they were missing two instructors who had taken leave time to go climbing. The climbers were believed to be attempting a new route on Mt. Bryce, a formidable 11,000 ft. peak on the southern edge of the Columbia Icefield. This surprised Clair Israelson, as he knew one of the men from a previous rescue, a "moderately experienced mountaineer" with more experience in being rescued than succeeding on big face climbs. Clair was amazed they were attempting such an intimidating climb, but he let Jim know and notified Cliff White, the only experienced public safety warden he could find on short notice. It was too late to go in that night, but they planned an early start the next morning for a reconnisance flight. That evening, Tim Auger was also notified and was able to fly in with Jim when he left Banff.

The first helicopter search revealed the climbers had approached Mt. Bryce from Castleguard Glacier and were definitely headed for one of the biggest faces in the Rockies. The north face ice route of Mt. Bryce is an extremely ambitious climb that requires moving fast over steep terrain in the few hours of the day when the face is not bombarded with rockfall. In this case, the pair was not able to escape the steeper part of the face before afternoon warming turned the route into a constant barrage of ice and rockfall.

As a result, one of the men was hit by a large rock, which resulted in a compound fracture of his left arm and a badly bruised hip. Unable to go up or down, the two dragged themselves to a relatively protected rock outcrop where they set up a bivouac and prepared to wait for a rescue.

After two days without food, and not knowing if a rescue was coming, the unhurt climber continued on to the summit ridge to see if he could climb out for help from there. Even with luck, his journey out would still have been a two-day marathon, as there is no easy way off the mountain. By this time the weather was deteriorating and the winds were getting worse.

The rescuers flew in early that morning. The clouds were thick around the summit, but as they descended down the north face it cleared up enough to spot an injured climber waving at them. He was alone right where they feared he would be: well up on the face on the hardest part of the climb. The weather had been poor and was getting worse, but it was not the clouds that were the problem as far as Jim was concerned, so much as the intensely high winds. The clouds were too low around the upper part of the mountain to find the second climber, so they returned to the Icefield Chalet to set up a strategy. They took one last flight to the summit of Mt. Bryce, hoping to find the missing climber. Fortunately, a break in the clouds revealed the second man on the summit waving like crazy, determined not to be missed a second time. They were able to evacuate the grateful survivor, who told them where he had left his partner. Clair decided he would need all the help he could get. He contacted dispatch with word to round up the best rescue wardens available.

Success would largely depend on what the pilot and machine could handle. The enormous size of the mountain, particularly the vast expanse of ice and the profusion of steep gullies barraged by rocks and ice, were going to make flying in very tricky. Jim, however, had to return to Banff to attend to another rescue, which had been on hold for some time. Fortunately, Gary Forman, on standby, was able to take over.

With an experienced team on deck, Clair asked Gary if he could sling directly in to the injured man. This was wishful thinking, as the storm had not abated and in fact was worse as the wind picked up. Gary was not going to fly into wind conditions that would toss the helicopter around like dead leaf. The rescue team was faced with having to climb in to the man, and the day was spent organizing gear and personnel with the idea of establishing a base camp as close to the victim as possible.

On a reconnaissance flight later that day, Clair and Gary found a small shelf about four rope-lengths from the stranded climber, but at the same altitude. Clair quickly had the rescue team flown in. Clair was partnered with Cliff White, while Tim Auger and Darro Stinson were flown in as backup. Wasting no time, Cliff set off across the face. The plan was to establish a fixed line,[62] to use if they needed to move the man back to the staging area. Cliff remembers the traverse from the staging area to the injured man was very steep, difficult and bombarded by rockfall. The storm that had been plaguing them was now pounding the team with gales of stinging snow. Cliff had no idea how they could safely haul an injured climber back across that nightmare.

Tim was leading the second rope, with Darro on belay, when a large rock hit him. As he dangled from the belay piton[63] he wondered if his back was broken. After recovering, however, he was able to carry on the rest of the way.

Once there, Cliff, Tim and Darro splinted the man's arm and loaded him into the Jenny Bag. There was serious doubt about whether they could get the man back to the small ledge, when suddenly the weather broke. A calm voice came over the radio saying, "The weather is clearing. I'm going to see if I can get you off from there."

The blessed whop-whop of the approaching helicopter was like angels singing in the heavens. The red O-ring at the end of the sling rope came in through the cloud, they clipped on, and the Jenny Bag swung gloriously into the void against a backdrop of darkening summits on the far side of the icefields. The weather held until they were all off the mountain. Then it closed in permanently for the next two weeks. This was one rescue where they came seriously close to losing a rescuer as well as the victim.

× × ×

The national parks in the western region convened annually to review rescues in each park, the state of the equipment, potential policy changes and programs for the next year. This Public Safety Committee concluded in 1981 that "several directives related to public safety in national parks ... were badly out of date, weak in content and in need of a complete revision." The policy for mountain rescue broadly stated that all parks had an objective of providing aid to all visitors feared to be in distress or in potential danger.64

But just as the Public Safety Committee was starting to look more closely at the problems of rescues on increasingly technical terrain, management in Ottawa was waffling on the idea of even having a rescue service.

By 1983 the federal government had created several new northern parks that also had a public safety mandate. This coincided with drastically escalating helicopter costs (from approximately $150/hr. to $400/hr. in a matter of a couple of years). The assistant deputy minister for Parks Canada was asked to review the matter.

He created a Program Management Committee to investigate the allocation of money, announcing, "Concern has been expressed that the program may be overextended in the provision of search and rescue services to the public, particularly in relation to high-risk activities such as mountain climbing." The committee wanted to know what other countries were doing about similar problems; whether there was an alternative organization (for example, the Calgary Fire Department or the RCMP) that could replace the public safety wardens; how they could recoup costs from people who needed rescuing if they were engaged in a high-risk activity; and if it was possible to develop a long-term policy for search and rescue.

By the early 1980s many of the keen young wardens of the 1970s had settled down with families and homes, and began to look for a transfer to a safer function in the warden service. Though the wardens assigned to public safety did not drop their standard, it was becoming more and more difficult to maintain enough expertise just to keep up with the climbing standard of the day.[65] After a decade of service, many had seen a lot of death, most often in dangerous territory where mistakes had bad consequences. Just the sheer number of rescues dictated the sobering probability that time and exposure would eventually catch up to them. Some helicopter pilots felt the same way. Todd McCready, who took over flying rescues for Gary at Yellowhead Helicopters in Valemount, BC, made an early rule for himself that he would retire once he was 35 or had reached a certain number of accumulated flying hours.

On the other hand, new personnel with climbing backgrounds helped relieve the mounting pressure of the growing number of call-outs for rescues. Teams were reaching their full potential, streamlining and refining the work, which can only be accomplished with time. The rescue specialists of Alberta and BC's six mountain parks remained the only professional mountain rescue unit in Canada. A good portion of their success was due to the skill and knowledge of pilots flying for them. One of the reasons the public safety unit had been so successful was that they had largely been left alone to perfect their skills.

In compliance with the 1983 federal committee's disquieting inquisition, the superintendents of each national park across Canada were asked to submit a set of recommendations.

The Public Safety Committee submitted a report to Ottawa stating that several significant advances had been made in the mountain parks with regard to avalanche forecasting and control, the development of an effective double cable system facilitating rescue on difficult rock faces, and the effectiveness of helicopters in rescue and backcountry search operations. It also recognized that a public safety program was much more difficult to maintain in newer parks in remote locations, especially in northern Canada. More significantly, it pointed out, "Parks Canada policy provides no clear direction on what levels of mountain search and rescue service should be provided to the public. This omission was not deliberate, as all rescues were assessed according to the degree of difficulty to accomplish the mission without unacceptable risk to the rescue team."

A good example of this was the scenario played out on Mt. Deltaform,[66] where it was considered too dangerous to send in a ground team when the helicopter could not get a warden close to the stranded party. After assessing the big north ice faces, the public safety team accepted the fact there could be situations where a rescue was not feasible. There was plenty of risk to rescuers even without going into a place where success was unlikely.

Though there were questions about legal responsibility and cost recovery, most of the field personnel just wanted to know if the program was going to continue and, if so, under what direction. After evaluating whether any other agency in the region could do an adequate job (and concluding they either could not or would not), and admitting that some form of public safety program had to be maintained, the six mountain parks' Public Safety Committee analysis promoted the second of three recommendations: that the status quo continue, with limited resources to be provided in parks located at the extremities of normal visitor travel.

Ottawa allowed the public safety program to continue and even expand to meet the demands of increased recreational activity, but some wardens, and some of the climbing community, were alarmed that rescue services had ever been questioned. In addition, the inquiry brought the use of the helicopter into the spotlight. Over the years, there had been a growth in work for the ever-evolving helicopter industry, but costs of buying, maintaining and operating helicopters were also going up. All of this was examined in the federal committee's deliberations.

By the mid-1980s it was apparent that rescues in the national parks would not be handled by any agency other than the warden service.

× × ×

The volume of incidents continued to rise with increased tourism. As a result, helicopter use was increasing as well, not only for rescues but also for routine jobs. This made the park contract appealing to several newly forming helicopter companies. As early as 1981, the superintendent of Banff informed chief park warden Gaby Fortin that competitors were questioning the exclusivity of the contract with Okanagan Helicopters.

Jim Davies was hired on what was called a single-source contract and the work was not put up for bid. Parks was able to do this because the contract specified that the company supply a certified rescue pilot, and Jim was the only one available in Banff. Other companies were told they did not have the skilled pilots to do the job. Rescue work was critical to the parks, and the very thought of having to fly with an unknown pilot unnerved most of the wardens, who knew their life was in the hands of the man flying the machine. The bond between the pilot and the rescuer was vital to the success of every operation.

One event that Cliff White recalls helped prolong the continuance of the single-source contract. The incident was a night rescue on Cascade Waterfall in winter.

Two young men had completed the ice climb and were descending when an avalanche hit them. One man was seriously injured with a broken leg, but his partner was unharmed and able to go for help. By then it was pitch dark.

Normally, the rescue would be left until morning, but in this instance doing so could mean the man might not survive. Cliff discussed the situation with Jim, and they decided to try to sling in that night. Jim remembers: "I had a landing light [that shone] straight down and one that [shone] ahead and once I got over the waterfall, I was able to put the lights on and go straight in. I followed the trail this kid made on his way out and we found the victim that way. I was slinging the wardens at the same time, floodlighting the whole area with the helicopter ... and it worked very well. There wasn't even a moon that night. It was absolutely black."

This was the second night rescue using a helicopter in the mountains, and it was a success. The first one had occurred years earlier, involving Eddie Amann and Peter Fuhrmann on Mt. Hector near Lake Louise. Eddie remembers flying back to Banff in pitch dark conditions. But Cliff noted the second one came to the attention of Jim Raby, the director general of Western Region in Calgary, in an unexpected way. The director was driving to Banff that night and happened to see "the light show" on the side of Cascade Mountain. He came over to find out what was going on and, as Cliff says, "got an earful about why they needed a rescue pilot who can do this work at the top end of his game." The discussions about putting the work out for contract were put aside until more consideration could be given to pilot expertise.

Nevertheless, Raby was dealing with Ottawa on the matter and did not have enough clout to convince people who rarely climbed a hill, let alone a mountain, that this was a necessary component of the warden's job.[67] He could not (or did not) defend the need for a specialized pilot hired on exclusive terms. Jim's company had an MOU arrangement with the government rather than a written contract – usually required by law to be open for tender – but the argument for trust and expertise only stalled the bureaucrats for a few years. As the competition grew hungrier, demands to open the contract for bid intensified until the wardens were forced to produce standards by which other helicopter pilots could be tested.[68] This case was one of the first indications that Parks Canada would be run from the top down in the future, by people who had very little experience or knowledge of any of the western national parks for which they were responsible.

By this time, flying using vertical reference was becoming more commonplace as pilots learned the skill while long-lining logs or moving equipment to gas well sites. It was not so much a technical leap as a mental one for new pilots to go from flying static objects to live cargo, and they were eager to test themselves. The competing companies were finding it easier to hire young men who had the potential to do the work, as well as an inclination to do so.

One of the government requirements for contracts was that the lowest bidder had to be accepted, as long as they met the terms of the contract. All the companies needed was to certify a pilot by some government standard. The day came, Tim Auger recalls, when "Fuhrmann came along and said, 'well we're going to have to go out and test these pilots.'" They had no recourse but to consult Jim, as he was the only one who knew what was required in a pilot.

There were other standards besides technical skill that could be considered too, such as thorough knowledge of park geography. This actually worked one year when Peter asked the nominated candidate to verbally describe the location of several well-hidden

218

backcountry lakes. Candidates lacking this type of local knowledge kept the wolves off for a while, but it was a rather poor fence. Finally, one company complained to Ottawa, and Banff administration was told to solve the problem.

In Banff, near panic and rebellion set in as wardens realized they might have to commit their lives to an unknown pilot. Jim had provided confidence and safety for years and it was unthinkable to put that in jeopardy.

Interestingly, Jasper was not going through this dilemma. Gaby Fortin, the chief park warden of Banff, was not wrong in saying Jim Davies was the only certified pilot in Banff, but he was not the only pilot working for Parks. Gary Forman in Jasper had gone through a simple test with Peter Fuhrmann shortly after he moved to Valemount, BC, and began to fly rescue missions for Jasper National Park in 1980. Jim was quite happy with this arrangement, as it was too far for him to go to Jasper for rescues, and the workload in Banff would have prohibited this anyway. Yellowhead Helicopters also gained a second qualified pilot when Todd McCready joined the company. Don McTighe in Golden filled in for Jim on occasion as well. Ultimately, Banff had to provide a test that was impartial to any company wishing to submit a pilot for certification.

The wardens needed help, and they got it from a person working for Parks Supply and Services who was responsible for helicopter services for Canadian government jobs. He was in full sympathy with the wardens and was one of the few individuals who seemed to understand they were asking a lot from the pilot: they were asking for commitment and ability to bond in a team environment where lives were at risk. The Supply and Services employee was able to advise the wardens they could be choosy as long as they were very specific in the terms of reference in the contract.

Knowing that the future of a safe program now hung on the outcome of establishing a valid test, the wardens carefully outlined the flying parameters. For this, they relied on Jim's assessment of the skills required to do this job safely. At the same time, the rescue service had to be careful Jim was not so involved in creating the test that the competition could claim conflict of interest. However, Jim set the de facto standard that had to be met. As Tim Auger recounts, "We dreamt up this test that had these various components that you would have to be a Jim Davies to get through."

With the doors now seriously open to rivals, the companies marched in with their pilots – and their lawyers. The debate, by now, had even reached Canada's House of Commons. With a seriousness that was never a part of the heyday of the 1970s, Tim, Clair and Peter laid out the test requirements, knowing that if they failed a pilot, they'd better have good, documented reasons. At the same time, their lives and the lives of casualties depended on their decisions, giving them a strong "bucket of blood" argument for those who objected.

The companies, of course, did object strenuously, to the point that Transport Canada sent in inspectors to see what the problem was. One inspector was "sent out with orders to make sure the thing was cleaned up." The wardens had to show him precisely what they needed. The inspector was flown on a rescue scenario to the north face of Mt. Victoria over the "Death Trap" in semi-whiteout conditions. The flight was enough to convince the man they really did need the best pilots they could get.

Quasar Helicopters, run by Jim Bickerstaff, was one of the

companies bidding for the contract, and Bickerstaff wanted Jim to come and work for him. Jim did not like either the company or Bickerstaff and had no intention of doing so. He questioned Bickerstaff's integrity and didn't think they had a long-term future in the helicopter business. Nor did he trust Bickerstaff, who he felt had undue influence in the bidding process.

But Quasar came forward with one pilot, Jim Stone, who was outstanding. After going through the routine test, they had Stone fly through a scenario on Cascade Mountain that Tim Auger described as having "a bit of a sting in it." The required sequence looked easy from the ground, but Peter asked Stone to go into a location that was prohibitively dangerous due to gusting, quirky winds. Stone waved the flight off, saying the location was too dangerous to get into.

But to be certain, Jim Davies was asked to fly the mission as well. When he called the exercise off, Parks knew they had a pilot who met their criteria. In the end, one good result of the process was the establishment of a testing program that would ultimately save lives.

Banff Park rescue service had held off the bidders as long as they could, but the bottom line was that the wardens might be flying with pilots other than Jim Davies, and that took some adjustment. Jim told Okanagan what to bid, as it was an important contract. By then, however, Okanagan was growing into an international company and decided going lower than Quasar was not worth their while. What was so hard to understand was that the Quasar bid was only $10/hour lower than Okanagan's. For the amount of flying Jim was doing, this difference was a drop in the bucket for a government that could absorb far larger bills. But Jim Stone, working for Quasar Helicopters, passed the rigorous test and the wardens had to honour their commitment to the process they had established. With Okanagan Helicopters unwilling to underbid their rival, the contract went to Quasar.

One consideration Jim never took lightly was being connected to the people on the line below. He and he alone was responsible for their life and safety until they were on the ground. He reflects: "I think the biggest psychological thing in sling rescue was the fact that you were hauling live cargo. And again, I guess it's funny how your mind works. You could do a recovery of somebody who is deceased, and you could fly them, and it was totally a different mindset because that person is dead. And then you go back for the rescue team and they are wandering around and you pick them up and fly and again…. It's live cargo…. It's not really like a light switch that you turn off and on but there is definitely a difference."

When Tim and Clair were looking for that sensitivity in a pilot, they had good reason to look hard. All they had to do was recall a frightening incident that happened in the Bugaboos to Peter Enderwick, a warden working with Hans Fuhrer in Kootenay National Park.

Tim and Clair had been called to help Peter to look for a person who had drowned in a stream crossing on the way to the Bugaboo hut. Kootenay relied on a local pilot for most of their work, including rescues, as he was capable of executing rescue sling operations. Most of the operation of finding and flying out the victim was completed when he went back to sling Peter, who was still at the recovery location. As he approached the lodge, he was contacted by the RCMP about details of the drowning. The radio communication to Peter was now cut off. In fact, the communication with the RCMP was so distracting that the pilot

forgot he was slinging a live person. As they approached the
buildings at the lodge, Peter realized that the pilot was coming
in too quickly and far too close to the ground to put him down
safely. He began madly trying to detach from the sling line, as
his legs brushed the top of a fence. At the last minute, the pilot remembered Peter was still attached to the line and pulled
up just before the warden would have been slammed into a low
building. From that time on, all communication, except with the
person being slung, was eliminated until the rescue was over.

Tim and Clair knew they needed stable, careful pilots with
enough confidence to go "into situations that can be very, very
difficult." The pilot had to be able to make decisions about when
to go and when not to go, even as the bar was raised for what they
could do as a team. As Tim realized, not all pilots had the ability
or desire to fly into dangerous terrain in bad weather with a live
cargo solidly attached to the machine – and for brief seconds,
also connected to a mountain. "Our test had to ... recognize that
there are some situations that some people can [handle] and
some can't as well. We want only those people that can." The
emphasis from the beginning was that the pilot would be part
of a team working together under difficult conditions, where an
individual's actions affected the safety of both team and victim.
Many pilots flew well, but not all were able to work as a team
member under those conditions.

Still, the change in contract was a watershed moment. Tim
Auger understood. His days of flying with Jim were over. "The
world became a new world at that point."

In fact, the rescue service entered into a nightmare world where
pilots came and went with alarming frequency. In the mid-to-
late 1980s, everyone seemed to have a company that only lasted

for a few years before being bought out. The contracts Banff signed automatically affected both Kootenay and Yoho national parks because all three came under Peter Fuhrmann's jurisdiction. This was frustrating for the wardens in Yoho, as they found it quicker to fly with Don McTighe, who worked for Okanagan Helicopters in Golden, BC.

Meanwhile, new pilots would show up for rescues on a regular basis. Whether it was the bureaucracy of fair play or simply greed that led to the new condition, the fallout left a field of bitter feelings. The willingness of upper management to dismiss so cavalierly a critical component of a mountain rescue team left Parks staff feeling they could be dismissed just as easily.

Peter may have insisted that the new pilots know their way around Banff, but they didn't know the backcountry of the other two parks. One incident illustrates the importance of this knowledge.

After a mauling incident at Lake O'Hara, wardens were monitoring the bear's movements, often employing the helicopter. Kathy Calvert was flying with one pilot she had never met before, but – justifiably – assumed he knew the mountains from the air. They were flying up MacArthur Creek when the pilot asked where he had to go to fly back to Lake O'Hara. She looked at him for a moment, only then realizing he was unfamiliar with any of the country. Looking around (instead of for the bear), she could orient herself by recognizing familiar mountains. They were returning from the north of Mount Odaray when they hit very dense fog. Fortunately, Kathy recognized the slope leading to the upper Odaray Plateau but was unnerved when the pilot hugged the ground, asking if Kathy could still see the ground. The pilot at least was keeping good vertical reference with the slope, which was gentle enough to not endanger the rotors. They did fly safely down out of the fog and back to the compound, but Kathy never did see any sign of the bear.

Wardens were not the only people shocked and opposed to the sudden loss of a pilot they were fortunate enough to have trusted for the previous 20 years. The *Canmore Leader* published several articles protesting this development, particularly when it became known that the monetary difference between Quasar and Okanagan was only $10/hour. The impression among the locals was that upper management did not put much value on the life of public safety wardens. Karl Jost, who was well up in the hierarchy of the Canadian Ski Alliance, wrote, "Let us see the new helicopter company perform a daring rescue off Mount Deltaform at night in conditions in which an eagle would not fly. Jim Davies did it! No one else would or could!"

Jim was justifiably upset at the whole outcome.

Flying rescues for Parks had been a way of life he enjoyed, and in which he took a great deal of pride. Anyone who knew him well realized what a jolt it was to have the contract lost to a company he thought was only marginally good enough to do the job. He had no quarrel with any of the wardens he had worked with, nor with Peter Fuhrmann, who remained a good friend.[69]

This was not a mega-corporation with nameless numbers of staff he was leaving. He was part of a small community, most of whom he knew or who knew of him and were proud of his achievements. Jim had been a central figure in a small but dedicated public safety function that relied heavily on his skills, but he also flew a lot of the park staff on routine jobs that could turn dangerous for any number of reasons. Only a few years earlier (1981) he had received the Alberta Achievement Award for excellence in helicopter flying, which recognizes individuals whose accomplishments in their career, the community and the profession have brought honour to the occupation.

For both Jim and his warden colleagues, it was like losing a good friend – yet with no closure, because they had to continue on as before. This left a hollowness that was hard to live with. The loss did not seem much removed from a corporate organization disposing of a valuable employee without cause, saying "don't take this personally, it's only business." In this case, however, it was much more than business. To those involved, it felt personal.

Part of Jim's identity was taken from him, and this took time to accept. Flying for Okanagan Helicopters meant relocation, as most of their business now was commercial and they had no base in Banff or Canmore. They did have a subsidiary base in Golden with Don McTighe as the manager. Jim was offered work there, which he took for a short while until a better offer came along

Life, however, is often enigmatically reinventing itself, with lines of connectivity that go beyond coincidence. Lance Cooper, who had been mentored by Jim, was instrumental in establishing his own helicopter company with Keith Ostertag and Guy Clarkson in Canmore. This was a successful venture when they started, but it is expensive to run a small operation against large companies with deep pockets. Lance and Keith sold out to Alpine Helicopters, of Kelowna, BC, which was heavily involved with providing pilots and helicopters to the now mushrooming heli-ski industry. As a former climber and mountain rescue specialist, Lance insisted that rescue work be part of the job. When Jim was free from Okanagan, it did not take long for Alpine to ask Jim to fly for them. Jim welcomed the opportunity where he could return to work with people he knew and trusted. It was conveniently close to home and his life transitioned to the new arrangement with more ease than close friends would have expected.

Quasar got the contract in the fall of 1984, but soon was having problems: two crashed helicopters. One occurred on the side of Mt. Grotto when the pilot was flying a survey crew to the top. He was flying up the side of the mountain when the engine quit. Apparently, a fuel line had detached, causing the failure. The helicopter fell 40 ft. onto a steep scree slope and rolled downhill. Though the occupants all wore seat belts, it was a rough tumble, terrifying the passengers. The machine came to a halt when its mast jammed into the snow, stopping the craft just short of a major cliff.

No one was hurt and a second helicopter was dispatched to bring them down. In the newspaper coverage, credit was given to the pilot, who used impressive skill in minimizing the potentially serious consequences of engine failure in such a hazardous location. And luck certainly had something to do with it.

Though it was technically an unforeseeable accident, Jim chalked it up as a mark against Quasar. The incident might have gone unnoticed if a second crash had not occurred shortly after, on Fay Glacier near Moraine Lake. In this instance, Joe Meyers was flying a crew in to the hut but misjudged the landing. Helicopters require flat surfaces to land on, particularly in snow where support is questionable. In this case, the skids on the helicopter sank when he landed on a slope, again causing the machine to roll.

Jim heard about the accident over the radio and immediately got a newspaper friend to fly in and take pictures of the crash.

Though they stayed well away from the site, Bickerstaff was incensed, and complained to Transport Canada about Jim causing interference in the recovery. Jim was suspended from flying for two weeks by the department. But he had made a point. After less than three years, Quasar could no longer fulfill the contract when it went bankrupt in 1986. In the meantime, Jim still had plenty of work sitting at his door.

9

No Lack of Work

The need to develop a specialized public safety function involving heli-sling rescue started in Banff because of the spiking rise in accidents in that park and, later, throughout the other mountain parks. Banff also had a far-seeing alpine specialist in Peter Fuhrmann, who quickly grasped the importance of the helicopter; and they had Jim Davies, a pilot with the flying skills to help develop an increasingly sophisticated rescue program. The agreement Parks had with the Department of Transport restricted the use of the sling rescue system to the national parks, and to begin with, the wardens stuck to that restriction.

But Banff was more of a haven for mountaineering and hiking, with skiing added in the winter, than a rock climber's destination. The iconic Mt. Yamnuska, located at the entrance to the mountains, which unavoidably greeted the public before they got to Banff National Park, was a more attractive goal for dedicated rock climbers.

When a young Hans Gmoser settled in the mountains, this classic hunk of limestone struck him as "a silent and graceful silhouette, massive and yet so elegant. In one straight line it rose to the sky." Yamnuska stands as sentinel to the mountains beyond. This "beautiful rock face" fascinated Hans, who was surprised no one had put up a route on any of the graceful lines that snaked their way to the top. It would have that effect on many climbers once Hans, Leo Grillmair and Heinz Kahl opened the door to the climbing possibilities.

But as climbers became attracted to Yamnuska's potential, it was not long before accidents happened. This steep mountain face laced with overhangs and rotten rock, battered by high winds funnelling through the Gap, was not an easy place to conduct a rescue.

Banff park got its first call for assistance on Mt. Yamnuska in 1974 for a man and his dog, stuck on the east approach on the back side of the mountain. A second call was much more serious, on the classic "Red Shirt" route. Since slinging directly in to this steep, overhung route was not feasible, the only alternative was to fly the rescue crew to the top, where they used a cable to reach the victim. Here they were faced with another problem. The ridge overlooking the route consisted of loose scree and they could not find anything solid enough to hold a cable anchor. They finally opted to use the helicopter as the anchor. Ludwig Gramminger was visiting from Austria and went along with Peter as an observer. The team was nervous and uncertain that this would work, but Jim assured them it would hold. It did, much to everyone's relief.

Peter was concerned about extending Parks resources for rescues beyond its borders. This was not for bureaucratic reasons, as it is hard to argue against saving lives. His concern was the possibility of being responsible for rescues in a sizable section of the eastern slope mountains. A precedent had been set with an upgrade on Highway 40 to Kananaskis Country, enticing greater public use of this area. This was resolved when most of this region was added to the provincial park system.

In 1977, Peter Lougheed Provincial Park and Kananaskis

Helicopter on Yam acting as anchor
(KATHY CALVERT COLLECTION).

Provincial Park were created when Highway 40 was still a poorly maintained gravel road. The latter park was included in the Kananaskis Planning Area (Kananaskis Country), also created that year. In 1979 Kananaskis Village added a world-class golf course, hotel and convention centre, using new-found Alberta wealth from oil and gas revenues. It also allowed forestry practices and had the hydroelectric dams on the Spray River.

Since the wardens were already stretched in handling their own rescues, Peter lobbied the Alberta government to hire an alpine specialist for Kananaskis Country to set up their own rescue program. In 1982 a five-year management plan outlining the development of future operations was completed and included a search and rescue component.

Peter had the ideal candidate in mind to run the program: Lloyd "Kiwi" Gallagher. Lloyd had ample background for the job, and he was Peter's first choice as an alpine specialist for Kananaskis Country. Peter met with the director of provincial parks in Calgary and recommended "Kiwi," and he was accepted. Peter had to phone Hans Gmoser and ask him to release him as

Lloyd Gallagher in Kananaskis
(KATHY CALVERT COLLECTION).

manager so that he could take up the new job. It made things easier that the Gallagher kids had by then reached school age.

Lloyd was born in Leven, New Zealand, in 1939, and one of his earliest memories was of his father carrying him on his back in a pack while hunting red deer and wild pig for the growing family. By the time he was ten, Lloyd was part of a local "tramping club," and by the age of 16 was leading two-week treks in the mountains. Being a member of the hiking club meant there was a chance of being called out for search and rescue work, and by age 14 he had been on a number of call-outs, never realizing that decades later, this would become his full-time profession.

At 21, Lloyd became a licensed mechanic and headed off to New Zealand's South Island. For the next five years he hunted deer for the government, climbed mountains, crossed torrential streams on foot and skied pristine slopes. But Lloyd wanted to see the world and felt Canada was a good place to start. He earned the money for a one-way ticket by working on the famous Milford Sound trail system two years prior to leaving in 1965. He told his parents he would be back in two years, then boarded a boat for a month-long voyage to Canada. Lloyd had no hesitation about where he was going. He hitched east from Vancouver, drawn like a magnet to the Canadian Rockies.

When he arrived in Calgary, Lloyd joined the Calgary Mountain Club and the Calgary Mountain Rescue Group, where he met a host of climbing enthusiasts and helped on local search and rescue calls. His first job as a mechanic, at the Banff Springs Hotel, led to working for Hans Gmoser as a mechanic up in the Bugaboos. Hans realized Lloyd had great potential to do more than fix snow machines and suggested he get his guide's licence and come to work for him in that capacity.

But Lloyd was hungry to move on and see more of the world, especially Yukon, Alaska and Greenland – and possibly Europe. He hung around long enough to get his guide's licence and then headed north. To help with expenses, he did seismic work and led geologists and surveyors from the Arctic Institute of North America up Mount Logan to the research station there. Lloyd spent the remainder of the summer of 1966 and early winter on the Greenland ice sheet before returning to work for Gmoser at his fledgling heli-skiing operation in the Bugaboos.

Lloyd remained with Hans for the rest of the 1960s and most of the 1970s, watching Canadian Mountain Holidays (CMH) grow. In 1972 Hans cast his eye on the Premier Range in the Cariboo Mountains northwest of Jasper, where he had found excellent skiing in the past. He decided it would be a prime location for expansion of his heli-ski business. After the unfortunate altercation with ski guide Mike Wiegele was resolved, Hans began to look in earnest for a new lodge site. Lloyd accompanied Gmoser and architect Philippe Delesalle into the upper reaches of the timber-choked Canoe Valley. There they scouted through bush and around muskeg before finding a site for a ski lodge.

Lloyd was put in charge of construction of the lodge in 1973. As he put it, "I had built an outhouse once and it wasn't a very good attempt, so the lack of construction experience made the job challenging." He found time to get married and built a suite in the lodge for Fran and himself with the idea that someday they might have a family. The first skiers arrived in the early winter of 1974 just as they were laying the carpet, and Lloyd assumed his new responsibility as manager of the entire operation.

The planned family soon arrived, however, and Lloyd realized he had to consider his future with children in mind. They needed a stable community that provided schooling. When the chance to work as alpine specialist in Kananaskis Country came along in 1979, he gladly accepted.

The challenges of Lloyd's new job were similar to the ones faced by Walter Perren nearly a quarter of a century earlier. Many park rangers brought in from various parks throughout the province to make up the Kananaskis staff had no mountaineering background. It reminded Lloyd of the problems Walter had had trying to teach park wardens, many of whom were ex-army or ranchers, to climb. Some of the more colourful motivational comments Walter employed amounted to a gentle chiding such as, "Stand up – you won't bump your head on the sky." Or "I could lead a milk cow up here!" One story, not easily verified from a third-hand source, claimed that Walter even carted horse manure onto Victoria Glacier, where he strategically placed the droppings higher and higher, thinking, "If they won't go anywhere except on a horse they can look for them up here."

Some of the younger rangers had just come from college or

university with little outdoor experience of any kind. With patience and understanding, Lloyd set out to mould his crew into a professional mountain rescue team. Lloyd accomplished this by exposing them to as much training as possible. In this, he was lucky in having the experience of the Banff public safety team so close by. They provided the rangers with additional training opportunities when they invited them to attend Parks Canada regional schools, both summer and winter.

It took an average of roughly five years to bring a person up to the standard set by the public safety team in Banff. Lloyd took them out at night, and he exposed them to long trips in all sorts of bad weather to build stamina. He also had to convince park managers that the schools were not a frivolous waste of time spent having fun. His experience in this regard mirrored the same problems national park wardens butted their heads against.

During these years, Lloyd relied on the Calgary Mountain Rescue Group to provide seasoned mountaineers to help with rescues, especially in their capacity to run complicated rope and cable rescues on Mt. Yamnuska. There were also a number of dedicated and highly proficient cavers among the Calgary group who could be called on to help with difficult cave rescues. To bring select managers onside, Lloyd would often invite one of them out on a week-long trip to one of the well-appointed park huts situated in some spectacular location. It made his job much easier once the managers understood what he was trying to accomplish.

In the early years, Lloyd was also blessed with a generous budget. The government at the time had a lot of oil money in its coffers earmarked for the new park. It took a long time, though, before he was comfortable spending it. Lloyd had come from the private sector in the heli-ski business where accountability was paramount and funds lean, so he was careful with his spending. He admitted it took him much longer than it should have to buy cable rescue gear, because the equipment was so expensive. Contrary to what some thought, helicopter slinging was often cheaper than ground rescue because it usually entailed only the helicopter, a short flight and two rescue personnel.

Lloyd was a firm believer in the team approach and decided that if Kananaskis Country were going to be successful in different types of rescues, he needed to know each person on his team very well. Lloyd's convivial personality assisted greatly in accomplishing this. His strategy was to give every ranger good basic training and then, when they arrived at a rescue, decide where each person would work best. This functioned for simple rescues in the early years, while he worked on establishing a dedicated team of rescue specialists, similar to Banff's.

Each time there was a rescue call-out, Lloyd did not know who was going to show up at the staging area; it depended on which rangers were on shift. As he put it, "Every rescue is like a damaged house; you need to learn to work with the pieces you have. I had to decide who I would lower over the rock face, which person would be on the rope, who would operate the radios, who would be on the gear, and because we worked so well as a team, that would give me all the combinations I would need to pull off a rescue as quickly as possible."

It took time to build the public safety program with people who were just getting comfortable in the mountains. His goal of putting together a team initially just involved bringing the rangers to a skill level where they felt comfortable responding to rescues that did not exceed their ability.

The rescue program moved along swiftly for Lloyd. "The reason why Kananaskis came on stream so quickly was because of the co-operation that existed between the two organizations [Parks Canada and Kananaskis Country]." It helped that Lloyd already had the respect and friendship of Peter Fuhrmann, Willi Pfisterer and Tim Auger, all of whom he had climbed or skied with. He had also climbed with many different wardens over the years but especially with Auger, whom he'd accompanied on two expeditions to the Himalayas. He also had a sound relationship with Jim Davies and looked forward to working with him again. They had worked together in the fledgling Bugaboo (CMH) heli-ski business in British Columbia and trusted each other.

While Jim was working in Banff, Lloyd was fortunate to have Lance Cooper, a former member of the Banff rescue team, as his helicopter rescue pilot.

Lance had arrived in Banff in 1973 after joining the warden service in Kootenay National Park in 1972. He saw better opportunities in Banff with public safety and was happy to bring his creative mind to early equipment development. But he was particularly entranced with the flying end of the job. He developed a close association with Jim Davies, who introduced him to all aspects of the helicopter. In fact, Lance chose to go into the public safety work mainly because of the helicopter, though his role in rescue work was important as well. It also meant specializing in this field, working with a small group of people, which he preferred.

Lance came to flying helicopters in a roundabout way by flying with Jim on early rescues. From the moment he got into the helicopter he watched every move Jim made. He was probably the only rescue warden who often carried on a long conversation with Jim, who habitually had little to say when flying. Jim got along well with Lance, as with the rest of the public safety wardens, whom he respected for doing what he thought was the hard part of the job. When he realized Lance was really interested in flying, Jim encouraged him to develop his talents. Lance had some of the same qualities as Jim, being normally quiet but especially cool and concentrated when on a rescue.

By 1980 Lance had made up his mind to quit the warden service to follow his dream of becoming a helicopter pilot. He must have saved up for it because he marched into the Healy Creek warden station where he lived with Linda and his two kids, Todd and Tanya (both young at the time), and told Linda they were moving – now. Keith Ostertag, a pilot who'd worked for Okanagan Helicopters with Jim Davies, had moved to Edmonton and was working for Shirley Helicopters, largely in the North. The small company had a training position open if Lance could get there right away. The whole family was uprooted and moved to Edmonton in two weeks.

After Lance got his licence, he spent a couple of years flying in the North and learning the skills of long-lining. But his family wanted to return to Canmore, where they'd lived all their lives, and he was restless to get back as well. Keith, Lance and Guy Clarkson, a fellow pilot and photographer, decided to form a company in Canmore, but kept it simple when they adopted the name Canmore Helicopters. They did quite well for a few years until Keith pulled out and Guy went on to other adventures.

Knowing there was considerable potential for tourist business on the edge of Banff National Park, Alpine Helicopters offered to buy Lance out in 1984. Based out of Kelowna, Alpine

Lance Cooper slinging practice
(JIM DAVIES COLLECTION).

Helicopters had long eyed Canmore as a desirable location for a small subsidiary base. Lance could see the advantage of working for a larger company that could absorb a certain amount of deficit and he agreed to stay on a base manager.[70]

Alpine's managers were happy to have him involved in rescues, but their basic niche was touring flights and providing pilots for the heli-ski industry, which was rapidly expanding. Lance's return to Canmore was fortuitous for Lloyd Gallagher, who needed a rescue pilot he knew and trusted. Lance spent many hours flying with Jim, learning the finer points of flying into places only climbers could get to. When Okanagan left Banff in late 1984, Jim worked out of their base in Golden for a short time. But he was unhappy with the company that lost the Banff contract and did not appreciate going to Golden every day. Okanagan was moving into more lucrative work with large companies bent on finding and extracting sought-after resources. When

Alpine offered him work in Canmore, he dropped Okanagan and went to work for Alpine.

Lance was happy when Alpine Helicopters did not bid on the Banff contract that was awarded to Quasar in the fall of 1984. He knew there were good people like Tim and Peter who were determined not to lose the standards Jim had set as pilot. The long, drawn-out struggle to keep Jim and the standard he set was fraught with squabbling that threatened long-time friendships and left the wardens mistrustful of the government. Lance was glad Alpine (and therefore he himself) was not directly involved.

Jim was happy to continue to mentor Lance, which made a huge difference to the growth of Lance's expertise. Lance was appreciative of this unique opportunity and credits Jim with teaching him skills that were not common among helicopter pilots. Lance still did a good many sightseeing flights with tourists,[71] but it was not long before he was called out on his first rescue. For Lance it was pretty straightforward.

A young woman had taken a bad fall on one of the harder routes on Yamnuska and Lloyd wanted to get her off the mountain before dark. Lance slung the rangers to the top with their rope rescue gear, but had to leave them there for the night, and actually flew back to Canmore in the dark. He picked them up the next morning and took the woman to the hospital.

Climbing incidents were not the only type of rescues Kananaskis Country faced. Lloyd relates:

> In the rescue community there is a tendency to automatically think that rock rescues are the most challenging, but in fact when I look back, the biggest challenges were, of course, the big

searches where you have many people out there searching, especially if a child is involved or a plane is missing. There is much
more work involved as the rescue coordinator. Climbing rescues
are really simple things to do, usually. You get a call, someone
is hurt, you know the climb, you go up there either at night or
in the daytime, you fly in and hopefully within an hour or two
you've wrapped it up and you go home.

Even though from the public and media's standpoint [climb-
ing rescues] look more challenging, exciting, more scary ... in
actual fact it's a very easy thing to do. They're clean and simple,
whereas you have to plan a search more thoroughly. You don't
know where it's going, for it can go in a hundred different directions, and when it progresses into day three and day four, you
now have the media involved. You've got the public involved
and the family involved. You have everybody on top of you and
by then you're tired because you're the head honcho making all
the major decisions. So, searching is the most demanding and
the most costly, and we've had our share of big searches.

One of the reasons Kananaskis Country tended to have large
searches was the added terrain of the foothills that many mountain national parks didn't have: it's easy to get lost in the featureless timbered hills. Aircraft went down or people wandered off
in forested expanses riddled with lakes and rivers.[72] In addition,
the close proximity of a large city (Calgary) also brought out a
diversity of people trying their hand at every form of outdoor
adventure, from hang gliding to horseback riding. The area also
included a fairly dangerous cave on Grotto Mountain.

Lloyd felt the rangers and wardens in public safety were a small
community of their own and encouraged joint rescue practices.

He often invited park wardens from Banff to take part in training in Kananaskis Country, especially in search management, where ranger Doug Hanna was developing an unprecedented expertise. Doug was fascinated by the dynamics of a successful search and the anomalies that could make even the most straightforward searches a puzzle. It was an interest that would eventually lead him to consulting work. The warden service was, in fact, behind in this area because they had fewer large searches.

Lloyd became adept at dealing with agencies and jurisdictions inside and outside of Kananaskis, including many volunteer search and rescue organizations. He developed a reciprocal arrangement with the Calgary Fire Department because of the number of water rescues the park was becoming involved in. He went into Calgary to teach members of the fire department how to rappel down high-rises and office buildings, and they in turn would train the park rangers in water rescue. There was no money exchanged; much as with Parks Canada's involvement with the RCMP in training their dogs and handlers, the only exchange was of knowledge and ideas.

×   ×   ×

Alpine Helicopters chose not to bid on the Banff helicopter contract when it was put out for tender, knowing they had all the business they could handle. This made it easier for Jim to accept their offer. Being close friends with Lloyd Gallagher and fellow Alpine pilot Lance Cooper was a special bonus. Although he felt ripped apart from his community in Banff, he would still be working with people he knew well and liked. Though Jim did not know the individual rangers in Kananaskis, he had flown on some of the joint rescue practices (held either in Banff or Kananaskis). As Lloyd collaborated frequently with Parks Canada, for Jim, flying rescues for Kananaskis Country was not a leap into something new.

The struggle over the helicopter contract in Banff could not help but bring the whole heli-sling program to the attention of the Department of Transport. They quickly focused on how helicopter slings were attached to the machine, which they had never been very happy with from the early days. The helicopters being used by this time were far better than what Jim had started with and DOT insisted on a three-tiered release system. Suddenly the rescuers had to face the possibility that they could be released if the pilot activated three components. However, most pilots would immediately go to autorotation mode and look for a landing spot before taking the extreme measure of dropping someone from the sky. The new attachment was expensive ($3,000) and could not be put in every helicopter. Quasar might have counted themselves lucky, as they went bankrupt before they were forced to install the pricey system.

× × ×

During his early years with Banff National Park, Jim did not spend a lot of time with his son, Morgan, who lived mostly with his mother and thus migrated between Assiniboine Lodge and Vancouver. He also had flying commitments that took him away from home for long periods of time. Though Morgan spent his elementary and junior high school days bouncing between Vancouver and Banff, he stayed close to his friends in Banff. Siri thought it was important for Morgan to stay in touch with his father as much as possible. It also gave her a bit more free time to travel abroad.

Morgan had a ping-pong school history, spending grades 5, 7 and 9 in Banff with Jim, and grades 6 and 8 with Siri in Vancouver. His final high school years were completed in Vancouver, where he started to get seriously into mountain biking and kayaking. Siri sold Assiniboine Lodge to Seppi and Barb Renner in 1983, the year Morgan graduated. It was a time of change for all three members of the Davies family, as Jim knew by then that his future in flying for Okanagan in Banff was in question.

When Morgan graduated from grade 12, he was young and fit, the outcome of a life devoted to strenuous physical activity. Those pursuits gave him a sense of what he wanted to strive for in his adult life. Academics were important but did not leave him with an overwhelming desire to go on to university. If he were to go in that direction his interest lay more in teaching kids' outdoor pursuits than picking up a profession that would leave him tied to a desk five days a week. If Siri, a free spirit herself, or Jim thought he might head straight for university, he dispelled that fantasy by hopping a plane to southern California with a friend and biking back to Vancouver.

Siri herself rediscovered her passion for travel and took off for Africa as soon as Morgan was out the door. She had no problem travelling on her own as a woman, despite an uncertain political climate. She started in North Africa and made her way to Zimbabwe and Botswana, where Morgan met her. They travelled on to South Africa and then Siri pushed on to South America. Morgan also joined her there later with his girlfriend, but then returned to Vancouver to further his education.

Siri was not done, however. She spent the rest of her travels in Australia and New Zealand before finally settling in Kaslo, BC. She never remarried after her divorce from Jim but did have boyfriends. The small town of Kaslo, situated on Kootenay Lake, provided lots of activity in the summer and skiing in the winter. It must have suited her, as she spent her remaining seven years there, before she died in 2001.

After Morgan returned to Vancouver, he taught kayaking and guided hikes. One thing he particularly liked about guiding for the kayak company he worked for was the places he got to see. Some trips went to the Baja, Mexico, and Tonga in the South Pacific, while others were in the North around Pond Inlet, Greenland and Ellesmere Island. Morgan took after his mother rather than Jim in having a desire to see as much of the world as he could before settling down. After Jim went to Europe at 17, his travels were restricted to the United States, with a swoop down to Mexico with Sue on a long-deferred honeymoon.

From the time Sue and Jim were married and settled in Banff, life was busy for Sue, who kept track of both the company and Jim. But work never took Sue away from what she loved doing best: hiking the high mountain passes, exploring new country rarely visited by other people. By the time Sue was working for Jim, she had been in the mountains for five or six years and, with her extroverted personality, had made plenty of friends. She established a women's hiking group that went out every Wednesday and only let the weather interfere when not even the dog would go out. Such trips were always polished off with hors d'oeuvres and the appropriate wine at someone's house. Marg Gmoser became one of Sue's closest friends and was grateful for these reprieves from the kids and keeping a home going.

Sue remained the consummate party organizer. She knew

246

The girls' hiking group
(JIM DAVIES COLLECTION).

everyone. Marg remembered Sue organizing an all-women's dress-up party she felt would keep the town buzzing for days – which meant that Jim (who was not invited) had to find another diversion for himself. One party had a medical theme, and attendees were required to find an appropriate outfit. Marg dressed up as old Doc Brett[73] – a good friend of hers who had worked at the Banff hospital so long he was familiar to everyone. Others dressed as the doctors and nurses they had known best in Banff and Canmore. When the party really got going, they took to the streets and blitzed the hospital, causing more amusement than most residents had seen on the streets of Banff for years. Parties were even more fun for Sue if a piano was handy. She was a good player with a wide repertoire, and the music spurred everyone to dance and sing.

Freda Odenthal, a staunch member of the hiking club, remembered numerous trips to Skoki Lodge or Assiniboine in the off-season. One particular trip to Skoki brought out the wilder side of Sue's personality when she tackled the piano after a dinner well lubricated with wine. It must have taken her back to the

The after-hike party

days when the Mickles ran the lodge and she was working for them. By the end of the evening, she was on the floor playing the ivories with her toes.

When Marg's kids were older, Marg and Sue liked to get away for longer backpacking trips in the summer. They looked for appealing routes that avoided the regular trails, and often snuck off to camp in non-designated sites. On one trip in Kootenay National Park, they were caught camping up on a ridge by warden Hans Fuhrer. He laughed and told them to be up and gone early, as the helicopter would be arriving the next morning bringing a work crew for the trails.

On another occasion, when flying to Assiniboine, Marg spotted a new route to the lodge over a promising-looking pass but could not get a good look at the far side and failed to spot a small cliff band they would have to negotiate. She convinced Sue to go anyway, but as soon as Sue saw the little cliff they had to scramble down, her language became less than polite. Sue was a great hiker but no climber. Marg managed to help her down, where they faced another challenge. A steep snow slope dropped away from the cliff to the valley below. Sue also anointed this slope with colourful descriptions of hell. The rest of the trip was worth every step, though, leaving the women feeling they were the first to experience the awe and quiet beauty of this unknown country.

× × ×

Because Kananaskis was now a park with attractive tourist destinations, it was seeing a great deal of increased use, and therefore regular work for Jim. Though he begrudged the Ottawa bureaucrats for dismissing his achievements for a few dollars in savings, he was adjusting to the Canmore move. As Canmore was only a 15-minute drive from Banff, working for Alpine did not require Jim and Sue to relocate.[74] Little changed for Jim, and he even enjoyed doing sightseeing tours.

Because of increased helicopter activity, Banff imposed a flight restriction zone over the park. Machines could fly at a certain elevation from points A to B on flight plans, but unplanned landings in the park were strictly prohibited. Therefore, all Alpine's tourist flights took place over the eastern slopes of the Rockies and in to Assiniboine.[75]

Meanwhile, Kananaskis Country was keeping Jim busy. The summer of 1986 was momentous from a public safety standpoint, with significant rescues occurring from Mt. Robson in the north all the way to Kananaskis Country in the south. Even accidents on the Trans-Canada Highway increased dramatically, with an unprecedented number of people driving west to take part in Expo '86 in Vancouver.

For the rangers in Kananaskis Country this "summer from hell" was defined by major searches and difficult rescues, many resulting in fatalities. Both wardens and rangers found themselves dealing with accumulated stress that came with exposure to non-stop call-outs. In 1986 there was little recognition of how adversely trauma could affect those involved in rescue work. The backing and encouragement of teammates, and a chance to debrief, was all the support harried rescue personnel received. Lloyd Gallagher, however, was a pioneer in recognizing the importance of dealing with cumulative stress and the impact it had on individuals and families.

Lloyd became aware of the effects of trauma after one particularly casualty-filled search. A small plane had lifted off from the Springbank airport, with a pilot and an Alberta government biologist, to do a survey of bighorn sheep and cougar. When they failed to return by 3:00 p.m., the military was notified. They sent aircraft to the area but failed to pick up the plane's emergency locator beacon. In the meantime, executives of the company that owned the missing plane began their own search by small plane, leaving Calgary International Airport at 4:40 in the afternoon. They were not heard from again.

With two planes missing, the search took on epic proportions. Nineteen aircraft joined the search. A team of 30 military personnel flew in from the Canadian Forces Base at Namao airport, just north of Edmonton, to oversee the air search. They based their operation out of the old McCall Field, adjacent to the international airport in Calgary.

Lloyd Gallagher was contacted in Kananaskis Country to

organize and direct a ground search. The area to cover was huge, and he called in everyone – rangers, park employees, national park wardens, volunteer search and rescue groups and members of the old, disbanded Calgary Mountain Rescue Group. Hundreds of people showed up, many not used to rugged terrain but willing to help, either as spotters in aircraft or as searchers on the ground. Those with limited backcountry skills were teamed with more experienced individuals who dragged them over ridges and peaks, looking for anything resembling a plane or a body.

It was the ground searchers who first found one of the missing planes. Ranger Dave Smith was heavily involved in the search and recalls: "My task was to walk Mt. Allen from Ribbon Creek to Dead Man's Flats on the Trans-Canada Highway. The fellow with me was really slow so I decided to go down into the valley bottom. We glissaded[76] down a snow slope and when I got to the bottom I stopped and looked back up for the volunteer and suddenly, 15 feet away, I spotted an airplane tire." Sure enough, aircraft debris and body parts lay scattered about. It was the third day of the search and the first plane to be found was the one flown by the volunteers who went looking for their missing friends.

While the search for the first plane continued, the rangers had to bring the bodies from the located plane out from its remote crash site. Jeff Palmer, one of the rescue pilots regularly used by both Kananaskis and Banff, observed, "It looked like [the plane] had sheared off the peak [Mt. Lougheed] and then blew over the top into a steep long freefall. It's a real mess." Rangers had to climb above the crash site and lower themselves into some very tight places to complete the recovery.

By Thursday, June 12, 350 people were taking part in the most intense phase of the eight-day effort. The search was growing extremely difficult to direct. With the army now involved as ground searchers, just assigning people to new areas was monumental. Media coverage was intense and often reported inaccurate information. This made it difficult for search master Major Mike Barbeau and ground search leader Lloyd Gallagher to keep abreast of developments when they got conflicting reports through the media.

And of course, the two men had to coordinate efforts between them. As Kananaskis Country public safety specialist George Field later recalled, "You put an extravagant outfit like the military together with a cost-conscious outfit like K-Country and you have a definite difference in attitude and style." He went on to say, "It was an incredibly huge search. We had 300 volunteers in front of the emergency centre in Calgary who just wanted to come out and help and we didn't know what their abilities were. I had done lots of smaller searches with groups of people and that wasn't a problem, but this opened up a whole new search management arena for many of us in the business. We were going, 'holy mackerel, this is a big one.' Then before it was over another aircraft went down."

The day after the wreckage beneath Mt. Lougheed was found, the air search had to be called off because of high winds. When the winds calmed the next day, Major Barbeau addressed the media, saying, "I have a good feeling. There are a lot of people out and the weather is good." The fateful words were spoken too soon, however. A military Twin Otter with three airmen and five volunteers from the Civil Air Rescue Emergency Services (CARES) organization went down near the top of Cox Hill in the frontal range.[77] The pilot gave no indication of problems beforehand, leaving the impression that the crash was entirely unforeseen. This was one wreck no one had problems finding.

One of the soldiers first on scene was quoted by the media as saying: "When I arrived, the plane was just a great ball of flame and debris scattered all over the place. To me it seemed the plane had tried to turn between three mountains and just hit the top of one of them." He then said, "How many more people have to die before the search is called off?" Another soldier early to the scene reported that someone had managed to briefly survive the crash and subsequent explosion. "He was the only one who suffered. You could see the marks where he tried to drag himself out of the burning plane."

According to the *Calgary Herald*, it was a stunned and weary Canadian Forces spokesman, Major Wally West, who broke the news to the reporters. "There were no survivors." It was the members of CARES who were stunned and horrified the most by the crash, but they vowed to continue the search. It was also the first time in their ten-year history that they had lost a worker. Suddenly, they had lost five.

Two days later, 13 days after it went missing, the first aircraft was found on a routine workday for pilot Jim Lipinski as he flew an Initial Attack fire crew to their work site. Jim Davies flew RCMP constable Jim Krug and Public Safety Specialist George Field to the mangled plane below Mt. Kidd, and they could now understand why the plane had taken so long to locate. Field and the coroner would have to rappel 45 m down a cliff to get to the site.

Jim was kept busy; everything – bodies, pieces of the aircraft – had to be airlifted out. One of the largest air searches in the history of western Canada was over, with an appalling toll of

13 deaths. The standard search procedure used successfully by the military on flat ground did not work when employed in the mountains. Ground searchers located two of the crash sites and a pilot found the other one from the air.

The prolonged, massive search with such a dramatic cost showed on every searcher's face as they tried to deal with the trauma of this experience. Lloyd was certainly aware of the toll it had taken on him and decided it was time to address the possibility of his staff developing PTSD symptoms. He approached the Calgary Fire Department for advice and they referred him to an excellent therapist. He left the door open to his staff to attend a debriefing with an expert in the field and encouraged all to at least give this approach a chance. Many took his advice and it soon became a part of their debriefing program.

10

The Coast and Home Again

Jim's return to flying with Parks Canada was like slipping into old shoes. He had been away for almost three years, and although many of the faces were the same, many were new and younger, bringing with them a different set of skills.

Though the regime of training and emphasis on teamwork still prevailed, park wardens – particularly in Banff – were becoming more dedicated to specific functions where they had an interest and an aptitude. The "jack-of-all-trades" warden was becoming a rarity as the roles (public safety, law enforcement, backcountry, fire management, environmental assessment and wildlife) grew increasingly complex. One of the effects this had was the loss of the unified camaraderie they had enjoyed in the past.

When Walter Perren began to give the wardens additional training in mountain rescue in the 1960s, it hadn't been his intent to just give them another responsibility to add to the other functions. He always said he did not want to lose the great depth he found in the warden service and that every warden should get some training in all aspects of the job. At that time, rescues were uncommon and did not interfere with the other functions.

A decade later Tim Auger, like Walter, did not want to see the average warden he trained lose ability in the other functions. But he realized the generalist warden role was only possible at the expense of having a dedicated rescue team capable of responding to rescues of high-end climbers. By the latter half of the 1980s the era of the "jack of all trades" was slowly disappearing.

But rescuers burn out, or they age out of peak performance, so managers were always on the lookout for replacements or additions, depending on the money. The goal remained for each mountain national park to run its own show and handle most aspects of rescue without needing additional help from other parks every time someone got into trouble. But the reality was that small parks simply did not have the manpower to accomplish anything more than a simple heli-sling extraction. Tim Auger and his replacement, Mark Ledwidge, knew it was inevitable that one fully trained unit would respond to all call-outs, covering all the mountain parks. This transition was slow and confusing to most wardens, who did not know what role they were expected to play in even simple scenarios.

Eventually, new standards would require public safety applicants to have a full guide's licence,[78] which sharply reduced the number of wardens who qualified. This created problems for the parks faced with pouring a huge amount of money and time into training those who showed potential. The new guiding standards were daunting and the courses they put on were becoming prohibitively expensive. The requirement to qualify for a full guide's licence[79] was as demanding, expensive and time consuming as applying for a PhD in medicine. At least a doctor could expect to be eventually remunerated for all that time and money. Wardens who qualified for public safety did not have that satisfaction on the pay scale for the warden service. The real downside was for wardens who had worked in public safety for years who were told they no longer qualified to be on the public safety team. Resentment and bitterness began to creep through the halls, growing behind closed office doors, reinforcing the rumours of abandonment – a factor that added to the slow disintegration of a proud service dedicated to protecting the park.

Jim did not have a problem working with this new breed of warden, though he may have noticed there was more of a perfunctory atmosphere around the office or that some of the former camaraderie among everyone as a whole was less evident. Even Jim was experiencing a bit of ennui in returning to his old job, though it was good to be working with Peter and Tim again. But it was just not the same after the contract dispute that had tainted his enjoyment of the job. With all the radical changes occurring in the service no one seemed happy.

By the end of 1989, Jim was contemplating retirement.

Though he was still young at 51, the saying "there are old pilots and bold pilots but no old, bold pilots" may have given him pause. However, the main reason Jim decided to retire was Sue's health.

That winter, Sue began to feel poorly and could not keep warm on any of her outings. She felt cold even in the house. When she started needing extra sweaters or toques and gloves just to go to the front door, both she and Jim were at a loss to know what was wrong. Eventually, it became serious enough for her to see a doctor.

She was told she had scleroderma (overproduction of collagen), an autoimmune disease that is hard to diagnose, as it affects so many areas of the body in different ways. Scleroderma had no direct treatment other than pain pills to relieve discomfort. If the scleroderma was mild, it could fade away within three to five years. The doctor recommended moving to a warmer climate where her body did not have to fight the cold all the time. Neither Sue nor Jim wanted to leave Canada and especially the mountains, but Canada does not have a lot of choice when it comes to finding a warm climate all year round. And they weren't sure how long they'd need to stay away until Sue would be well enough to return to Banff.

At the time, Jim did not want to work himself into a desk job. In addition, new flying restrictions strictly imposed by the warden service no longer allowed fuel caches located at different backcountry sites. Also, landing in the park (other than landings specified for the designated job) was forbidden. These constraints took a bit of the fun out of the flying that had originally given him such a sense of freedom.

Since the flying contract for Banff had become available to other companies, the number of pilots capable of doing the rescue work was increasing. When he and Sue looked at it critically, there were no pressing commitments tying them to Banff. Jim was financially secure, with two houses in Banff, which meant they could afford a nice place in southern BC where they could stay for as long as it took Sue get better.

On March 25, 1990, Jim accomplished his last mission for Banff as an employed helicopter pilot when he flew a survey for wolf and bear radio locations. By that spring, he and Sue had found a beautiful house with a southern exposure and a view looking toward the bay at Saanich Inlet on southern Vancouver Island.

×   ×   ×

Jim was an exceptional pilot. Over the years, he was recognized by his peers and colleagues in the mountain community for his pioneering work, phenomenal skill and limit-pushing that saved lives without endangering rescuers. In 1988 he was honoured with the Summit of Excellence Award presented annually by the Banff Centre Mountain Film and Book Festival.

The Summit of Excellence Award, given in memory of Calgary climber Bill March, was first presented at the Banff Centre festival in 1987, to Bruno Engler, guide, ski instructor, pioneer in avalanche safety, photographer and filmmaker. In the past the festival has recognized individuals who made significant contributions to mountain life in the Canadian Rockies. It was an award that was especially important in the Canadian mountain community, and the list of recipients reads like a "who's who" of people who have contributed to that culture in some significant way: Hans Gmoser, Don Forest, Peter Fuhrmann, Willi Pfisterer, Chic Scott, Sharon Wood and Tim Auger, to name a few. Jim was among fine company.

Before he escaped Banff, Jim also received the Helicopter Pilot Award from Canadian Helicopters, in recognition of 12,000 hours of accident-free flight time.[80] It's no wonder the public safety wardens did not want to lose him.

×　×　×

Both Sue and Jim loved the house they found at Saanich Inlet, and it was not long until the warm summer months alleviated many of Sue's symptoms. They could lie on the deck, putter in the yard or go into the small town of Saanich for shopping or just to meet people they knew. The area was full of people from Banff who had either retired or spent part of the winter there.

As Sue regained her stamina, she returned to social mode and they held a lot of dinner parties. She was also able to bike the six km to Sidney, and often the two of them would pedal into

House at Saanich Inlet

(JIM DAVIES COLLECTION).

town on a nice day for breakfast at Philapanos, where they met old friends or new acquaintances. Jim kept in touch with the latest happenings in Banff through close friends who came for a visit, such as Roy Andersen, whose parents resided in Victoria; he and Jim also knew the Grey Campbells, another set of close mutual friends.

Nearby Victoria offered a wealth of things to do, with its endless gardens, bistros, markets and museums. The island was new to Jim and Sue, and they explored it endlessly, driving the winding country roads and exploring the beautiful beaches of the west coast. They did not have a dog of their own at this time but had ample opportunity to look after friends' and neighbours' dogs while they were away.[81]

Jim also had a chance to get back to his art. He created a number of watercolour sketches before undertaking the mammoth task of painting a mural in the basement of his home. The mural, a scene from the Rockies that stretched along one whole wall of the family room, may have been some of the best work he ever did.[82]

If Jim thought he was through with helicopters, he was wrong. By chance or fate, a very wealthy man from the United States owned the house next door to Jim and Sue's Saanich Inlet home. Dave Freeze and his wife came to the first party Jim and Sue put on shortly after they moved in, introducing themselves as "the neighbours next door," and all four became good friends. Dave had his fixed-wing pilot's licence but never had the time get his licence to fly the helicopter sitting in his backyard. With money to purchase the best, he'd bought a dual pilot Bell 206B-3. Dave was allowed to fly as long as he had a second qualified pilot to fly with him.

Jim qualified with Vancouver Island Helicopters so he could use one of their machines if Dave's was in for service, and on September 18 they set Dave up for training.

When Jim and Sue moved to Saanich Inlet, Morgan was living in Vancouver, teaching kayaking in the summer and skiing in the winter. Saanich was close enough for Morgan to visit them fairly often. When Jim started flying with Dave, they would meet Morgan in Vancouver and bring him on board for some sightseeing, usually making it a point to stop for lunch, assuring Jim that Morgan was getting at least one good meal.

Both Morgan and Jim enjoyed the chance to see more of each other. These flights also gave Morgan the opportunity to see what island living was like. He found Saanich to be a great place to escape from the city, with miles of small paved country roads perfect for road and mountain bikes. The area was excellent for kayaking, with enough inlets and bays to explore for a lifetime, and, being in the rain shadow of the central mountain range on the island, it was considerably sunnier than the mainland coast.

Jim found flying with Dave a great way to see Vancouver

Island, as well as the Gulf Islands with their quaint restaurants providing breaks for lunch. They dropped in on friends, such as Doug Robinson, a former coach for the Banff Ski Runners who'd moved to the island, or hopped over to Spokane to give Dave the chance to clear customs and get in a round of golf at the same time. Stormy days and cooler winter weather were spent working at home or visiting friends, but as soon as March rolled around, Jim and Dave were back out with the helicopter.

By 1991 Dave was gaining confidence as a pilot and was ready to fly long distances using just the GPS for navigation. Their first direct flight using GPS was to Kelowna, where they spent the night and flew back the next day. The training and flying continued through August, when they started to throw in more trips based on golfing or fishing. By the end of the summer, Jim convinced Dave to fly to the Bugaboos to get experience in flying more serious mountain terrain. They stopped at the ski lodge for lunch to visit and see the improvements the heli-ski company had made, just missing Hans by a few minutes.[83] On the way back to Saanich, they set down in Dave's brother's backyard for a two-hour visit. Telling Jim or Dave to drop over for coffee any time was quite literal. Jim, in fact, was amazed at how many people lived on small farms or acreages where this was possible.

As Dave's expertise grew, so did his wanderlust. That same summer, he and Jim took a tour of the north coast. They skipped from Sidney to Bella Bella to Terrace (to stay overnight), then on to Stewart, BC. There, at the local air base, they learned the weather forecast was for several days of clear skies. North of Stewart they had spectacular views of the mountains and the glaciated coastline glimmering below. They pushed on to Atlin, a small, colourful town full of history, nestled on the northeast shore of Atlin Lake. Taking a break, they decided to fish the Nakina River, where they seemed to catch fish all day. The following day was rainy, so they explored the town and surrounding area, resting up for the last leg of the journey north before heading home. The many glaciers they flew over highlighted the flight to Skagway, Alaska, the infamous gold-rush town, now overcrowded with tourists.

Bad weather flowed in, cleared, then threatened again, but they were able to make their way to Wrangell, Alaska, via Juneau. The weather improved by the time they reached Prince Rupert, and from there it was a good flight back to Sidney, where they landed on the 3rd of September. That final day took them over the high, glaciated coastal range, flying over spectacular peaks like Mt. Waddington. It had been an impressive trip, seeing some of the most beautiful country in some of the remotest parts of Canada and the United States. Both Jim and Dave would remember this trip for years to come.

Jim continued to fly with Dave through the early 1990s, mostly visiting friends or going fishing. Sue did not go on long flying trips with Jim, as they were fairly arduous. But she did not mind Jim being gone, as she kept busy with biking, gardening and visiting friends. She was happy to be at home and enjoy the break from the hectic days of running a helicopter business in Banff. It was a tranquil time for Sue, doing what she felt like on any given day. The lack of stress from not managing a heavy flying schedule or dealing with Parks Canada probably contributed greatly to her recovery.

During their stay on the island, Jim and Sue took several trips back to Banff to see friends and to see how Sue responded to the colder weather. Remarkably, by 1997 she was showing little of the reaction she had before, and her doctor said the disease seemed to be in remission. Since it was an autoimmune disease, there was no guarantee it would not return at some later date, but Sue was still young and vigorous, and had a formidable determination to regain her fitness and strength.

Though Jim had been happy at Saanich, Banff was his home[84] and he ultimately wanted to return. However, though the town of Banff had been released from Parks control in 1990, it still upheld the "reason to reside clause," limiting who could own a home in the town. Jim had sold the two houses he'd owned in Banff before they left and worried he might be refused the privilege of buying a house. With Sue's scleroderma under control it was a good time to press the issue, but in the end, they didn't have to worry.

Sue too was happy to return where she could renew her old friendships. Jim bought a fourplex from Craig Allen, where they lived with friends. Not long after that he commissioned work on a new house. He had a fair amount of experience in building houses (and knew the best contractors to use). In 1997 they moved into a large, open-concept house and adopted a dog.[85]

Sue resumed the role of directing the hiking club and entertained the idea of writing Jim's biography – a large project that would keep her busy during the winter months. Sue had become a fairly proficient downhill skier, having learned the basics when she worked at Temple Lodge on the back side of the Lake Louise ski area. But she preferred cross-country skiing now, which gave greater access to the park's backcountry and which she considered better suited to staying in shape. Jim had never done much on cross-country skis and for the first year they skied at Sunshine or Mt. Norquay. This lasted until snowboarding began to overtake the skiing. A couple of close calls involving young kids more eager to go fast than to turn convinced both of them that trail skiing on "misery sticks"[86] was safer and ultimately more enjoyable. Jim even put in a ski track from his house down to a small pond, which gave them a decent outing and provided good exercise for the dog.

Jim and Sue cut back on entertaining, happy with a life quieter than they'd enjoyed on the coast. The Banff School of Fine Arts (the site of Jim's first year at kindergarten), now known as the Banff Centre for Arts and Creativity, had grown in international standing in the arts and had numerous programs, as did the Whyte Museum of the Canadian Rockies. It was rare for a month to go by without some event of interest put on for the public that Jim and Sue could attend. The only thing to mar these years was an eye infection Sue had contracted on the coast that required constant medication and never did heal completely.

Jim enjoyed his retirement. He put his talents as an artist, rediscovered in Saanich, to use painting watercolours from charcoal sketches of the park and its resident fauna; he also undertook a new mural in his basement. Jim enjoyed meeting the "guys" – old friends down at the Cascade Hotel. Though Sue had objected in the past to the influence Jim's old friends had in luring him down to the bar, this was less of an issue when they returned from the coast, as Jim had no flying commitments anymore. Staying connected with old friends was important and he stayed current with what was happening in the rescue world.

×　×　×

When Sue and Jim moved to Vancouver Island, Morgan was travelling with his mother in Europe, but he took a break to return to Canada to do some kayaking and visit some friends in Victoria.

As he walked through his friends' door, Morgan spotted a woman he did not know. Marie immediately attracted him, and he was delighted to find out she loved kayaking. He kept coming back to Victoria as often as possible to see her. They never dated in the ordinary sense of going out for dinner and a movie but got to know each other kayaking around the various small islands close to where she lived.

With a blossoming relationship that looked like it would last, Morgan realized he wanted the stability of a career. A university degree might satisfy the demand from employers wanting credentials for guides taking people on interpretive trips, and lead to lasting employment. Since he enjoyed the teaching aspect of his work, it seemed sensible to strengthen that side of his résumé. In 1998 Morgan enrolled at the University of British Columbia to obtain his Bachelor of Education degree.

But Vancouver had become an exceptionally expensive place in which to live. Finding a roof without a long commute from the city's outskirts proved to be very difficult. He solved this problem by purchasing a motor home and parking it at the university.

The back and forth between Victoria and Vancouver took a toll, and it came to a point where pursuing the relationship further meant either Morgan or Marie had to move. Morgan was committed to living in Vancouver until he finished his degree, so Marie got a job in Vancouver working for the province's auditor general. But the combination of living in a motorhome and dealing with the snarly traffic in this overgrown, rainy city quickly ruled out the idea of living there permanently.

Morgan had always kept in close touch with Siri, especially after she moved to Kaslo, BC, in 1994. Kaslo was a good place for Siri, as it gave her a chance to slow down. Throughout life she had burned the candle at both ends and now she was tired. Again, she made friends easily and enjoyed the quiet security of the small lakeside town, but her years there were difficult, as she was dying. Her life had been hard at times and wasn't up to the pace she liked to keep.

In 2001, a year before Morgan finished his degree, his mother died in the Kaslo hospital. She was 61 years old and had packed those years full of adventure, living in some of the most beautiful places in the world. Morgan's adventures, accompanying her on some of her world travels, opened his eyes to a huge variety of life and lands of awesome beauty he would always treasure.

But no matter where she went, no place would mean as much to Siri as Assiniboine. Though she had many friends, the only family she had was Morgan, his partner Marie and her grandson, Niko.[87] Siri had opted to be cremated so her ashes could be spread in the place she loved best. It gave her some peace knowing her ashes would be released to catch the wind where, for a while, they would float unhindered and free. These small fine particles would begin their journey in the alpine meadows below the crowning heights of Mount Assiniboine. Perhaps some would even reach the summit to rest among the small rock crevices looking down on the valleys and meadows and the home she had known for so many years.

It was a small party that flew in to Assiniboine Lodge in 2006 to say goodbye to a spirit that never lived by the conventional rules of life. Morgan, Marie, Niko and Hans-Peter Stettler landed at the lodge, where Seppi and Barb Renner greeted them.[88] Then

Morgan and Hans-Peter hiked to the top of Mt. Strom and released Siri's ashes to the wind. Morgan knew she had lived as she wanted and, though sad at her loss, also felt relief to know her suffering was over. Morgan and Hans-Peter brought with them a simple stone plaque marking her life and death. It now resides on the summit of that small peak.

Siri had embraced the roller coaster of her life and did not want a mournful dirge to mark her passing. The small group stayed at the Naiset Huts[89] the first night and had dinner in the lodge. The second night, Marie was delighted to stay with Niko in the teepee, also meant for guests. Niko was even allowed to have a bath in the sink, which livened up the party. Still, this was a quiet gathering that lent itself to reminiscing about the years they'd shared under the spell of Mt. Assiniboine. In all, as Marie said, "it was a lovely trip."

× × ×

After Morgan finished his degree in 2002, he and Marie moved to Victoria with Niko, where they bought a big white house. Shortly after moving, Morgan had an opportunity to buy into the Pacific Rim Paddling Company, which allowed him to take tours in many parts of the world. Working for them, Morgan spent his winters guiding kayakers on day tours, whale watching or just exploring the seacoast. In addition, he went on some of Pacific Rim's longer trips around Tonga in the South Pacific, Pond Inlet in the Canadian North, and extended tours to Baffin and Ellesmere islands.

While Morgan and Marie were living in Baja,[90] Jim and Sue took the time to go down to visit. Sue was happy just to be in a hot country, but the trip was a highlight of their retirement years. They paddled leisurely for two weeks on a kayak camping trip along the coastline from Loreto to La Paz, exploring the rugged countryside and snorkelling in the warm, clear water in the Sea of Cortez. Morgan was the guide. He had snooped out the best places to camp and knew where to find the migrating whales. The trip was remembered fondly by both Jim and Sue. Jim also valued the chance to spend time with Morgan and Marie.

×　　×　　×

In the fall of 2000, Sue and Jim decided to hike the Iceline Trail in Yoho, which starts at Takakkaw Falls and switchbacks 1,400 ft. up behind the youth hostel to high alpine meadows. From there it heads north toward the Little Yoho Valley, running over rock-laced scree slopes beneath Mt. Michael and the President and Vice President peaks. It is one of the most spectacular hikes in the mountain national parks, especially in the fall when the sun illuminates the gossamer foliage of the brilliant yellow alpine larch – a display that lasts for a brief few weeks before the needles drop, leaving the trees bare for the approach of winter.

It was a demanding loop, but Jim was still surprised when his normally very fit wife lagged behind and often sat down to absorb the view. When they got to the car, Sue announced she did not feel well. Her even saying something like that was so out of character that it alarmed Jim. She had been a whirlwind, hiking with her friends on their weekly outings and averaging 500 km a summer.

When she still felt bad after a few days, she went for a checkup and her doctor brought her in for tests. The results were dismal. She was diagnosed with leukemia, and Jim was stunned.

Sue went to the Tom Baker Cancer Centre in Calgary for treatment. Chemotherapy and radiation kept her confined to her bed at home or the hospital for the first 145 days. For Jim, it seemed like only days had gone by, rather than four years, since her scleroderma had gone into remission and they'd moved back to Banff. He thought they had paid their dues in life and looked forward to an extended retirement among friends in his hometown. Sue had always been careful about living a healthy life by eating well, keeping fit and getting a good night's sleep. Cancer was not part of the program, and it baffled both of them.

But other factors beyond her control may have impacted whether she would develop cancer. Heredity could have been one of these factors. Suppression of her immune system for treatment of the scleroderma may have been another. Whatever caused the cancer was irrelevant, however. Sue had to face the reality of the steps it would take to get better.

Her friends could hardly believe it. Both Freda and Marg remembered Sue as having an outgoing personality and tremendous vitality. She was tall and strong and often spent long days in the mountains. She was a confident woman who took on projects and work goals with gusto and determination. She was the last person to whom any who knew her expected this to happen.

Jim was very concerned, but he knew Sue's determination could be formidable when she tackled problems or setbacks. She confronted the "terrors" (her name for the cancer cells in her body), employing all remedies that might help. The doctors told her if she kept up her rest and eliminated stressful hiking, she had a good shot at remission after two years. It was the grail she needed. She embraced her recovery by getting a T-shirt saying "I'm bound to go to Heaven; I've already been in Hell."

Roy Andersen remembers Sue stopping in for a chat whenever he was out in the yard and she was cycling by. She had to discontinue her trips with the hiking group, but the women always came around to see how she was doing. When recovering from the chemotherapy sessions she was too weak to do more than stay in bed or sit in the living room swathed in blankets, but as the drugs left her system, she could get out and be more active.

Sue had always been extremely attractive, so losing her hair was a blow, even though she knew it would happen. However, with a scarf or a hat she still looked good. On Sue's low days, Freda would pop by for a visit, usually with a casserole or baked items because she didn't consider Jim much of a cook. Bruce McTrowe could testify to that after Jim told him the story of how to make banana flambé. Jim gave him the ingredients and the steps to make a spectacular entrance with flames dancing lightly over the banana. But he also added a warning not to add too much brandy. Apparently, Jim's concoction had wound up almost setting the house on fire.

Sue and Jim probably could have lived off all the food people brought by. Freda always found Sue cheerful and engaged in some activity as she sat in a chair by the window. Sue was a letter writer. Even in the age of computers, she preferred to keep everyone up to date by writing long, insightful letters that probably did more good for her than for those to whom she was writing. She also worked on her slide collection; it connected her to the people in her life as she saw them engaged in activities she loved. Sue was so positive that Freda always returned home feeling uplifted.

Sue knew chemotherapy was necessary, but she never over-looked alternative ideas if she thought they would help. She had heard that Dale Portman had overcome malignant melanoma, which had progressed to his lymph nodes, and that he embraced meditation as a tool for well-being, so she asked him about his experience.

In 1990 Dale had been given a 50 per cent chance of surviving his cancer. His melanoma had spread to the lymph glands under his arm and from there might quickly metastasize to other tissues in his body. The whole mass had to be removed. The good news was that the doctors found no evidence of it having spread further. The bad news was that melanoma was a slow-moving cancer that did not respond to chemotherapy or radiation. His doctor could only put him on a program that introduced brucellosis bacteria to his body to boost the immune system.

But Dale had come across articles explaining how meditation could help, so he asked Dr. Gerry, his oncologist, what he thought or knew about it. In 1990 meditation was considered quackery and most doctors would have discouraged this practice. Doctor Gerry, though, was familiar with the power of the mind and supported Dale in pursuing this therapy. He introduced Dale to a tape he'd made that took the patient through the steps of relaxation, body scan and visualization.

When Dr. Gerry discussed the powers of meditation with Dale, he closed his office door and asked that Dale not mention this nebulous concept to other doctors.[91] He did not want to get labelled a quack. Dale took the therapy seriously and meditated every day for several years thereafter, and the cancer never did return.

Sue was inspired by this and asked Dale to explain it in detail.

Giving Sue a tool she had control over probably helped her engage her body to fight the disease. It also helped her feel she was taking responsibility and not leaving her recovery solely up to her doctors.

Her efforts paid off when she went into remission. No one knows how the remission came about, but as Dale said, "You can't ignore the chemo and radiation, and the meditation would have been at least comforting and empowering to her." She must have felt like a boxer who'd made it to the last round still standing. When she could, she resumed her old activities with the hiking group. And Jim was happy to have her back as her old self.

The reprieve lasted three years, but a day came when Sue found she could not get her breath. Both Jim and Sue were dismayed to learn the leukemia had metastasized into her lungs. This development meant more chemotherapy and radiation. It was a disheartening blow to go through the whole process again, back to Calgary, and to the Tom Baker Cancer Centre at the Foothills Hospital. Radiation was the least intrusive, but it did affect her appetite when even a morsel of food gave her heartburn. Again, there were small remissions from the pain but not enough for Sue to return to an active life.[92]

Though her condition was relieved somewhat by treatment and painkillers, nothing prevented the rapid spread of the cancer. Sue became housebound, dealing with her illness as cheerfully as she could. Jim would do anything for her, but for the most part all he could offer was to be with her as much as possible, doing little things to cheer her up or finding some diversion to get her mind off her illness for a while.

Jim had all he could handle as a caregiver, but his friends stuck by him for support. This was a task in itself, as Jim is a very private person and prone to be stoic when people offer to help. Evenings at the bar telling tales lost their appeal when people with good intentions kept asking how he was doing. Nevertheless, support for both of them never stopped, particularly from Sue's hiking group, who brought food and sat with her so Jim could get out of the house for a while.

But even the most optimistic person could see that Sue was not getting better. She was listless and thin and surviving on painkillers. On a particularly bad day she woke up coughing and found it hard to breathe. This time Jim took her to the hospital in Banff where she could be kept on oxygen and closely monitored for medication. All anyone could do after that was visit her in the hospital while the staff kept her as comfortable as possible. She was not in the hospital for long.

Freda was there when Sue died, and she phoned Jim to come down, knowing he would not find her alive. Jim knew logically that this day would come but found it hard to believe anyway. He remembered massaging her feet, puzzled that they were so cold and stiff. As he looked down, the reality of her death sank in: the lifeless feet were not her but part of some metamorphosis to a cold clay statue. Freda gave Jim a tearful hug – there was little else she could do.

Jim remembered going home alone to the house, knowing no one was there.

×   ×   ×

Jim had Sue cremated, but held no funeral or memorial. Rather, with a small group of friends closest to her, he took her ashes up to Sunshine, spreading them throughout the high alpine meadows she loved. They all had a shot of scotch, Sue's favourite drink, and toasted her life.

Not long after, the hiking group also scattered her ashes at Assiniboine, possibly the place she loved best. Jim kept the remaining ashes and planted them under a Norfolk pine newly planted in their backyard. It was Sue's favourite tree and she would point them out every time she saw one.

Despite her illness, Sue had lived a good life. She loved Jim deeply. She'd had wonderful adventures, but most of all she maximized her time in the mountains, absorbing their peace and beauty. She revelled in the life she felt; in the strength of her body; in striding through meadows and cool deep forests.

×　×　×

After Sue's death, time weighed heavily on Jim and he kept to himself despite numerous invitations from friends to come for dinner or an evening's visit. He was rarely seen in the Cascade Hotel and only saw a handful of close friends who would drop by to see how he was doing.

Though Jim did not sell the house full of memories, it took five years before he could face cleaning out Sue's things. However, Jim did get a dog. At least the house would not be hauntingly silent when he came home.

Freda Odenthal remembered that, for a while after Sue's death, Jim would come over for dinner when she asked, trying not to make it an imposition. But over time, he came less often. She reflected that Jim and Sue did not have children outside of Morgan, who was busy catching up with his own life, and so the two relied on each other for comfort and support. The saying "time heals all wounds" may be true in some cases, but more often it doesn't. The task of daily living gave Jim some respite, and the dog gave him a reason to get out of the house, but it was some time before he ventured far from home.

Jim knew he had to get back to living his life without the order and structure Sue had provided. An old friend, Mo Vroom, helped significantly in getting Jim back on his feet. Mo had lost her husband, warden Bill Vroom, in 1998 under difficult circumstances, but had been able to overcome this tragedy by remaining at work in the Banff warden office as dispatcher. This was the best thing she could have done, as she was in contact with the warden service, many of whom were close friends and staunch supporters.

Jim had first met Mo years earlier at Mt. Norquay when he was skiing for the Banff Ski Runners. Mo and her friend were new to skiing and didn't know how to use the rope tow. Jim and another friend were happy to help out the pretty young skiers and they became good friends. Later, when Jim was flying for Parks Canada on contract, he saw Mo frequently when she was the warden dispatch operator, and they remained in touch after she retired.

At the time of Sue's death, Mo had retired and was living on her own in a small condominium, which kept her challenged to remain connected to the community. She encouraged Jim to drop over for visits and soon they were taking walks or going for coffee with old friends. They also took in all the events Jim and Sue used to attend. Mo lived at the opposite end of Banff from Jim's lofty house but thought nothing of walking the distance to visit with him and his dog. The visits brought Jim out of his self-imposed retreat, and to his surprise he began to learn how to overcome the worst of his grief.

With time, Jim began to make it a point to get to as many functions as he could and re-establish ties with old friends. He also kept an eye out for his neighbours and helped them when he could by looking after their house when they were away or acting as a dog sitter.

Morgan was relieved to see his father healing.

Morgan's life had become more settled when they moved to Victoria. Although kayaking had been a large part of his life, he did not want to spend the winters in Baja. It was a troubling time for Pacific Rim Paddling, which was facing more and more competition from other kayaking companies in Baja. Though Baja was becoming increasingly popular as a tourist destination, pressure was coming from the Mexican guides who had worked for several kayaking companies and begun to realize what a gold mine they were sitting on. After years working for North American outfitters, the guides began to set up their own kayak expedition companies, a natural progression in a developing industry. On top of this, Morgan's business partner was looking to move on from full-time kayaking. They decided to sell Pacific Rim Paddling to a fellow guide, ending a footloose but challenging period of Morgan and Marie's life.

Now together in Victoria full time, Marie and Morgan started to consider their next stage of life, where to raise Niko with good schooling, where to find decent accommodation and where to find work that would satisfy both of them. Marie's father had recently passed away, leaving her mother alone on a large piece of property with a large house in Procter, BC, but her health was not great, and she was moving up in age. She clearly needed some help if she wanted to remain living there.

With Morgan no longer working full time as a kayak guide,

there was nothing stopping them from moving to Procter, on Kootenay Lake near Nelson, BC. They made the move in 2010 to look after Marie's mother and take over the upkeep of her property. Marie's only worry was that Morgan would not like living in such a small town away from the excitement of the city and his friends. They would also not be near the ocean that had provided Morgan with a great job in an environment he loved.

But Morgan agreed that Marie's mother needed help and would do poorly if moved to a seniors facility in Victoria. Marie had a strong attachment to Procter, where most of her extended family lived and where she had grown up. Living in Procter also gave Morgan a chance to drive up to Banff more often to see Jim. Marie had no problem finding work, which led to her becoming a partner in a CA firm with a friend from Castlegar. The accounting work could be done mostly on the computer, which meant Marie could work from home.

Morgan resumed the work he had done earlier on the west coast – guiding kayaking trips to Gwaii Haanas National Park Reserve located on the southern island of Haida Gwaii. He also had work as a hiking guide for a mountain wellness retreat nearby where he worked on a part-time basis.[93]

When Morgan moved to Procter, Jim was happy to see more of his son and family. When Morgan was young, Jim was away flying for months at a time, and both felt they saw too little of each other. But, as old friend Roy Andersen pointed out, Jim always took his responsibility as a parent seriously. Now, it comforted Jim to see his son happy and settled with Marie and Niko, and to know Niko saw his parents every day.

Morgan and Marie, to this day, are not officially married, but the only thing stopping the ceremony is not agreeing on where

Marie, Morgan and Niko at Procter
(MORGAN DAVIES COLLECTION).

it should be held. They would have a hard time prying Jim out of Banff, though he might surprise them.

Only a few years ago, in November 2015, Jim made a trip to Vancouver to accept the Carl Agar/Alf Stringer Award "in recognition of his outstanding contribution to the Canadian helicopter industry." It was a chore to get him there. His cousin Nelda found out about the award and insisted he go in person to accept it. Despite his reticence, she skilfully manoeuvred him to pack up and get in the car where her husband was waiting to drive them to the ceremony.

In the end, it was a very enjoyable trip.

Appendix

Public Safety in Parks Today: Improvements and Problems

It was 58 years ago when Jim began his career as a helicopter pilot flying in the North for Bullock Helicopters, taking geologists over the land to spot mineral outcrops. At that time, pilots had to make do with piston-driven machines under a low ceiling limitation and minimal carrying capacity. Helicopters were used primarily to get people to and from remote locations. The limitations of these early helicopters were sufficient for helicopter companies to press manufacturers to develop machines with more power that could fly higher with a greater load capacity.

When Jim began flying for Parks Canada, the Bell 47G2 he flew could be used for pickups if the pilot had a level spot to set down on, but flying in mountainous terrain was nothing like flying over flat land. Training, such as could be had at Okanagan Helicopters' flying school,[94] kept pilots out of serious trouble in this demanding environment. One pilot notes, "Without this training it would have been impossible to work safely in the BC mountains; you are constantly having to deal with convection currents caused by warm air ... figure eights, reconnaissance, cirque and saddle landing techniques, updrafts, downdrafts and even bald eagles who tend to soar in the lower and upper flowing currents."

Jim did not attend this school when he started flying helicopters, as he was already experienced with the perilously tricky mountain conditions flying a fixed-wing Super Cub around Banff. He received additional training in the mountains from Evan Bullock, mainly around Moose Mountain, closer to the foothills. Once he began working in Banff, he familiarized himself with all the vagaries of the rivers, valleys and peaks of the park. He came to know what to expect on steep slopes under changing conditions and how to handle situations with an intimate understanding of what the helicopter could do and how far it could be pushed.

When Jim began heli-slinging, none of his machines had computers to automatically give him the information he needed on the instrument panel. He made modifications to the helicopter so he could look down to establish vertical reference, to accurately place the rescuer as close to the victim as possible. On the early rescues he resorted to removing the pilot's door so he could stick his head out far enough to see the people below, while manipulating the controls to make the adjustment to his position. At no time could he take his hand off the collective[95] while adjusting the rotor pitch and tail rotor. Such manoeuvres required a high level of hand–eye coordination. The disadvantage to this was the wind blowing in his unprotected eyes, made worse if the weather was bad.

Although this rescue did not involve Jim, it illustrates some of the precarious conditions aerial rescues faced with this unsophisticated equipment. In 1983 a Piper Comanche with four passengers on board had engine trouble as they headed into the coastal mountains south of Vancouver, BC. The pilot sent out a mayday just before they crashed into Chehalis Mountain at

Jim establishing his vertical reference
(JIM DAVIES COLLECTION).

5,330 ft. The Rescue Coordination Centre at Comox on Vancouver Island picked up the distress signal and sent it on to the North Shore Rescue personnel. The Canadian Armed Forces also picked up the signal, but it was too late in the day to send in help. They did send a reconnaissance plane that reported seeing people waving at them, so there was confirmation that some of the party was still alive. The following morning, the military flew a Boeing CH-113 Labrador helicopter into the site but could not get near the downed plane. The helicopter was too big to get in close and the pilot was concerned the wash from its rotors might start an avalanche. They needed a smaller helicopter, which was available at Okanagan Helicopters.

Okanagan sent in a Bell 206 LongRanger with cables and a Billy Pugh[96] with their best pilot, Terry Dixon. By the time the rescuers were organized and approaching the mountain, a storm had rolled in, severely reducing visibility. The two men from SARS riding in the Billy Pugh hanging from the heli-rescue line became nervous when they saw the ridge leading up to the crash site, 300 m above them. In order to get to the stranded people, the pilot had to manoeuvre extremely close to the rock ridge. The

gan a slow climbing hover, with the rotor blades about a
m the rock. It was delicate flying. Had the rotors hit the
veryone in the helicopter would have died.

However, the four survivors were located. The pilot set the
Billy Pugh on a ledge near the downed craft, and the rescuers
were able to climb out and assist the survivors into the basket to
be flown out. The pilot then made a second trip to pick up the
rescue personnel.

The pilot, Terry Dixon, later wrote an account of his experience
in the magazine *Rotor Tales*, published in 1983. He writes: "Flying
through those clouds and snow conditions was like flying inside
a ping pong ball. This is the sort of work that our pilots like Jim
Davies are doing routinely but it's certainly not the type of work
pilots normally find themselves faced with." At that time Jim
was flying a Bell 206 LongRanger, which seemed to him like
a Cadillac in the skies compared to the small, skittish, underpowered machines he flew when he first started rescue work
with Parks Canada.

×   ×   ×

The personnel currently manning the rescue services in the mountains of Alberta and southeastern BC have changed, but they are
nevertheless an interesting lot. In Kananaskis Country and Peter
Lougheed Provincial Park, the current rescue leader is Jeremy
Mackenzie, who manages a rescue team made up of four men.

Jeremy was born in Canmore and fell under the spell of the
mountains at an early age. By the time he was old enough to look
up in the sky and see Tim Auger or another warden fly by with
an accident victim attached to Jim's heli-sling rope, the rescue

program in Banff was well under way. In the romantic years of young adulthood when anything is possible, he was further inspired to make a life in the mountains when he heard a lecture by Hans Gmoser.

Jeremy is a proficient skier, and when his adventurous spirit led him to tour the backcountry looking for un-skied powder, he decided to become certified in Level One Avalanche Awareness and Control, the first level of training needed to stay safe in the snowbound backcountry. He didn't stop there. In 2008 he obtained his full guide's licence with the hope that this effort would be rewarded by a public safety position in either Banff or Kananaskis. Kananaskis popped up first, with a seasonal position leading to a full-time job running rescues for the park.

With three other qualified rangers, Jeremy has been kept busy with growing daily call-outs for assistance. Though the team has only four professional public safety personnel on call on any given day, the rest of the conservation staff is trained for heli-slinging. Since Kananaskis Country gets more call-outs for searches and water rescues, this additional ground support helps out considerably.

Kananaskis also works very closely with the Banff public safety staff supervised by Brian Webster. Banff has the luxury of employing nine personnel to cover the call-outs in Banff and the Lake Louise, Yoho and Kootenay (KYLL) jurisdictions. The rescue pilots from Canmore must cover both Kananaskis and the Banff/KYLL zone. These two groups train regularly together as a unit and can be called in to any rescue that is too complex or extensive for one unit alone.[97]

The rescue record for the mountain national parks and Kananaskis Country is so far unblemished by any deaths or serious injury either to pilots, rescuers or victims, though close calls have occurred. This is to be expected when the job entails taking the calculated risks inherent in rescue scenarios. Rockfall, wind and fast water are often cited as major objective risks, but gear failure (helicopter or rescue equipment) and human error are subjective risks the team tries to eliminate through excellent staff, constant training and regular equipment maintenance.

For the Kananaskis rangers, the Banff public safety personnel and the pilots, one of the most frequent yet difficult places to achieve a successful rescue is on Mt. Yamnuska. The number of climbers doing old or new routes has proliferated in the last few years. Nothing has changed on Yamnuska since the wardens first got called in for rescues. It still has loose rock, vertical rock pitches, overhangs and the unfailing winds that pour through the Gap to eddy unpredictably across the face of the mountain.

The closest a rescuer and pilot came to being killed recently was on one of the higher routes on this mountain. As often seemed to be the case, the victim was situated near the top but not close enough to lower a man to him. The pilot felt he could get close enough with the sling rope to get Jeremy directly to him. However, the effort took the pilot's attention away from the steep face and, without warning, the blades collided with the rock.

The rock ground off an equal 11 inches of metal from the tips of all four main rotor blades. Jeremy, dangling below the helicopter, wondered where the spray of rock fragments was coming from, when the pilot peeled off from the mountain, flying straight down to keep the air moving as fast as possible through the truncated blades. By the time they reached the staging meadow below, the pilot was in enough control to set Jeremy down and land beside him without autorotating. Jeremy was absolutely certain he would die that day. Other pilots who saw the damage were amazed the pilot could bring the helicopter down safely at all – certainly, his flying skills were in full employment that day.

Not all the qualified rescue pilots fly for the various parks (national or provincial). Mark Adams has been flying rescue missions out of the Alpine Helicopter base in Golden, BC, for ten years, working not only with nearby Yoho and Glacier/Revelstoke parks but with the Golden Volunteer Rescue Organization, responding to calls as far south as Kimberley, BC. This area takes in the Bugaboo Range, a popular area for climbers, hikers and skiers that can generate more high-angle rescues than most places in the Rockies.

The town of Golden became a subsidiary base for Alpine Helicopters in 1988 after Okanagan Helicopters quit the town. Don McTighe was the first certified rescue pilot in Golden. He initially worked for Okanagan, but when the company was bought out by Canadian Helicopters, rescues became a low priority in favour of larger, more commercial work. Don was not happy under this new administration and contacted Alpine Helicopters in Kelowna to propose they establish a base in Golden. Alpine was happy to do this, knowing they had an excellent pilot in Don McTighe.

McTighe knew Mark Adams when Mark was a young boy in Golden. Mark's parents, Dawn and Martin Adams, worked for Yoho National Park and were good friends with Don and his family. They arranged for Mark to go on a helicopter flight with Don, and from that day, Mark knew what his goal in life would be. Nothing deterred his ambition, and when his parents moved to Vancouver, he began his flying career for Airspan Helicopters in Abbotsford, BC. He got his class B licence[98] and honed his skills on commercial jobs working on power lines that required him to sling personnel to the top of support towers. When Don called one day, asking if Mark would come to Golden to work for him, Mark was thrilled. After sorting out his commitments, he arrived in 2010, already certified to fly rescues.

Though Golden does not get enough calls to dedicate a helicopter strictly for rescues, Mark gets enough to maintain his expertise in this capacity. He also trains with the rescue teams in the national parks, as well as the GVRO.[99] Though Golden gets fewer call-outs than Banff or Kananaskis, Mark has also seen the rise in the number of people coming to the mountains. For instance, the world-renowned high-level ski traverse from the Bugaboos to Rogers Pass now sees up to five or six groups attempting it each year. Despite its extremely challenging nature, people tackle this traverse without the expertise to complete it, relying on blind luck, and knowing they can call for help with a satellite phone or spot locator.

× × ×

A number of technical and regulatory changes have dramatically altered aerial rescue since Jim's day.

For instance, one major impediment to slinging people safely under a helicopter was lack of communication between rescuer and pilot. During the first training sessions in Banff, none of the wardens used a radio. When Peter Fuhrmann flew his first rescues, he was forced to carry a large box radio that sat in his lap,[100] similar to radios used in the Second World War. Before Jim stopped flying for Banff after the contract dispute in the mid-1980s, wardens only had to speak into a small microphone attached to their clothing.

In 1990 the regulations for Helicopter Flight Rescue System came under the purview of Canadian Aviation Regulations. As noted in chapter 9, in 1986 the regulation governing the slinging of external human cargo changed to require the rescue helicopter to be equipped with a release capability as a backup to be employed if the helicopter became hopelessly tangled with the line. This change went a long way with insurance companies. The first ejectable system required the pilot to employ three steps to release the load, which could eat up precious seconds. The system in place as of this writing only requires two distinct actions to release the load. This is more efficient and is used for all external human transport. However, to date, this release system has never been used in Canada. Jim always thought most pilots would look for a place to land before they would release the load. Todd Cooper, a rescue pilot and manager at Alpine Helicopters in Canmore, says he cannot think where he would use it. He did admit that if the line got tangled in some trees where the helicopter could not land, releasing the line might be the only way to save the helicopter.

When Jim retired, each mountain national park was responsible for executing its own rescues, and it was the responsibility of the rescue leader to make the call to bring in the helicopter if warranted. However, in 1998 the park system became a business unit, and six years later, in 2004, it became an agency with a CEO. The changes, in essence, made Parks a corporation without direct oversight by any government department. Currently, a single public safety unit in Banff handles all the rescues in Lake Louise, Yoho and Kootenay (KYLL) national parks.

Today, though there are still wardens who are given park support if they show ability, most wardens in Banff's public safety unit have their full guide's certificate, paid for out of their own pocket. But achieving full guide status is costly and can take from four to six years to achieve.[101] The smaller national parks of Kootenay and Yoho no longer have public safety wardens and rely on the Banff team to handle their rescues. Jasper still runs their own rescues and have separate arrangements with the rescue pilot. The standard set for aiding another park in the event of a large search or rescue will still see parks working together.

Kananaskis Country, under Alberta provincial jurisdiction, also has a select group of rangers just to perform mountain rescue, and they do train their staff in heli-slinging, as well as in ground and aerial searches.

Another departure from the earlier days is that pilots now take part in the debriefing after a rescue is over. The pilot's observations provide insight, help the individuals become a more unified team, and help the managers better understand what can be changed for the better and what is working well.

To truly assess the difficulty or "do-ability" of any given situation, the pilot will do a flight reconnaissance before bringing in rescue personnel. Often one of the trained rescuers will go on this flight to assess the terrain and decide on the best approach to retrieving the victim.

With increasing numbers of people climbing more difficult routes, accident rates in Kananaskis, Yamnuska and the mountain parks are rising steadily, while the number of trained personnel to carry out the rescues has remained static in Kananaskis Country. Brian Webster, who supervises public safety in Banff, has not found this to be a problem yet but acknowledges they work hard to keep abreast of more people and higher climbing standards. New sports like paraponting can lead to people getting hung up in the most unlikely places.

Liability management has also changed. In the 1970s and 1980s, pilots and wardens could get away with a lot more. Gone are the days when Jim could land on a peak or drop someone off at a lake. Managers are strict about night flying, too, allowing only twin-engine helicopters to work after dark, and helicopters cannot ignore aviation regulations. Wardens heading up units such as public safety are now personally liable for the proper training of their staff.[102]

Because more people are using the park, including in the backcountry (and they all have cell phones and cameras), a public servant's error can easily blow up in a very public way.

Helicopters too have evolved since Jim's day. Their capacity for flying higher, faster and heavier has increased considerably with more powerful engines and better designed machines.[103] Still, the skills of flying a helicopter have not changed. Pilots must manage the same five controls and make utmost use of their training and intuition. In the mountains, and particularly on the eastern slopes in Alberta, unpredictable winds remain a critical factor, particularly in the often tight confines near cliffs, found in rescue flights. Pilots can easily encounter conditions where their helicopter may get into a site but can't get out.[104]

Statistically in aviation today, the helicopter is safer than the pilot flying the machine. Helicopter accidents can still happen as a result of mechanical failure, but this is due to sloppy maintenance, which is still an aspect of human error. Crashes that happen now most often come down to pilot error or communications error.

More and more often, a longer line is used in rescues where communication is essential. Mark Adams once used a 500-foot line to extract a body from the Plain of Six Glaciers near Lake Louise, but at that distance the pilot only sees the load as a small speck. For this extreme long-lining, pilots rely heavily on the rescuer to report their position accurately. If a helicopter is operating on a steep rock face, the rescuer can use a throw rope to toss to the victim so the rescue line with the rescuer can be pulled into the face. A longer line gives the helicopter a much greater capacity to hover in one spot until the victim and rescuer are ready to be slung off. The rescuer releases the short throw rope as the helicopter takes up the slack and flies directly away from the face in a downward plunge – a plunge that must be more gut wrenching to the victim than the hairy climbing that put them there.

The most recent challenge pilots must deal with is the effect of climate change on weather. This issue was considered important enough to be a main topic at the last ICAR (International Commission for Alpine Rescue) convention in Europe in 2019. Mark has noticed that the warming temperatures around Golden are causing more fog to develop – a pilot's nightmare. He has also noticed a change in the winds, which are becoming more frequent and violent, making a big difference to where the helicopter can go.

The latest innovation in aerial mountain rescue, still in its infancy, is the use of drones. Brian Webster is a proponent and hopes to move ahead in this field as Banff has the resources to buy drones and employ technicians to fly them. This is still very new and the team will have to determine where they can best be used. Hopefully, drones will be able not only to assess flying conditions but to drop food, supplies and communication equipment. As with most machine-driven developments, it is possible to envision a day when some rescues will be done by drones. But that is not likely in the immediate future.

Despite superior technology for both helicopters and communication, though, the flying still has to be done by the pilot. It is interesting to note that helicopter pilots must still pass the flying exam designed by Parks in 1984, in order to qualify for rescue work. This test must be completed flying the original Bell 206 LongRanger used by Jim. Such an experience gives new pilots an appreciation for the helicopters flown now.

The challenges in aerial mountain rescue have become more complex, with greater numbers of people attempting extreme sports, technological innovation, regulatory and liability issues and a changing climate. There are few pilots who have the ability and disposition to take up the challenge of heli-sling rescue flying, but for those who do, the reward is significant. The helicopter rescue program started by Peter Fuhrmann and Jim Davies is now in the capable hands of younger people who continue to attend yearly ICAR conferences and remain updated with the latest developments. Gerold Biner, one of the world's most respected rescue pilots, with experience in both Switzerland and the Himalayas, recognizes only two other countries with the same rescue capabilities: Canada and New Zealand. He states: "I dare to say that, along with the Canadians and New Zealanders, our mountain training methods and standards here in Switzerland are among the best in the world."

Like today's rescue pilots, Jim Davies is not alone when he says flying rescue missions was the better part of his job. Flying home each night, he could be sure he was earning his keep, knowing

Bruce McTrowe, Jim and Brian MacDonald
at 2009 warden centennial celebration
(JIM DAVIES COLLECTION).

his flying resulted in a successful mission despite the outcome, be it closure for loss of a loved one or jubilation at their safe return.

Endnotes

1   There was a dump near town, but it had no fencing, allowing access to bears and other scavengers, including people. One resident in Jasper actually made a living from valuable things people threw away.

2   Of Banff's Whyte Museum of the Canadian Rockies.

3   Her mother was quite strict and did not like her children to associate with the faster crowd.

4   Jim did not think this was administered.

5   Operators eventually built a tramline to the top of the mountain but it only ran during the summer.

6   The Snowcat is a modified skidoo but looks more like a tank. It is used by various backcountry ski lodges for transporting skiers and clearing snow.

7   Despite the high mortality rate for helicopter pilots at that time.

8   This would eventually lead to his groundbreaking heli-skiing enterprise with Jim's help.

9   In the end he based his ski trips out of the Stanley Mitchell hut in the Little Yoho Valley in Yoho National Park.

10 At the time, Jim had only 78 hours of flying under his belt.

11 As part of his ski business promotion, Hans presented this film to audiences around North America.

12 In fact, Jim had landed there often when the Whites ran the lodge. If they knew he was coming, they would sometimes ski up there and stomp out a landing area for the plane.

13   Erling Strom had established himself at Assiniboine, running ski tours from the lodge built by the CPR. Jim could actually land on Lake Magog and avoid the risk of damaging the supplies by air dropping them.

14   A tree well is a deep hole surrounding a tree in the spring when snow next to the tree melts.

15   When Bert quit the warden service for his new trucking business, he'd often hired Bruce's dad to work for him, and the two men had become good friends.

16   At 17,150 ft. above sea level, Mt. Lucania was the highest peak in the Centennial Range.

17   To provide food for the settlers flocking to the island at that time.

18   Necessary to develop the skill of vertical reference.

19   Later investigation pointed to the toxicity of the lead solder used to seal the cans as a possible explanation for the fate of the lost expedition.

20   Sue and Grace were both in university down east and came out as summer students. Grace was getting her degree in fine arts and thought Sue's major was history.

21   Ultimately leading to a lifelong career in public safety in Banff National Park.

22   Willi, on the other hand, found Fred's direction abrasive.

23   It wasn't until the 1980s that this problem was finally cleaned up.

24   Jim flew an Astazou Alouette II, which had a turboshaft engine but was still underpowered compared to the newer Bell 206B JetRangers. Jim used it initially but heard that it crashed a few months later in British Columbia.

25   Because the wardens could deal with any law enforcement problems that cropped up without the use of an airport.

26   The turbojet engine helicopter was new on the market, but expensive.

27   When he tried to get a helicopter from Calgary, they either did not show

up or went to the wrong place. If they did come, they generally had no idea what Peter wanted.

28 Rockfall hazard increases as the sun rises and melts the snow, releasing rocks that may have fallen into a chute from cliffs above.

29 A modified canvas rescue stretcher designed to fly injured persons beneath the helicopter on the sling line.

30 A bivouac is an impromptu night spent on the mountain.

31 If the situation was serious enough, wardens from other parks could be called in.

32 Later, Don McTighe, who worked for Okanagan helicopters in Golden, would be the designated heli-sling rescue pilot.

33 The range of peaks dividing North America's eastern and northern watersheds from its western watersheds.

34 Peter was a high-end climber, and in 1986 became the equipment manager on the first Canadian Everest Expedition.

35 Banff had a policy of rotating wardens on a two-week basis between the backcountry and the town. It took considerable training to do backcountry patrols safely, as well, considering the nature of horses and the isolation of the remote cabins.

36 Most of her neighbours were wealthy doctors and lawyers.

37 Who had considerable influence with the public safety program, having pushed it through Regional Office, as well as Ottawa.

38 Peter Whyte worked with Peter Fuhrmann on structuring a rescue plan from a command centre down to the field rescue teams and support crew.

39 The stress put on the loaded carabiner gate caused it to jam when the protective sleeve kept it from opening.

40 A serac is an ice pinnacle.

41 Jim noted that just finding him was amazing.

42 A belay is a secure point from which a stationary climber can hold a partner's climbing rope in case the climbing partner slips.

43 Dr. Boyd was working at the Banff hospital during this period.

44 Sernalyn was soon abandoned, becoming illegal for any use.

45 Wilf worked in Banff for the Canadian Wildlife Service.

46 Anectine only paralyzes the bear's muscles and does not make it sleep.

47 Bill actually had the camera knocked out of his hand by the bear.

48 Jim went one step further and bought up a few handguns when he went to the United States. He never left home without the gun stashed in the helicopter.

49 This is also the title of book written by Sid Marty surrounding the event.

50 A survey of waste in tourist towns revealed that waste from restaurants was 55 per cent food.

51 The mystery of how and why it was stashed there was never solved.

52 In fact, the thief barely glanced at the signs, wondering why people were screaming at him not to go in there.

53 Jim's role with rescue dogs was to take the dog and its handler to a location from which the dog might pick up a lost hiker's scent, to begin the dog's part in the rescue operation.

54 To "quarry" for a rescue dog is to enact the role of a lost hiker as part of the dog's training or as a demonstration.

55 Called monsoon buckets.

56 The moniker was a parody of the movie *The Eiger Sanction*, starring Clint Eastwood, who ends up having an epic adventure on the north face of Switzerland's Eiger Mountain.

57 A vertical crack in a rock face can be more straightforward to climb than the face itself. This vertical crack is referred to as a "chimney."

58 Sue kept an account of Jim's work and what was required each day.

59 Just inside BC's Assiniboine Provincial Park.

60 Jim added a bit of a tour of the area.

61 Despite the trend toward specialization, however, almost all wardens were still trained in mountaineering in the early part of the decade.

62 A fixed line is a rope stretched over a route and anchored at multiple locations. A climber clips into the fixed line with a carabiner as he moves along the route, which will hold him in case of accidents.

63 As a climbing leader progresses, he hammers pitons, similar to large spikes, into cracks in the rock and fastens his rope to these with a carabiner. In this way, should he slip, the piton will shorten his fall.

64 In more recent years they decided that this aid should be extended to those outside the park, if requested.

65 And in fact upgraded their ability by attending warden climbing schools and by climbing with friends on their own time, often beyond the level of difficulty encountered in the climbing schools.

66 Described in Chapter 6.

67 If a park invites persons onto park property, the park is responsible for their safety. This is a very grey area that affects the liability of park personnel.

68 Initially, such pilots were directed to Peter Fuhrmann, who demanded the pilots prove they were skilled in mountain flying and have an intimate knowledge of the park.

69 To this day.

70 In 1997 Lance's son Todd also became a rescue helicopter pilot, which, in Lance's words, was "one of the things I was most proud of."

71 Tourism flights were becoming more popular.

72 Swift water rescue was another field that the rangers would become adept at handling.

73   Dr. Brett was a permanent resident of Banff who was well known about town.

74   It was the exception for the Canadian Rockies to have two major tourist towns so close to one another. Jim and Sue loved Banff, where all their friends were, and the drive to Canmore was easily shorter than most commutes elsewhere. In fact, Canmore, Harvey Heights and Banff formed a very strong Bow Corridor community. Not far from this were also the communities of Exshaw and Dead Man's Flats.

75   Jim was still flying to the lodge until well into the late 1980s.

76   To glissade is to "ski" down a snow slope on one's boots.

77   An unrelated plane crash on the west coast of British Columbia acted as a catalyst to finding missing men as soon as possible, because the individuals on the west coast had survived the crash but succumbed to their injuries after struggling through the thick BC bush. The fact that the west coast victims had not died on impact gave everyone renewed hope the missing men in Alberta might be similarly fortunate.

78   Or close to it, with the intention of completing all the courses.

79   The standards for achieving the full guide's licence had also risen. No longer could a candidate pass two exams (summer guide and winter guide) for a full licence; by the late 1980s, five courses were required (summer assistant, summer full, winter assistant, winter full and rock climbing), and examiners passed only the best of the best.

80   Prior to this he had also been recognized by the Helicopter Association International, who gave him the Pilot Safety Award of Excellence for having more than 10,000 consecutive accident- and violation-free civilian flight hours in helicopters.

81   Both of them loved dogs and they rarely went long without one.

82   Jim never called attention to his creative streak, and now only those who currently live in the Saanich house enjoy the mural (if they were smart enough to not paint over it).

83 Hans was happily enjoying the summer part of CMH guiding, which now extended to taking hiking groups into spectacular alpine terrain.

84 He had been born and raised in Banff and had spent his entire life there, with the exception of the years spent on the coast.

85 At one point Sue was reluctant to get any more dogs, as it was so hard on her when they eventually died.

86 "Misery sticks" was a derogatory term wardens used for cross-country skis.

87 Niko was born in 2001, the same year Siri died.

88 Seppi and Barb had purchased the lodge from Siri in 1983.

89 The five Naiset huts were built in Assiniboine by A.O. Wheeler in 1925 to accommodate hikers on his walking tours. Naiset means "sunset" in Sioux.

90 Morgan and Marie lived there for three months in 2001. When Marie became pregnant with Niko the couple moved back to Victoria for a more stable life.

91 Dr. Gerry eventually convinced the cancer unit at the Tom Baker Cancer Centre that meditation could be helpful in cancer treatment, and today it is recognized as the leader in starting the mindful-meditation program in cancer treatment in Calgary.

92 At the time, they had a dog named Smokey, and Sue loved to go on long drives through the mountains, letting the dog out for short runs.

93 Morgan now owns and manages a number of rental properties and is part owner of a small hotel currently being renovated near Red Mountain in Rossland, BC.

94 Established in Penticton in 1951.

95 The collective controls the height of the hovering helicopter above the ground.

96 A Billy Pugh is a basket that attaches to the helicopter long line that can

be used to sling people and equipment to a specific location. It is often used for water rescue.

97 As of this writing, Alpine Helicopters is the only company working in the Banff–Canmore and Golden, BC, areas with trained rescue pilots. Their main mountain headquarters is in Canmore, where they handle all of Kananaskis, Banff and the KYLL (Lake Louise, Yoho and Kootenay) zone parks.

98 A Class B is needed to qualify for flying to transport human external loads.

99 Golden Volunteer Rescue Organization.

100 Most people envision the rescuer slung under a helicopter as being held by the rope in a standing position. In fact, they have a chair and they sit in it, creating a lap for the radio.

101 In addition, rescue wardens perform a dedicated job that revolves around constant training and being called out day or night to attend rescue missions.

102 Banff does have liability insurance but cannot cover individuals who might be named in a lawsuit.

103 Some rescue helicopters can fly up to five people at once if absolutely necessary, though it would have to be an extreme emergency to do this, as having that many people could cause a lot of problems with load management.

104 The accident with Kobe Bryant was an instance where the pilot lost vertical reference, leading to the death of all on board.

Bibliography

Biner, Gerold. *Flight for Life: Mountain Rescuers between the Matterhorn and Everest.* Zurich: Orell Füssli, 2016.

Calvert, Kathy. *Don Forest: Quest for the Summits.* Surrey, BC: Rocky Mountain Books, 2003.

Calvert, Kathy, Leonard V. Hills and Richard D. Revel. *Waste Management in Jasper National Park.* Ottawa: Parks Canada, 1995.

Calvert, Kathy, and Dale Portman. *Guardians of the Peaks: Mountain Rescue in the Canadian Rockies and Columbia Mountains.* Surrey, BC: Rocky Mountain Books, 2006.

Grant, Douglas M. *Vertical Horizons: The History of Okanagan Helicopters.* Madeira Park, BC: Harbour Publishing, 2017.

Hare, Jannis Allan, Douglas Hare, Louise Schulz and Banff History Book Committee. *We Live in a Postcard: Banff Family Histories.* Banff, AB: Banff History Book Committee, 2005.

Sandford, Robert. *The Highest Calling: Canada's Elite National Park Mountain Rescue Program.* Canmore, AB: Alpine Club of Canada, 2002.

———. *A Mountain Life: The Stories and Photographs of Bruno Engler.* Canmore, AB: Alpine Club of Canada, 1996.

Scott, Chic. *Deep Powder and Steep Rock: The Life of Mountain Guide Hans Gmoser.* Banff, AB: Assiniboine Publishing, 2009.

———. *Powder Pioneers: Ski Stories from the Canadian Mountains and Columbia Mountains.* Surrey, BC: Rocky Mountain Books. 2005.

Strom, Erling. *Pioneers on Skis: Tales of High Adventure from Norway to Lake Placid, the Rockies and Mount McKinley*. Central Valley, NY: Smith Clove Press, 1977.

KATHY CALVERT grew up in the Canadian Rockies. In 1974 she became one of the first female national park wardens in Canada; in 1977 she was a member of the first all-women expedition to Mount Logan and in 1989 was on the first all-women ski traverse of the Columbia Mountains from the Bugaboos to Rogers Pass. She is the author of four books: *Don Forest: Quest for the Summits*, *Guardians of the Peaks: Mountain Rescue in the Canadian Rockies and Columbia Mountains*, *June Mickle: One Woman's Life in the Foothills and Mountains of Western Canada*, and *Ya Ha Tinda: A Home Place – Celebrating 100 Years of the Canadian Government's Only Working Horse Ranch*. She and her husband, Dale Portman, live in Cochrane, Alberta.